Winds of Change

Original Manuscript

by

Robert Ghost Wolf
and the Mountain Brotherhood

LIBRARY OF CONGRESS

CATALOGING-IN-PUBLICATION DATA

Original Manuscript for:

Winds of Change

ISBN: 0-9660668-4-7

ORIGINAL MANUSCRIPT EDITION OF WINDS OF CHANGE
by ROBERT GHOST WOLF and THE MOUNTAIN BROTHERHOOD

Volume 2 of "Last Cry"

Mistyc House Publishing · P.O. 10196 · Spokane · WA 99209

Cover Art and Illustrations by Robert Ghost Wolf

Special Art Contribution by Robyn Ryan

Cover and interior design Robert Ghost Wolf / Cindee Delgado

Editing by Cindee Delgado

Special Literary Contributions by The Mountain Brotherhood

Printed in the United States of America

Table of Contents

Preface

by Robert Ghost Wolf and the Mountain Brotherhood

That which I have presented to you here has been shown to me. This writing is not intended to frighten or intimidate you, but to make you aware of the intensity of which these events will occur if we do not change consciousness on a global level. As I have said again and again, the Mother is tired. She is ill. She is about to purge herself as her children will not do it for her. We can draw from her energy grids endless resource, only is it is done with the intent of nurturing her dream and her children as a whole. It is the law of the giveaway ... the white buffalo.

I, as have countless others, have tried to awaken you to that which some perceive as our eminent demise. I have also tried to make it clear to you that this purging is leading to a re-birth, which is not all bad! What you do with this information is up to you. If you go forth and make the changes in your own consciousness, the 'I' which is the all, which is the we... which is the 'I AM', then you become part of the solution. If you return to the consciousness of "I, Me" then you become part of the destruction.

We of the Mountain Brotherhood can only give you the tools. We can not control how, or if, you choose use them.

In the light,

Ghost Wolf and the Mountain Brotherhood

Forward to the Reader

by Laura Lee Mistycah

As with *Last Cry*, there has been much counter intention to getting the information in this book to the public. Working behind the scenes on *Last Cry* was enough to give someone hives and a good case of paranoia if they weren't well grounded with a good sense of humor. With both books there have been interferences ranging from communication glitches to electromagnetic mishaps to blatant physical sabotage.

Following Wolf's appearance on the Art Bell Show last December, 1996, the volume cranked up in our already challenging lives and the "shift started hitting the fan!" Hundreds of letters, e-mails, phone calls and orders started pouring in. But before many of them could be responded to, our systems were hacked into and the information was deleted. ☹ Cindee, our web master, office manager and miracle worker had just begun her 18 – 20 hour days for Wolf Lodge. To keep ahead of the hackers, she was having to change access codes and site locations every 24 – 48 hours, as they went so far as to break into our site and delete web pages! The real cruncher came when someone actually *cancelled* our web site! We had to do some fast and tricky maneuverings to keep things going which included a decoy site that is still floating around in cyber space! To add insult to injury, they set up a virus that came into our computers when we went to download our Internet orders. Not only did we loose the orders, we lost the computers!

To further complicate matters, Wolf and I were in the middle of moving with our four children to another location, Wolf Lodge had just undertaken a complicated rescue mission and our financial resources were at an all time low. Had it not been for two Angels by the names of Michael and Partice Brown coming to our rescue and financing two replacement computers, *Last Cry* may never have gotten out! (Thank God for Angels!)

Back on the road again, new challenges continue to arrive daily. One of the most prevalent (and annoying) targets is our ability to communicate. Having our phones tapped became almost mundane, though quite irritating. The echos and reverberations when trying to speak to someone and other oddities, like hearing the phone ring *while I was talking on it* and having the phone dial numbers other than those we would press! One time, Wolf dialed a local number (seven digits) only to get Art Bell, whom he'd dialed hours before! Bizarre occurrences with phone and fax lines have not limited themselves to just our main phone line. They have also made residence in our voice mail systems, Cindee's phone and our fax and computer lines. Sometimes calls would go directly to voice mail, or not come through at all, even though no one was on the phone! Then, someone changed our voice mail service to dump all messages every 24 hours. We didn't catch on to this for some months, so those of you who did not get a call back, well... We even had an instance where someone actually placed a clear, gooey, gelatin/silicone like substance *into* the outside box the lines run into!! (No wonder the lines went out that time!) The phone company has been just as confused. When we moved again in September, (a house gets really small with this many kids!) the lines took forever to be installed and when they were, the fax line was installed in the family room, so we were without fax service for over two months! So if any one tried to fax and couldn't get through, well...

To top all of this off, (though there is more that followed, so I guess I should say something like "the icing on the cake" etc...) we were forced to request an unlisted phone number. Not because of people making inquiries or wanting to speak with Wolf or I, but because of threats. Yes, hard to believe, but we actually began to receive threats of violence should we release the information contained in *Last Cry*. The last straw came when one of our children answered the phone in Wolf's absence, and upon informing the caller that Wolf was not in, he asked to take a message. With pen in hand and anticipating a name and phone number, I watched as my son grew pale and wide-eyed. I immediately snatched away the phone and listened. I can only imagine that my expression was the same for the words that I heard were of the ugliest one could imagine. This caller was actually threatening, through a child, the lives of our entire family. Stunned, I called Cindee who in turn called the authorities and had a new and unlisted number working within an hour. Since that time those of such ill intent have had to resort to threats by e-mail, letter, personal messenger or Internet postings. Thankfully, none of which our children are exposed to.

As I said, there is more... the computer saga, for example! It seems that no matter what computer we use, or who we have do computer work for us, strange and bizarre things occur. We are not talking about the average computer glitch or hiccup. We are talking down right unexplainable impossibilities. Even Cindee, who has done computer work since 1982, reports that the weirdest things happen when working on just about anything for Wolf Lodge! So much so, that for a project to go 'without a hitch' is unusual! She has had files move on their own, sometimes to totally different drives. Graphics have been the most fun(?), after hours of work tweaking, perfecting and saving them, she would go back and they would have reverted to a previous format, if they were there at all! These events occur over and over, each one a little different than the last, but just as frustrating, none the less. While editing *Winds of Change* from a Zip Disk, the disk decided it would format itself as a 'read only' disk, no longer allowing changes to be saved to it. I jokingly told her that she was witnessing Alchemy at a high tech level! Wonder why she didn't laugh? ☺ Then, still during the edit, came the 'battle of the computer screen.' It began when she was editing *Etherean Relationships*, and half of the screen went blank – the entire lower half of the screen. No task bar, nothing – just white! This escalated to the point she was just about convinced a nymph had taken up residence as every now and again (but only during the edit) the entire computer screen would turn white and the computer would NOT respond. What really threw her was when this happened during the wee hours of an all night edit and she, in total frustration, shouted out loud "That's enough. I've had it. Knock it off or else!" She no sooner had restarted the computer and had begun editing when the screen turned completely white ... except for one word ... "there." As if to, *so there, take that!* Which was immediately followed by a cold whisp of air across her cheek (and no doubt a shiver down her back!) Enough was enough and out came the sage, the Aurauralite, the Power rock and the white light!!

As you can imagine, there are several metaphysical words that are not used in every day language and thus are not present in every day dictionaries. After editing two books, *Last Cry* and *Winds of Change*, Cindee had built up a considerable custom dictionary. Apparently, the resident nymph took exception and there are no longer beginning letters to any of the words in that dictionary. For example, "Aho" is now "ho" and "Alchemy" is now "lchemy," rustrating, er, I mean frustrating, to say the least! Needless to say, she persevered as your are now reading *Winds of Change!*

I should mention that though Wolf created the artwork for this book, his computer has acquired a similar nymph. But we know that one came in the form of a 'bug' attached to an e-mail, so Cindee wound up scanning in the artwork. At the time of this writing, we are still waiting for a tech to figure out how to re-configure the hard drive so Wolf can get back to the finishing touches on *Eye of the Shaman* and *Sacred Circles.*

Throughout all of this we have managed to maintain our sanity and humor. We've even coined a phrase for all the craziness... "Welcome to Wolf Lodge!" ☺ Well, now you have an insight as to what we have been up against and why 'target dates' are so ambiguous around here. In closing, I would like to thank all those who have stood by us and behind us, and the many of you who have been so patient with us. We are all in this science fiction movie together, so let's keep a sense of humor and our ♥ in place as we move through the shift. Remember the immortal words of The Cat in the Hat, "It's fun to have fun ... but you have to know how!" so ... if we're going to 'do the shift' let have fun doing it now! **Love, Light and Laughter, Laura Lee Mistycah**

Winds of Change

Trust Spirit

top the Andes Mountains near the city of Cuzco, Don Lobos turns his yellow eye towards the midnight blue canvas of the celestial tapestry woven by the Spider Woman. He watches the heavens and the movement of the stars above him. A deep understanding of the turning of events that will follow, as the season of man changes in its foreverness comes over him. The celestial clock is nearing midnight. He watches in silence like the Panther, as humanity awaits the final moments of the dream called reality. He is burdened with knowing it will unfold in accordance with the ancient knowledge remembered by the Inca. What contemporary man may call *the prophecies*, was to the ancient Inca the knowledge of the Divine Laws from the original teachings of the indigenous peoples of this Earth.

Below his mountain hideaway, in the city of Cuzco and its valleys, one can begin to feel the energies of a different world. A world of more ordinary men, a world of those who walk amongst the fallen Angels, a world of those who are sometimes called the Gods in amnesia. Gods who dream walk through their sometimes silent and sometimes not so silent slumbers. They stumble through life, falling into their path rather than walking with purpose toward a point of destination. Unaware that they are as eternal as the light itself, believing that the conditions of the holographic game are the laws of reality. But this evening, the energy throughout the heavens is churning with a strange intoxicating resonance. The seasons of man can be felt churning deep within the belly of the cosmos, as well as within the bodies of the little Terrans below.

The sun will rise in the morning over the little city of Cuzco, as it has for eons. This rising is a signal of our eternal nature to those of us who still hold the ancient knowledge, a signal that the spirit of man shall triumph through the darkness of ignorance and pain which exists at this moment. Let them recognize this symbol lest they be consumed in the ashes of their deeds. Each morning we are reminded of the eternal nature of the universe, of which we are but a small part in the web of life, as Grandfather Sun sends his eternal energy to all that grows upon this little jewel in the cosmos, sometimes called the Emerald of the Universe.

Don Lobos sits beneath the celestial canopy of the jungle sky, amid the Cathedral of the Moon as the fragrance of flowers mixing with the salt air of the below fill the air around him. He finds himself traveling through veils of human wondering. *We are travelers through the void, with eternity as our final destiny. Ahead of us lay the uncharted waters of a million unknown potentials, and behind us we shall leave all our past dreams. The deeds we have done are like the ripples in the tide, sometimes shimmering, sometimes as formless as darkness. Our passion, it seems, is in moving as the tide, ebbing and flowing, sometime thrashing upon the rocks of unseen shoreline.*

Mankind's ultimate destiny lies in the stars from which we have come. For as it was in the beginning so shall it become again. The whole of the Earth and its people has entered the gateway of the *Winds of Change*. This entry occurred October 10th through November 15th of `97. Kate-Zahl, the Pale Prophet, told his visions of the future for mankind to the ancient Toltec People approximately 2,000 years ago. Those visions are now becoming the living dream.

The Ancient Ones seem less and less hidden in some obscure past with the passing of each day. Their presence can be felt at the ceremonies. You feel the actual, physical presence of a person next to you, intuitively. Like when a stranger walks into a room. Upon turning, you are startled to find that there is no physical person there. You are left wondering whether or not to mention this to other people participating with you, only to find in your hesitation that they also have had a similar experience. Occurrences of this nature are becoming more and more common place as the gateway swings wide open.

This phenomenon is being experienced regardless of cultural background, lending to a greater intuitive understanding that the flesh is only a vehicle through which we are born of light. We pass through only for the sake of Earthly experience. Visions of the Crystal cities and halls of learning are more and more frequently coming to my door, as people come to me seeking explanations for their visions and dreams. Experiences that they have no cultural reference for. In other words, there is no cellular memory to connect to within their present body physical. It is a memory of the light being they are, which has had multiple experiences in many cultural and tribal dramas, along the wheel of reincarnation.

These appearances and mental or spirit messages from the old ones is a global occurrence at this time. We cherish and honor the old ones who taught so much to those first courageous beings that ventured from beneath the surface, upon a virgin land as they emerged from Middle Earth. The Shamans and the seers tell us that the season of the Dragon has indeed returned. Grand teachers, wizards and healers who have been here before have come again unto this plane to help mankind make the transition into the Fifth World. Some awaken late in life's experience, still others claim to have made an arrangement with souls who have grown tired of their Earthly Sojourn. Thus an exchange of sorts is made.

When one encounters one of these beings, it will be noticed that there has been a radical change in the person's life, which can effect sudden changes in interests, relationships, or career. Moving to a different area after years of apparent sedentary patterns have been followed methodically. A complete change in personality also accompanies this kind of arrangement with 'Walk-in's.' The reason for this happening with such frequency at this time is that there is simply not enough time before the major shifting of realities begins to allow for the process that has been the norm for eons of our evolutionary experience here upon Earth. In summary, there simply isn't enough 'time' to 'wait' for anybody to 'grow-up' before the changes hit. It is yet another affirmation of *the Quickening*.

Dragons are often seen in visions as the Phoenix hatching from its embryonic rebirth. The Eagle is also a form through which the Dragon has manifested upon this plane at this time. So yes, Eagle dreams connect to this level of consciousness. When we have this kind of vision our memories are stirred by voices that seems to be speaking from somewhere deep within our cosmic consciousness. The real us that is eternal and exists through many life experiences, and knows the greater truth to our human expression upon the physical plane. These voices have begun once again to speak to us from our now not so distant past. Sometimes through feelings, and sometimes heard as songs that could only come from spirit beings.

They speak of knowledge long asleep in the icy consciousness of contemporary mankind. The question of our need to exercise discernment comes into play here, as 'they' can be others that are around us, perhaps while involved in a ceremony, that are from another time. You see, time is collapsing, and there is a merging occurring, as time itself seems to be liquefying. Later as the changes progress, this will actually transcend to the physical plane and things that have been created in this consciousness will then begin to liquefy. For all things are but an expression of our consciousness, emotional, as well as physical. We are magnets for thought as well as senders of thought forms. This occurs through the process of creation known as manifesting into physical experience, or physical form. Thought forms can manifest into physical experience or physical form i.e.: when one is trying to manifest abundance, if such abundance were to manifest as 100 pieces of gold, that would be manifesting into physical form. If, however, one manifested abundance and their suddenly appears in the individual's life business opportunities that lead to financial success, this would be manifesting into physical experience. Here, the experience leads to the desired results, which is abundance; abundance that is created through circumstance.

This understanding kind of gives you a new insight into relationships, doesn't it? What goes out will return to its creator, so there is really no one to blame for our life experiences, is there? It is really a matter of learning to get control of the wheel in an ongoing dream. Life is an experience that is manifesting into physical and emotional reality that never stops, hence the term *the River of Life*. Remember that *thought manifests the nature of reality, as* we discussed in *Last Cry*.

The breath of the Dragon is once again being felt upon the land, as our brothers from the stars make once more their presence known amongst us. The promises of the old ones are being kept as the unfolding of what was once prophecy is being experienced as current events. North in the states they say you can feel a queer chill to the air as old man winter makes his presence known throughout the highlands. A chill that, before it is through, will not be able to be denied by even the most closed minded of our kind. For even they are being affected by comic churning of the universe which moves through their beings like the magma beneath the stones of the Earth. Memories of a truth still felt within their longing hearts, remembered in the games of innocence their children play.

Our Appointment with Destiny

I have heard tell within the hearts of the people there is a clear sense of despair that can be easily witnessed. It is in fact, like a plague that is spreading across the globe at alarming speed. Our dreams are dying. Youth no longer sees its place in what appears to be a bleak future, at best. It is The Great Malaise -- The Great Nothing. It is attitude, which is manifesting a maligned thought projection of reality. Illusions are very real in appearance, but very thin in substance. Subtle, yet all consuming of the spirit caught in the labyrinth of ignorance.

What are being missed in the subtleties are the sounds of magic, they are also in the wind. Some are hearing tones in the winds that carry across the land the songs of the human spirit, which have continued to be sung through the nightmare. Is it not true that young mothers still hold within them the hope for a future world? As their babes suckle on their breasts, the human story continues. In this continuance, they have let their songs loose to be heard even unto the crystal peaks that shine in the last vestiges of wilderness, and Mothers dream lives yet upon the wind.

The Eagle knows the dream is still alive, flickering in the darkness of mans mind. The beasts of the field and the winged ones that play above us are aware of the change. They have already evolved. Some remain here to assist us, as once again we are invited to join them, in yet another New World. They hold a very big key to our knowing the proper timing for the turning of the pages of an as yet little understood calendar. It can be seen in their eyes as they watch us, waiting for recognition, a signal that they know will come from us and us alone.

As I wrote in my book *Eye of the Shaman,* we are at the edge of time. We are well within the energies of *the Quickening.* We stand alone now in the Alchemical Garden of creation watching the beginning's of a process that until now was witnessed by a very few and only those who moved through the final stages of initiation. Now we are all upon this globe experiencing the Final Initiation. How amusing must we seem to the Elfin Folk, who observe us stumbling through our darkness, cursing the gifts that are being cast forth before us from the world still unseen by flesh caught in time. How amusing to the few amongst our own kind, who dared to awaken before the call is realized by the masses. For this is *our appointment with destiny* that will be kept by all. For no stone shall remain unturned as the wheat is shaken from the shaft.

It is both a time of blessings and a time of woe, depending upon ones attitude of perceptional worth. Those who are true of heart, who remain in reverence of the Sacred, will find the path made easier. Those who are caught up in their addictions to the illusions of a material world, who no longer are capable of feeling the Sacred, will find the path shall become an inescapable labyrinth of doubt and fear. They shall be caught up within their own webs, as the power of the old dream fades. For all things potentially, yet no thing materially, shall they find across the bridge between worlds. We can bring no thing from this world except that which is born of the Father- Mother within us all.

Those who loose the dream will see only emptiness within the endless myst. The Emergence of *the Fifth World* will continue to unfold like the petals of a flower before their eyes. One can not stop the seasons, any more then they can live with out consequence to the universal laws of Creation, the laws of Love. Creation can not be un-created, it can only be transformed into another expression, except when the fire within dies. *Five* is the number of man. This is his star, and his destiny. For 666 is but a tally of gold, while *555* is the tally of man. And his numbers shall be counted amongst the stars. For all are coming home in this time that we have come to call *the Quickening.*

Strange and abstract shall more become the order of the day. In many ways we are going to experience a sci-fi reality. For these changes you experience shall not be born of linear mind. Rather they shall be based upon creation from a limited reality by a being that is not acting from the whole of itself. Nor shall these changes be comprehended and therefore neither will they be embraced by the logic that man holds so dear. For what thoughts one embraces as the clock nears its appointed time, so shall it be.

What is being exposed presently is the mechanical manipulation of the time space continuum by man. In their madness to own the Earth, and control all her people some have attempted to control the very conscious of the species. There is a story that will unfold within the next four years in our counting that will shake the foundation of all linear thought, for man has broken the code of the universal law. Contracts were made with the lessor Gods of other worlds as well. Man is not just of this form, nor just of this Earth. We are not even the form we hold as judgement before a universe of which we presently know little more than nothing about.

Revelations and the Hall of Mirrors

many revelations will occur which shall reconnect you to a particular time sequence in the twentieth century. An experiment being conducted by the then *Third Riche*, which has been kept from you by your world governments, went awry. Thus, those who were in charge took desperate measures. Not all the influences regarding their decisions were solely of this Earth. There were, and continue to be, many partnerships being made between yourselves and the Ethereans. For the most part, the Ethereans, or inter-dimensional beings have been identified and placed into one general categorization titled ETs. The natural order of evolution was grossly overlooked in the mechanical manipulation of your realities. The result of which we are now experiencing, is in reaction with those manipulations, and therefore quite predictable. Although the final outcome of events now set into motion can not yet be seen. The reason for this is to allow you choice.

The concept of *Future* and *Past* are an alagam of the same experience. Much of what is occurring is due to manipulation of events and technology by those who have the ability to time travel. Much of what we are experiencing is actually the manipulation of what has already occurred thus affecting the outcome of the future events. As stated, a law has been violated. Part of what has been set into motion is the Earth Changes we are presently experiencing.

Earth Mother, Terra, Gaia has taken action to remedy a malformation in her own process of self-creation. She too is going through this Quickening. She too is transcending to yet another level of consciousness, and in fact already has. But we have as yet not grasped the understanding that because time is nothing, she can and has encapsulated us within our own dream state, to put it very simply. In doing so, we have been allowed to evolve within our own dimensional reality. Remaining seemingly separate from the whole. This is due mostly to our experience in limited consciousness, which is in truth the greater experiment going on here.

This may seem confusing so if you need, please read what has been said to this point once again. Feel it rather than try to intellectualize it. Try to flow with it! Read with your heart, for it can not be fooled, rather than with your mind, for it can be tricked. We are talking about manipulation of time, space continuum. We are talking about simultaneous realities being set into motion at once. Many people are in a manner of speaking, experiencing artificial time sequence events fusing with their real time sequence of events. Others still are caught in time loops. What was not yet understood at the time of the initiation of the experiments was that this galactic change, the shifting of the cosmic clock, would be occurring, and the least that it would be occurring so soon. Whether this was a deliberate withholding of information on the part of those who gave so freely the technology which would lead us to this cycle of self destruction, is another story in itself.

We have been given a gift of non-interference for the most part, until recently. There are those who have broken a galactic understanding and pirated, so to speak, into our encapsulated reality. Which is where our present day problems arise. As written in *Last Cry -- the contracts made between world leaders, during the 50's is up. The consequences have already begun. Only there are new elements to the game that again were not foreseen by those in the position of world power at the time. They have become victims of their own limited perceptions. Certain technology was in fact allowed to pass on with the understanding that it would eventually backfire on its initiators.*

The Nature of Reality ... Once Again

The changes that we are now entering into the throws of are twofold. We are dealing with those born of the Mother of all Mothers to facilitate a galactic shifting that effects the whole of the universe. On the other hand, we are facing changes that are the result of our ignorance, or innocence, which is a matter of interpretation of events. We have been told that Spider Grandmother herself has been summoned by *Great Mystery* to spin the webs of this new reality that we ourselves are dreaming. She has not done so since the beginnings of this time, the time just prior to our emergence into the Fourth World. I say innocence because much like children asleep, we are unaware that we are dreaming. We think that that which is the dream is real, and know not how to awaken. And like children we cry out in our confusion of emotions into the night. While the Mother of Mothers stirs in her sleep, hearing her children waking from a bad dream. She rises and seemingly stumbles through her own slumber to reach the cradle that within holds her precious gift to life.

Guided by her maternal instincts she is already schooled in precisely what is necessary to resolve the child's dilemma. And we, humanity, like the sleeping child, sound our annoyance at the motions she makes while reaching deep into our dream time. She helps us transcend realities, back into the moment. Kicking and screaming, we shall be taken up into the warmth of her arms and overpowered by her presence of love.

Perhaps for some it will feel as though it is the first time they have ever experienced this feeling. For many are wanderers, and have become lost in the darkness of their own hearts. There are many that live in a reality devoid of the emotion of human love. Thus the emotion has been lost to millions, as if stripped from cellular memory.

It is our inner most thoughts that weave the nature of our realities. We have so long forsaken the great truths of this dimension that now we cry out that we have lost touch with the Earth, but it is ourselves we have lost touch with. We no longer know what it is that we are. We no longer remember from whence we came into the flesh. For we are children of light and not a particum of us came from the darkness. Illusions are born of lack and ignorance, which are manifested as fears in attempts to manipulate and control the weak and the innocent. Oh, and how have managed to build a world of fear my fellow lords of light? One that is so subtlety woven through time manipulation by someone's maligned intent to cage the spirit of our brothers and sisters.

We ourselves are caught in the webs created by a thousand unenlightened life times. We indulged in darkness for the sake of the knowing. We have fallen to our depths in the density of 3rd dimensional reality. Some of us have begun to awaken and hear the calling of the heavens. We must find our way out of these labyrinths of our own weavings, built of our actions as well as our denial. We have become caught in the turning away, lost in despair as the light turns to shadow. Helplessness engulfs us as the Dream of humanity fades from view. We think that all we see is the suffering, which in reality does not exist except in the thoughts we embrace, and the love we continue to refuse to embrace.

Choice is the order of the day. We can still wake up our will -- that which is divine and part of the eternal stuff we are made of. You have come to a grand and wondrous ceremony. The Goddess herself demands your full awareness and presence at this event. We are all participating in the Great Initiation. As with all ceremonies we shall be tested under the fullness of the *Coyote Moon*. We shall experience all the faces we have worn, and all the rolls we have hidden behind. They shall become weights upon your embodiment until we find within ourselves the courage to strip them from our shining beautiful self and stand naked before our own God -- unadorned, as the light that we are. For our trappings do not impress the Creator of all things, nor do our words that change like the wind in the canyon. Only purity and simplicity of our light impresses the Creator of all things. All the trappings of the material world that we now hold so dear are already a part of our past.

That which we have that is more valuable than Gold we pay no reverence to, in fact we go so far as to deny its presence. For that which is within us that is considered a treasure to the whole of the universe is called the human spirit. The Spirit is the part of us that is God. The physical expression was the Idea, which was birthed by God, in the divine act of creation. Can't you feel the tears of your ancestors falling from the heavens; did you think it was just rain?

The Ethereans Interact with World Powers

Do you think yourself less then that raindrop, or to be less than the flower in the meadow, than the Butterfly in the field? Less perhaps, than the stars in the heavens? Do you think that perhaps we are the only star in the universe? If these things were true, which they are not, why then would you sit around in your contemplation expecting the Angels to come down from the heavens and save you? Is that not what you are telling one another in your churches? If the former were truth, the latter thoughts would be an indication of pure madness. Are there *angels* in your night skies? If there are beings from other worlds, given all the present data accumulated, indications are that they have had a long history with our race. Perhaps, just perhaps, the only reason why they have not blown us off the planet we are destroying is because we are something slightly more than we have been allowed to believe. Just perhaps this scenario was truth? What thoughts for the future of our race would you hold then? How would you view yourselves under the new paradigm that indeed we were divine in origin? And in fact, were the descendants of those great beings of light that still dwell in our heavens. *Imagine*...

Well, the stark reality is that there is no one who is coming to save you. There, that's the worst of it. Take your medicine of being responsible for your own outcome and hurry up and get well. There is no ship that is coming down from the night sky to lift you off this planet of misery and suffering. It is not going to happen. You can bank on it. There will be intervention only if the situation gets so bad that the Earth herself is placed in danger of not being able to recover from the malady our thought forms. I believe that we are already past this point. The interventions have begun. Gently, without force and undo aggression.

Those of you who regard yourself to be less than the flea, would also it seems expect the *Father* of all that is to drop what *he* is doing within ten billion universes and come to save little old you. This is a paradox, is it not? The same you, who does not even care enough to save him or herself? What kind of reasoning is this? Again we have a clear case of contradictory belief patterns, what is referred to as insanity! You are the one who gets yourself out of this pickle. You are the only one who is coming. You are the only one who is leaving. But the problem is we are not sure if we are coming or going for the most part, is it not?

We have given up our courage. We did so when we surrendered our spirits to some unseen higher force; the government, our parents, the authorities, the UN. We can no longer find our own path, so we bread a race to follow as a slave race. "*Work For the Company*!" Rabbits have more sense of individuality! We are a dis-empowered people on the whole. A mere race of sheep, and the Wolves are being isolated and hunted down.

We are afraid to practice much of what we know is spiritual truth. We can not even light a fire in our back yard in a lot of places. We can no longer camp in our National forests without permission. Nor can we walk along the beaches without a paid fare to do so. We are afraid to speak out if it is not what the masses concur is acceptable reality. If we choose to stand alone, then we can expect to be attacked through our children, in attempts to force us to conform. Yet we hold onto a dream of living in the land of the free. Strange thinking when you look at it, is it not? The norm has become to threaten as a means of getting one's way, and trying to control you. If the Phone company should make a mistake on your bill, too bad! However, if you forget to pay one month you are often promptly shut off, and a huge deposit is required the next month to turn your service back on.

What is about to occur in the human drama, is we are awakening to the awareness regarding the consequences our own creations. We are going to have to deal with the results of an artificial reality that no longer works. We are going to have to deal with awakening to the fact that thought actually does create. We have entered the *Hall of Mirrors*. Conditions that were manifested by non-other than ourselves will meet us head on. Artificial realities, and cosmic realities. Yes there is a grand plan woven throughout it all. Yes, there is a way back home, Dorothy! Precautions have been taken in the event that we should ever fall so completely asleep that we would no longer hear the inner voices of our own being.

There are also those events that are part of the grand cosmic clock, so to speak, that will transpire and we shall address both sides of the matter here. Let us begin with the weather. That is always a simple thing for us to experience the effects of on a universal level, regardless of culture, race, and belief patterns. It is amazing how undiscerning the wind can be. A *tsunami* does not care who we think we are or are not, nor does a hurricane, or any other 'natural disaster.'

El Nino ... World wide Consequences

So disrupted and severely damaged are the layers that compose our atmosphere that at this time which way the tides will turn is still an unpredictable reality, employing the scope of science as we have know it. Here lies a major factor as to why direct intervention from our *Brothers beyond the Sun* has come about. For the sake of the planet -- rather than the politics of the situations (which is one of the reasons why they have remained anonymous.)

My *sources* have informed me that our world leaders have been given a time allotment in which to rectify the situation regarding Earth's environment. By the time this writing is published, that time allotment will be even shorter. Those who call themselves 'the watchers' know that to achieve this with the technology mankind presently has is possible. If a considerable change is not realized by the end of the allotted time period, there will be intervention from those who come from the stars, as well as those who come from the Inner Earth. Those within the inner earth have also been warned, both the terran races and the extraterrestrials who dwell there.

Yes, there is indeed an Inner Earth. It is an ancient place that is known to those from beyond the Sun as Agharta. It is a place where those who are often referred to as the "*old ones*" retreated to during the last holocaust, and have chosen to remain unto this time. You see, they are not of the violent nature of those who inhabit the surface world. They have evolved far beyond the warring beings that dwell upon the surface of this planet. They are the advanced races. Their abilities in the realms of higher consciousness are approximately three thousand years advanced from those of the surface dwellers.

They are directly involved with our brothers from beyond the Sun in the process that has become known as *the Quickening*. It is a last ditch effort to accelerate the evolution of your species, to develop mankind beyond the instincts of warring and the emotions of self-destruction before the great change is upon us. This shifting has happened before upon this planet -- only not to this extent. It is well known by those who are presently in positions of world power that the effects of the shifting will be permanent and unavoidable. These changes will effect those below the Earth's surface as well as those who create their realities upon its surface.

The Earth is a mobile of simultaneously existing realities. Some of them side by side, others far apart. Mankind is the furthest removed from any form of connection to the earth grid than any other species upon this plane. And there are many! When the balance of the inner universes of Earth become as disrupted as they have, the very core of the Earth spins out of balance. When this occurs, there will be many reactions upon the surface, as well as below the surface. There now exists an imbalance at the very core of the Earth! As a living biosphere, Spaceship Earth is in trouble. "Hello, Houston? We have a problem!"

Let us speak of this El Nino, which is directly connected, to the phenomenon of global warming. For years now, scientists employed by the government have all but denied the development of global warming, minimizing any potential for hazard. You have taken them at their word, up to this point. Now, however, they have reversed their public position and they are telling you that indeed global warming is truly a reality. Ask yourself, is it your scientists who have changed their positions of declared truths, or is it your spiritual messengers that shift with the conveyance of the times?

At first, this El Nino appeared to be a splotch of unusually warm tropical air that was lodged in the midst's of the Pacific Ocean. The size of this 'splotch,' however, has continued to grow at a phenomenal rate. Scientists, with understandable concern, are tracking its progress. This reflects that El Nino, that unpredictable spirit of the atmosphere, and its dance with the ocean is indeed gathering strength. Based on its present, unexpected rate of growth, there are no predictable limitations to its final state of maturity.

This El Nino, it would seem, is preparing to unleash its ire upon our planet, targeting the America's most specifically with meteorological havoc and mayhem. The full extent of which and the consequences thereof can only be guessed at the present moment. This El Nino, apparently, is to be experienced rather than patterned. The tropical storms in the Pacific at this time are of unusual size and power. Further, they are occurring outside of what we have come to call normal weather patterns, defying any existing methodology ... **Hurricanes in Phoenix?**

Traditionally, El Ninos appear every five to seven years. Lately, El Ninos seem to be forming every 16 to 18 months, another physical sign of *the Quickening* ... further testament to the extent of which we have placed things out of balance upon our planet. Yet, as a species, we continue to experiment with HAARP and other means of weather manipulation, particularly through our military installations, on a global level.

Storms causing torrential downpours have already begun in Chile and Peru, leaving them in states of complete disaster with continuing conditions of massive mudslides and the flooding of plains areas. Some of the flooding is so severe that at this point, isolated areas are seeing as much as 3 to 5 inches of rain within just a few hours. In these areas it is believed that many new lakes have begun to form. El Nino shows us it's reverse side in the draught conditions occurring in Australia and Indonesia. Eastern Brazil is experiencing a torturous draught, which threatens to devastate the economy. The entire Pacific Rim is feeling the effects of this El Nino. This translates to the fact that the entire weather machine of planet Earth is now under the direction of this El Nino as it nears a size of greater than 7,000 square miles or more than a quarter of the Earth's circumference.

Temperatures upon the Oceans' surfaces are rising so rapidly that they have already surpassed the conditions recorded in 1982 when that El Nino left thousands dead, hundreds of thousands homeless and greater than $13 Billion in economic disasters world wide. Scientists at Columbia University in New York recorded that at the time, this was the biggest El Nino in history. Already in Mexico Hurricane Pauline has left well over a thousand dead, with countless thousands of people homeless. This means that people who were already living under poor conditions are in an even worse situation, if that is possible! How do the homeless become more homeless??

We have already, as of November 1997, seen well over 2,000 people loose their lives, and tens of thousands become homeless due to the onslaught of this El Nino. Keep in mind that it has still not reached its predicted peak. What will happen when the next El Nino comes on the tail of this one in `98?

Devil Winds

It has been observed that El Ninos traditionally reach maximum strength in late December. Perhaps that is why the Peruvian fisherman and farmers dubbed the phenomena El Nino in the first place... A term which translates to "*the Christ Child.*" Scientist presently are predicting that if the heat coming off the Oceans' surfaces continues to rise, resulting temperatures could increase as much as 3.5° to 8°C. If this happens, the effects would be felt far into the spring of 1998. Among the most common disasters that we could expect around the area of the Pacific Rim would be extremely unpredictable weather such as; flash floods, landslides and droughts, resulting in traumatic crop failures. Blizzards will turn to Indian Summer conditions within perhaps days. We could see crop yield production reduced by as much as 75% over the next 7 months as a result of this El Nino.

We can expect the fishing industry to change radically on a global level as a result of this El Nino. Many of the waters to the South and North of the equator, which normally run cold, will see temperature increases of as mush as 15-20°C. Already we have had multiple confirmed reports of; Marlin being caught off the coast of Oregon, Anchovies being caught off Argentina, and tropical fish along the Oregon coast. Similar findings are now turning up on the East Coast with tropical fish being caught and sighted off Long Island, New York.

We must also realize that this heating of the Pacific Ocean, and now the Atlantic Ocean, will stimulate the growth of bacteria, both natural as well as that which is resulting from the dumping of toxic waste. Severe Red Tide Conditions can be expected. We will experience severe pollution as a result of this along the coastal waters from South America to Alaska, and from Florida to New England, which is already in serious trouble. And remember, what goes up from the Ocean forms clouds and comes down as rain upon the land. It is all connected, you know. This is part of what the Cogi Indians were trying to tell us years ago.

We will see unusual and radical shifts in the temperatures across the US, such as: Strange warm winds that bring about dangerous, killer lightning storms throughout the North West, ranging well into the Great Plains. Hail the size of golf balls or better. Snow falling in great Abundance upon the Glacial Peaks, only to be washed away by freak downpours a few weeks later due again to these strange warm winds, which will then bring on the flooding again. These 'strange warm winds' are what many of the Native Elders refer to as *the Devil Winds*.

Other odd and catastrophic natural calamities will occur, such as: Landslides are going to be common place. Many roads will be closed to travel due to these flood conditions. This means that trucks will not be able to get supplies into many of the rural areas that have become dependent upon food and supplies form outside areas. In many areas, the trucking industry will come to a standstill.

The Dancing Devils - El Nino, La Nina and El Viejo

Keep in mind that the rising and falling of temperatures will be severe, as much as 40° to 70° F in the space of couple of hours. As a result of the climatic chaos, we are going to experience the collapsing of many industries including fishing, agricultural, retail and transportation. People are going to be hard hit who do not have foods and herbs stored up. Medicine will also be hard to come by. Only private individuals with the abilities to produce tinctures, and who have access to stored grains will be able to bring things into many areas, or in many cases -- survive.

These are all results of our tampering with the atmosphere. Tampering undertaken without the slightest regard for the consequences of our actions. Yes... Atlantis, again.... Will we ever learn?

The El Nino, because of the nature of its character (see Illustration) is causing changes in ocean currents as well as the jet stream patterns. Therefore, we can expect weather to also be coming from unusual directions. If we look at the weather satellite maps up on the Internet or on our local TV stations, we can already see unusual things occurring in this area. There will be extreme

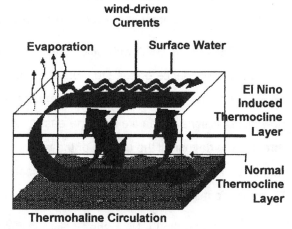

shifts experienced in these patterns as the oscillation of the Wind and Ocean currents meet head on. This oscillation is referred to as the ENSO cycle. What does this mean literally?

We will experience radical shifting between El Nino (the boy) and La Nina (the girl,) and sometimes the El Viejo (the Old Man.) The extreme oscillation of this ENSO cycle will cause a pendulum effect as the weather swings back and forth with increasing uncertainty, which will also contribute to crop failure, and not knowing when to plant crops. As the seasons will oscillate with the same irregularity as the temperatures.

There has begun a churning or stratification of the ocean waters. This process occurs naturally due to the physics of the ENSO Cycles. To get a better understand this, if one envisions in their mind a satellite picture of the Pacific Ocean...one would first observe strong trade winds blowing East to West, carrying water away from South America towards Indonesia. The resulting condition is that in fact the ocean is considerably lower (in elevation) on the Peruvian coast than it is on any point on the Indonesian coast. These conditions occur when the ENSO cycle is in its neutral or cold phase. This cycle is the La Nina, or little girl cycle.

The consequences of this are very dramatic in the overall picture of events though unnoticeable to the eye on the Earth level. The ocean, being a living organism, will attempt to replace the water the trade winds have blown off the Peruvian coast. The process the ocean uses in this effort creates what is termed *Thermohaline Circulation,* when the Ocean brings up very cold water from its depths, which creates the Thermocline layer. A mixing occurs by natural means creating a layer of cool water, which is then used to regulate the surface water tendency to heat up from the sun.

The waters that are found in the Thermocline layer are naturally rich with life sustaining nutrients. We also have another effect at play here. Because of events occurring beneath the oceans surface due to increased volcanic activity, this water is unusually warm thus creating an abundance of micro organisms living in the replacement water.

The obvious result we would notice is that at first the waters off the Peruvian coast will now support an abundance of sea life. But there is also a negative effect as well. Bacteria will now proliferate in the warmer waters. The concern is the underlying incubation of *Pfiesteria,* which is now killing billions of sea life from the east Coast of the US to the North Sea. It is a cancer that threatens to devour all the oceans of the world. A direct result of this is the millions of fish, aquatic mammals and other oceanic life, most noticeably -- turtles, developing oozing sores and tumors. These life forms are presently dying all along the eastern waters of America.

Following the La Nina, the El Nino shift occurs. El Nino acts up and the trade winds shift radically. ENSO is moved into a positive or warm phase. At first, the Trade Winds may dwindle, then actually start moving from the opposite direction, West to East. Therefore, the up-swelling of the ocean waters off the Peruvian coast stops, in essence, and the micro biotic life as well as the fish feeding off the micro biotic life move to a different area. We will observe a flip-flopping of oceanic environments, so to speak. Much like we surface two-leggeds will experience this winter upon the land. This constant flip-flopping can cause sufficient stress to sea life that, coupled with the conditions created by pollution, is causing many species that were in abundance just two years ago to now die off. I have received reports from friends in Alaska that there were almost no Salmon migrating into the Copper River Basin in Cordova, Alaska.

Coastal Peru is not by any means the only area effected by this action of the ocean. This effect is being felt from Argentina to Alaska. If all this were happening in the Pacific Rim locality alone, on a global map, it would be devastating to the overall balance of the Oceanic Eco-system. Instead, all this is happening globally. Can you see the potential for the enormous catastrophic potential? Normally, the Thermocline layer of chilly water separates the cold deep waters from the warmed sunny waters that reside near the ocean surface. This El Nino will alter that in-between the shifts, having a neutral effect on the environment – momentarily, everything goes upside down. This causes a downward effect upon the Thermocline layer.

Normally in the Pacific, this chilly water mixes with the warm surface water, cooling it. When the El Nino enters, this chilly water goes to very deep depths and the surface water then rises to noticeably higher temperatures, higher by as much as 10° to 15° C. Thus life cycles and conditions in these regions are altered considerably. Whale and Dolphin migrations, for example, have already been radically altered. Tropical fish have begun to appear in unusual waters, such as the Marlin off the Oregon and the Washington coast, the Anchovies off the Argentine coast, etc....

Perhaps this is answering how this El Nino will have global consequences?

Mitakyue Oyasin, We are All Connected in the Web of Life

We are now receiving reports that Pacific waters that are normally 50°- 60°F are, at the time of this writing, reaching temperatures of 70° – 80° F. These warm currents are moving Northward, warming the waters from the Oregon Coast up to Alaska. Hence, we see fishermen catching Marlin off the Oregon Coast. The Pacific's Thermocline is now far below the surface, throwing the entire ecosystem of the Ocean off balance.

The main factor of this phenomenon that is effecting the weather on a global level has to do with the heat. It is like when we place new logs on the Lodge fire, we are feeding the fire, causing it to grow even hotter, creating more and larger flames. So it is with El Nino. We now have storms that are unfamiliar. They are not like anything 'modern' man has encountered. They are more powerful and larger storms than have been seen before. The Winds are following the new currents, and we are experiencing new storm belts, larger ones at that! The heat is also rising, effecting the jet streams, which govern the movement of weather patterns globally. This rearrangement of the Pacific weather patterns has totally altered the global weather patterns.

We are seeing draughts in North Eastern Brazil, South Africa, and Australia as well. While the American Southwest is experiencing torrential rains and floods. Science is only beginning to map out the probable Climatological *Connections* to this *web of life* spun across the planet.

The jet streams act as connecting links to weather cycles around the world. A slight shifting of these tracks in the Northern Hemisphere can be expected to cause storms and very wet weather to move in a Southerly direction. Keep in mind that even a slight shifting in the other direction would be expected to cause severe snow as well as Arctic like conditions in the North. The shifts caused by the El Nino effect that we are presently experiencing are fluctuating so rapidly, they are resulting in totally erratic movements of the jet streams. The jet streams can no longer serve as predictable weather tracks, as they have for hundreds of years. This is going to make it very difficult for our friends who compose *the Farmers Almanac* this year to keep their predictions accurate, for sure!

The nature of the Storms we can expect this winter will be strange, to say the least. There will be hot winds that seemingly come from out of no where, while within a matter of hours we could experience radical drops in temperatures. Severe lighting storms will add to the chaotic weather patterns and have devastating effects. You could very well see 70° temperatures in Montana in February, blizzards in Phoenix, flooding in desert areas, and firestorms in rain forest areas which are coming under the effects of drought. All are real possibilities. The South West can expect better than a 50% increase in the amount of precipitation. For instance, in Northern Arizona we could see 200+ inch snow falls.

This El Nino's effect on world industries will go beyond farmers, ranchers and fisherman. We can expect commodity traders to loose, and in many instances, almost entirely. Water, and other natural resources will be heavy hit, water has already become a commodity. (Water for $1.59 a liter?!?) Not to speak of the overtime that insurance underwriters will be putting in until the funds are no longer available. Many insurance companies are already not underwriting insurance policies in certain areas that are proving to be climatically unstable.

Setting up stores of food, and medicinal herbs would be highly recommended. If you have not already begun to secure these items, **find people who have and start networking**. Seeds, **organic seeds**, are going to be very valuable this spring, and you had better plan on green house growing conditions. The price of foodstuff in the market place is going to go sky high...when it is available.

The planet is heating up with atmospheric gases, and we have entered *stage one* of *the Green house effect* you've heard so much about from environmentalists. A note of interest, which may be hard for your egos to take, is that from the aspect of the divine game of life, there is going to be a social experiment. The experiment is designed to see how well we interact under the coming climatic changes that are in store with the approaching millennium.

The Birthing Time - the Time of the Purification Begins

hile we are experiencing the chaos of the surface world, there will be equally severe climatic reverberations going on beneath the surface. These changes will be going on beneath the Ocean's surface as well, even below the tectonic plates. The egg of the Phoenix is fracturing, and the Phoenix is struggling to emerge. The shell (Earth) is fracturing, and the Phoenix (Fifth World) is being born. The New Earth in accordance with the prophecies is beginning to take form. The cosmic soup is beginning to boil. It is a time of

Birthing, and the groundwork is being staged for *the Purification* the Hopi have tried so desperately to warn us was coming.

The movement of the Magma below the Earth's surface is also causing a changing in the character of the Earth's magnetic fields. This 'new Earth' has within it new magnetic particles which are aligning themselves with the fluctuating magnetic fields. They are acting independently from existing Earth, and cause in this action a polar reversing in the energy fields of the Earth. That translates to confused geophysical communication, which will filter down the life chain and materialized as confusion in humans as well as animals. Thus the thinking process within the brain matter, which is conducted through electrical impulses, will fall into chaos.

We still have the ability to soften the effects of the outcome of this drama, or we can sit back and do nothing. The latter of which has its own consequences. So the crux of the experiment is to determine humanity's ability to work together in harmony, using technology for positive ends is up for utilization. If we do nothing, well, someone else might step into the picture... which will have its consequences, will it not? The warnings have been given out to the world governments. Now they are going to be brought to the people, those who are open to an alternative to decadence. It has been called the War with Valued Life. The message is a simple one, "Wake up and Live!"

Once quiet and pristine, the Andeluvean world beneath our oceans was where those beings who elected to live the more peaceful and tranquil life choose to explore. That was long ago in a world that is lost somewhere in legend. A world that was older even than the tales of Avalon, older than memory. It was when Dolphins and Humans parted ways, one to the ocean world ... the other to the world of land dwellers. During the bridging of this transition the legends of Mermaids, and Mermen came into fruition. There are many stories of these times written in the ancient texts, which have been, because of our amnesia, good material for Fairytales. Now we shall see the merging of these realities come into our reality awareness once again. For we have entered what could be called a new kind of Fairytale.

There is so much that could be said about the subterranean world, the land of the Smokey Sun, the inner Earth, known to many as *Agharta*. There are many of these *legends* that have been recorded down throughout human history. Once it was written in oriental text how even the great Ganjas Kahn was stopped along his trail of conquests by the King of the Earth. His men ran in fear as this magnificent being rose from an opening in the Earth. Having been disturbed by the ravaging of war upon the surface by the Kahn and his marauding armies, the Lord of the Inner Earth decided to do something about it. The Great Khan, it is told, was instructed to return to his homeland, and to find peaceful means to resolve the problems of the empire he had created, or face an unpleasant ending. If it were not for this intervention he most likely would have continued straight through Europe. No other explanation seemed feasible to the ancients as to why the march of this invincible army was abruptly ended and returned to their homelands.

I once was gifted with a copy of Admiral Bird's personal diary. In his dairy, Admiral Bird speaks quite plainly about the presence of a very advanced race he encountered at the North Pole. Regarding the question as to the validity of his story? You and I are left with the wondering of how exactly he did manage to travel all those extra hundreds of miles and return, when there was no physical way his plane could carry enough fuel aboard for such an extended venture. (Keep in mind, there are no fueling stations at the North Pole!) To every doubt there is an unexplained factor of physical validity. Legends do not come from the air. Birthed by unexplainable facts, this is why legends, more often than not, outlive the civilization that created them. We are finding more and more that those 'legends' are being validated as technology evolves.

Fire, Earth, Wind and Water ... Purging by the Elements

Throughout the Pacific Rim, new Earth is forming. This new Earth will form the new landmasses that are already rising to form the continental configurations. There is, resulting from the fluid character of the movement of the inner Earth matter, or magma, a rocking that is occurring. Present landmasses are rising and then dropping, then grinding up against each other. This is being caused by the movement of magma and the water that runs through and around, and in some cases through the tectonic plates themselves. This geophysical occurrence is also causing a flip-flopping of our environmental conditions, the reverberations of which are being felt from Australia to Alaska, as well as from Japan to Mexico.

We are experiencing a churning within the geo-layers of other regions with this active movement of the tectonic plates. There is a very active fluctuating movement occurring at this time from Central Mexico to as far away as the East Coast of America. No thing upon this Earth is fixed. Earth is a living organism that is adapting to its own growth, undiscerning of what the Human drama may conclude within its limited perceptions of physics. There is a fissuring and fracturing that is occurring which will most likely be first felt in the Nevada and Oregon areas. These areas are mostly built upon layers of basalt, which is quite unstable, and water solvent. In Central America, Mexico will be hard hit by geophysical change this coming year, as well as experiencing intense flood damage, due to the unusual storms that are already impacting the land.

It is now common knowledge, accessible everywhere, that there is great activity near the Cascades as Rainier readies itself to let loose some built up energy. There are many new *hot spots* being created hydro-thermally beneath the Earth's surface throughout these areas. Fissures are opening in the external crust of the Earth. This is a part of the Mother's process to relieve the pressure from below. New Earth is created through intense heat, i.e.: lava flow. This process is actually quite like what happens to the Human body when it is recovering from wounds. Although in this scenario, the presence of the intense heat in the body of man is experienced as a fever. The fever is a body's way of healing itself and destroying its enemy, or infection.

It does not take a trained scientist to notice that with this intensity of build up something is about to blow. The balance of alternative "release valves" which have been easing the pressure up until now, is being effected by the continued deterioration of the infrastructure which is made up almost entirely of basalt. On the surface, plants, as well as insects, are already going through very noticeable signs of transformation.

We are seeing many new species, as well as a noticeable degree of mutations in animals. In the Southwest we have four-eared jack rabbits, five legged frogs, fish and turtles with tumors, etc.… Crossbreeding of other species. In the Northwest I have even seen three horned deer! There have been occurrences of the dying off of millions of frogs, and honeybees in many areas. We are seeing species appearing in areas they have never been known to habitat before. The mammals that these changes seem to be especially noticeable in are the rodent families during these early stages of the Earth changes.

Regarding the geo-thermal activity, rock formations and the transformation of landmasses: Anyone who has ever had the misfortune of accidentally placing basalt into a lodge fire knows first hand how volatile this material is when heated. Gas pockets explode sending missiles hurdling through the air at such a high velocity that they could kill some one as quickly as a bullet. Take into account the heat build up that is occurring beneath the Earth's surface along the Cascade Range. Factor in the occurrence of some rocks breaking off beneath the Earth's surface (some larger than a football field.) Given this equation, even a rocket scientist can figure out that there is going to be some rumbling happening in 1998!

Underground streams and rivers are changing course very rapidly. There are reports that the course of some rivers has moved as much as several hundred feet. In other areas, like Sedona Arizona, they are simply disappearing, "drying up," where they have been a constant for centuries. Also, the depths at which wells have formally been functioning without a problem is no longer the case. Many farmers, ranchers, and homeowners have to dig down much deeper, or find a new well site completely, because the old ones are drying up. When this type of phenomenon starts to happen in widespread areas, it is very serious and needs to be looked at, at much deeper levels if we are to see the long-range potential outcomes.

The watershed in Northern New Mexico that has surrounded the Taos Basin and fed the western states of New Mexico, Oklahoma and Texas for untold thousands of years is rapidly reaching critical lows. In Nevada, up in the Virginia City Highlands, many of the old mining shafts are flooding, as new water veins seem to be opening up beneath the surface. Water tables have, in some areas of New Mexico, dropped as much as 750°. This is true especially in Clayton and the area that has been called the Kiowa Grasslands. Vast amounts of water being drained to feed new wheat and corn crops, that have replaced the traditional ranching as ranchers scramble to try to make ends meet and hold on a fast disappearing way of life, have contributed to this. Water is also being drained to feed the population explosion that is occurring in the Phoenix area, as Californians continue to evacuate *Paradise Lost* by the thousands each month, and others move in search of safe harbor. Some just abandoned their homes and former ways of life, simply counting their losses.

One of the geophysical factors that is resulting from the water movement beneath the Earth's surface is that there are a lot of hollow areas that once facilitated the water, which are now in danger of collapse, and some are filling with natural gasses. Heat alone is not the sole cause of underground gas pockets exploding. Build up in pressure between the layers of basalt, granite, and shale can reach such intensities that explosions will occur, as the pressure finds the weakest flaw in the infrastructure and seeks an outlet of relief. Also, lightning upon the Earth's surface can ignite the gas as it nears the surface of the soil and firestorms result, then it is a matter of chain reaction.

Throughout the West, especially Oregon, Montana and New Mexico, there are thousands of miles of tunnels and caverns which are the result of the last cataclysmic experience of the Earth Changes. Never mind the thousands of miles of man made tunnels and massive underground development by the military. These areas are literally honey combed with tunnels and are very unstable at this time.

The Salt Lake City area is also an area that is to be watched. The Great Salt Lake is steadily receding, leaving its own honey combed effect and the movement of plates in that area is beginning to pick up. Some cracks I've seen in the mountains around Kanab, Utah seem to have opened as much as two feet in the past few years. One could say the ground was walking Westward and Northward!

As the El Nino activity continues to intensify, and it will, there will be heavy flooding and severe fluctuation in temperatures. This condition will bring about the appearance of the *Devil Winds*. Sudden yet isolated winds storms that will have gusts of wind of 100 to 200 miles per hour. Situations with weather fluctuations will only worsen. The influx of spring breakup compounded by now weakened surfaces and the dying of vegetation that once held the soil together will leave erosion to take care of the rest. March will be a rough month for many. We can expect heavy rain and snowmelts to create conditions that will encourage massive flooding throughout the Southwest and the dessert areas, all the way up the Kootanies through Montana and Idaho.

Emotional Storms ... the Hall of Mirrors

This El Nino and its intensity are physical developments of our own actions. The direct results of the deliberate manipulation of the forces of nature without regard for the consequences. This El Nino is also a reflection of what we are already experiencing within the realm of our inner Emotional Storms. As with an El Nino, emotionally there will be a steady build up of chaotic energies. That build up will start in Mid October and have come to a head by mid November, 1997. This has to do with changes that are occurring throughout the universe. Until now we have been sheltered from them. With the Cosmic Clock ticking ever closer to midnight, and we are already well past the eleventh hour, we are talking minutes before the Shift takes on a character and motion of its own that can not be predicted by anyone from this dimension or the next.

The atmosphere that surrounds the Earth is much like the auric field that surrounds our physical bodies. Once there was a natural flow, a correct movement of energies, a Feng Shui that surrounded us. Just as there was once a natural collaboration of the elements within the atmosphere surrounding our planet that protected us from negative outside influences. Due to the weakened condition of the human spirit we hardly have enough energy as a species to keep ourselves in balance if conditions were normal.

Changes can be expected to be swift and radical in nature. Regarding the consciousness of the masses, the socially unconscious will move from one perception to another within very short periods of time. Trauma will be experienced on almost every social level as the fires of human emotional changes sweep over the globe. America, being less steeped in the cultural restraints that govern other regions of the globe, will be very hard pressed for peaceful emotions during this time as we enter the *Hall of Mirrors*.

The 16th Insight

We are being tempered in the initiation to develop our emotional strengths. We will find with increasing intensity, that we will be faced with the consequences of our deeds, both of action and of thought. The very foundations of our core belief systems are going to be tested. Many foundations, which have been built upon inaccurate or manipulated and false conclusions, are gong to collapse. Everyone will feel the *Winds of Change* tearing them apart emotionally, ripping them from their life patterns by the roots as they are removed from our consciousness. It is for clearing the field and preparing for the new paradigm that is coming, and coming quickly.

We will experience these storms and react to the shifting and flip-flopping of our emotional states much as the Ocean is reacting to El Nino and the *Devil Winds*. We will feel strange calms, almost neutral emotional states, as we are under the effect of La Nina, the little girl, then El Nino will come in and there will be very dramatic shifting in our emotional feelings and out looks. This will lend to very stressful human psyche conditions. The results of our reactions to how things effect us in the everyday occurrences of the dream will take a very heavy toll on the body emotionally.

We will go from this strange placid calm, which leaves us wondering if we in fact have any feelings about things at all, to heated impassioned reactions to situations as they come our way. Life is a constant river where we are going from one emotional encounter to the next without a break in the flow. But with the El Nino effect our reactions will be highly charged. So expect a lot of overreacting.

Allow yourself the grace to change. You are going to have to develop your adapters and be able to take control over your emotional freak-outs in a moment, or risk the chance of irreparable damages to your self and those around you. You are quite literally going to feel the *Web of Life*, like a robe over your body. You will need to develop a strong discipline to bring yourself to a place of neutrality, as well as the ability to catch yourself in mid flight of the drama and simply stop. Remember, you **are** the director of your life's experience, and not merely the actor.

We are not necessarily creating reality with each thought. Some thoughts are simply observation and never acted upon. Then again, we are not always in thought. What about those spaces in between thoughts, where is the real you then? When you have your eyes open you are in thought, but when your eyes are closed, when you blink, where does the conscious you go? When the heat of the El Nino effects your body, which is in reality a miniature encapsulated ocean, are you fully responsible for your actions? Are you in ownership of every emotion you have, or are you caught without power in a reactionary state of helplessness?

And when the old man, EL Viejo, comes knocking, will you be forced to deal with the extreme mood swings? Yes, you will if you have taken the time to develop your personal power and are in control of your emotions, if you are coming from the Father-Mother within your divine self. If you are, however, coming from ego, from altered ego that is, you will be subject to the laws that effect the existence of the ego in that altered state. Meaning, your perception of what is really going on in any situation will be warped. Warped to accommodate the limited ability of the altered ego to recognize its own existence.

The altered ego lives in a reactionary world, a world where it is constantly requiring the approval of others to justify its actions and decisions. It is a world where you are always living for the approval of every one outside of you, never being allowing of self, never accepting self, which is why its position on all matters is always shifting. Just like the flip-flopping of the El Nino. The altered ego is not sure of what it is because it is only the reflection of the real you. Therefore, it never knows where it stands on any issue. It will stand until the *Winds of Change* seem stronger than itself. Then it will compromise its position and sacrifice its *state of 'isness'* to comply with the pressure being applied from outside its reality. It is survival motivated and God ignorant.

When El Viejo comes he is like an old wizard, and has no caring for what is within the realms of your accepted reality. He is locked in his ways, and he has come to stir things up. This old wizard will do his job, only your intent can cause him to stop long enough for you to regain control over the supernatural forces he creates with his stirring of the *caldron of dreams*. El Viejo will remove all that does not belong, all that is out of harmony with the divine plan for the Mothers Dream. Perhaps you will even feel the effect of La Vieja, the old woman.

La Vieja will take your emotions and swirl them around until you are so wrapped up in them that you can feel nothing else. It is like an electrical current. Once it has a hold of you, neither you nor the current can let each other go, until one of you breaks the connection, usually through trauma, or you simply pass out.

You see, we think that everything upon this planet is cold factual science. We perceive earth as a thing with no consciousness of its own. I.e.: The Wind is just the Wind. Lost within our spell of limited reality we do not even have a clue as to what its true essence is. Never mind how it works. To all things there is a spirit, and essence of divine nature. To all things there is a degree of emotion and force. All that surrounds us is articulately alive, and filled with the life force. El Nino is a series of spirits, elements, reflective of the different ages and genders of us all.

Nature is playing with us according to what our roles of reality have dictated. We have denied her world, her plans, her dignity, and her laws. We are annihilation her world when ever we get the chance, by what ever means we deem necessary without regard of consequence. So we are now in the absence of balance. We are left with the world we created and all of its synthesis. A world dominated by human consciousness, where the game is played by human rules. The elements are within as they are without. That which man walks upon and through also moves within him.

Being caught under the spell of limited reality, we believe ourselves to be separate from things. We think that when we are in connection to their spirit essence, when we acknowledge the essence that is divine within them, they acknowledge what is divine within us. At that point an agreement of cooperation can occur, which when mastered, allows one to walk on water. It is a matter of cooperation, and not domination. Man has the ability to master the elements as Lord's of light. The elements, which possess their own consciousness, their own divine spark from the source, will respond with willing affirmation to those desires, but only when the message comes from the heart. Nature always has and always will embrace us in the Dance of life.

When you love the Earth she will respond with a reflection of what you are sending her emotionally, and what your true feelings are inside. We are composed of what she is. She has given us the gift of the body to experience the dream we call life with. The realization of this relationship owned can bring us to a state of harmonic convergence with the elements where, even though we walk through the storm we shall experience the calm around us.

To those who are fragmented and lost in the spell of limited reality, who allowed themselves to get stuck in the encasement of their altered egos, this will be a time of experiencing much emotional anguish. This time will have occurred between October of 1997 and April of 1998. We are going once again through an initiation, and the elements are the vehicle of the deliverance of that initiation. We are experiencing the full impact of our creations through thought forms. How we walk through these storms and the impact they have upon our lives is all a matter of attitude held. There are those that are the emanations, those that are the players, those who are the observers, and those that are the creators. Which one do you choose to be?

Many will experience situations where it appears as if their entire life were being scrutinized and placed on trial by those around them. Gossip and stories will come about out of nowhere that have no validity, for reasons that can't be understood. It will be almost as if your enemies were mocking, or taunting you to create within you internal levels of anger, and switch you to recourse born of violence. You must resist with all that you hold dear and fine within you. It is a test. Most of this will most likely be coming from those individuals who have no life of their own, therefor they would desire to live yours. And if everything is going wrong in their lives it must be your fault. They are those who are incapable of free thought and discernment of the heart.

You might discover through this process of experience that you have enemies who will seem to come out of the woodwork like phantoms. They are not real, the scene around you is not real. It is not personal. They are mirror reflections, but can you tell the reflections from the real experiences? Can you tell your real thought from the illusion? Remember that it is the *Hall of Mirrors*, and these are the tests. As consciousness continues to implode, you will find the experienced reality will take on more and more of a dream state quality. We must learn to make the transition to *anological mind*, as *binary mind* looses its hold, and life experiences born of binary mind become increasingly abstract. I talk about this, and many ways of revitalizing your own power in my written work *The Eye of the Shaman*.

Often it will seem that at times there had to be some covert plot to destroy you by your phantom assailants who now have a phantom conspiracy engaged against you. We are going to experience a synthetic consciousness, which we have created as our imprisonment. The *Hall of Mirrors* is a virtual reality game in every sense. So know if we do not have a strong sense of who we truly are, we will get caught up in the illusions created by our untruths. If we are not living the life we truly hold as our chosen path, if we are not walking that path with heart, we will be blown off course. This is what is required to walk the *Good Red Road*. If we have based our position, as a being, as a parent, as a lover, as a friend, as a woman, as a man, as a professional, etc..., upon illusions, we will fall and fall hard. Have you ever experiences sailing through a squall with your sails up and full, not knowing how to tack the boat into the wind? It can be rough going, and you could wind up out of control and upon the rocks or capsized very quickly.

Life really is very fair, although people can often seem not to be so at times. If we look to people solely for our understandings, we will more often than not find ourselves disappointed. That is equal to looking for solace of spirit, in the supermarket of human consciousness. The human mind is not always clear and its perception is not necessarily the reality of Creator, or of the Mother. **Is.** Does this mean that people are bad? No, not at all. We the People are all just children looking for the answers. Many simply just haven't found theirs. They may not even be real; they might be emanations of humanity. What to do, what to do.....

A big key to getting through this maze is to walk through our experiences as they come up and deal with each, one at a time. Then turn them around by owning our truth in each situation, taking our stand and drawing lines both within us and with others. We will be building self-empowerment, and creating a new image of ourselves, an image of ourselves that is clear **where** we are standing in the light. By our creating this energy within ourselves, we will radiate this to those we come in contact with, and all that is around us will respond to the light of the God within.

Consciousness is also a living thing. It is organic. Human consciousness, despite what the external expressions might appear to be showing us, wants very much to achieve the dream, also. Despite what our priests have been telling us for thousands of years, 'perpetuating the great lie' that we are separate from and unworthy of God. We are very, very loved. Every precaution is being allowed, every opportunity to turn human destiny around is being afforded us during this transition of consciousness.

Proper Attitude is essential! Do we have the ability to hold the attitude *of I am Happy, I am Beauty, I experience Joy? Everyone around me is the reflection of my joy and my attitude. I will enjoy this moment as if it were my last.* If one persists in making life a struggle, why not consider struggling for a just cause? Why not happiness? The state of happiness takes just as much energy to maintain as does the state of misery. Poverty takes just as much energy to maintain, as does abundance. It is a matter of what you choose. What we put out is going to come right back to us in manifested form and emotional experience. We are the *weavers of the web*. Yet for the most part, we accept the role of the fly caught within the web. Welcome to the *Hall of Mirrors*, it is a labyrinth that will take all your intent to be able to come out the other side whole and intact.

You are the game master. The gatekeeper, and the guide in your journey. Your feelings of separateness are the illusions that you yourself embrace. There is no separation, it does not exist in the cosmos. All is connected in the *web of life*. El Nino is the child that brings the fever that cleanses the sickness from our minds and our creations. Remember the story *A Christmas Carole?* Recall when Scrooge was confronted by the Spirit of Christmas future, and saw the faces of fear and suffering as children in bondage beneath Spirit's robe. This is what we have done to the human spirit, this is part of the *Seven Thunders* that will preempt the day of *Purification*.

During this next phase of *the shift* we might find ourselves laid down for a spell as with any high fever. But, it will be a temporary situation. The emotional fever is so that we might make ourselves a little purer, and a little lighter, so that perhaps we might become a little wiser in the use of our intent and realize the power we hold when we throw around our thoughts, words and actions. We are purging our own inequities through divine will of the Spirit within. These are the beginnings of the *Purification*. These are the first waves.

Did you think the Elders were kidding? Did you think the ancient ones wrote these things down so we could tell each other scary Halloween stories? I am sorry! They meant it with every tear that fell from their cheeks as they told us what they knew, even through their own pain and struggle to become free from the spell they were caught in themselves. They spoke from experience telling us about the impending disasters. In our indulgence with separation we have broken the chain that keeps us together. We are on our own now. We have for the most part, torn ourselves away from our roots.

What humanity has done in deeds, what we have created in thought, will now be experienced personally. Every person you were mean to, you will feel what they felt when they experienced your projection. But life is kind for life is living. It is the river, which constantly flows. There will be some flooding and raging of the river of life so that the spring will have new Earth to sustain the many new seeds that will appear as the Sun breaks through the icy grasp of winter's sleep. And you will be stronger for the owning of the experience.

Life is a hologram, and you are its creator. You are creating the game as you go. Remember past karma is no longer a life sentence. It is no longer a factor in your walk here upon the Earth. That was changed in 1995 at the ceremonies of the Spring Equinox. We spoke about that in *Last Cry*. But you are responsible for your present actions. You are creating your present karma this very moment by the thoughts you choose to embrace. By the way you walk your walk and talk your talk. By the experiences you choose to have or not have with your children, your career, and your inner child. Your success and your failures are all part of the condition's of the game yourself have created. *These are the principles of the 16th Insight.* You get to live it, and actually participate in the dramas you have created, with full awareness and feelings.

You have the power to change the conditions of the game in a moment. But remember it is a labyrinth. Not all is what is seems. You must go through the illusion and demand the reality to come forth. It is a game, a game that is very real. The consequences of the game are what you make them. Love is the secret ingredient here. If you have the ability to allow love to enter your field of awareness, unconditionally, you will pass through the portal into a world where you will possess ever growing powers of manifestation. We can measure love not in what we receive but by how much we give out. The Joy in love is in the loving. If you falter, El Viejo will push you onward, have no doubt! But do not get caught by La Vieja, she is a little more unforgiving.

Relationships that were not established upon foundations of love and mutual admiration will suffer greatly. It will be harder and harder to keep putting a Band-Aid on the wounds received and inflicted by harsh actions between souls. We are entering an energy where this kind of behavior will no longer be tolerated. It is the merging of Christ energy into every aspect of life, from the infinitesimal to the infinite.

We are experiencing a new aspect of our human consciousness with this influx of Christ consciousness. We have reached a point where the new consciousness itself is now taking on its own life force, and we are being made aware of the fact. Human consciousness has been established in the cosmos. That is no longer just the experiment. But this new consciousness needs to be developed into its highest form of expression in order to come into alignment with the Christ consciousness, which **is** the Christ. I speak not of the Christ as the individual who was the master born in Bethlehem. I speak of the Christ consciousness that is a part of the bigger picture. I speak of a consciousness that is enveloping the whole of the universe, which is also going through this change, this initiation of the human spirit. In this that we speak of so often, we are only an infinitesimal part. The entire universe is in the process of Christing; the whole universe is in the throws of *the Quickening*.

El Nino will blow through our lives and effect all upon the Earth. It is a global occurrence, not an isolated event. There are those who will tell you it was man who created this El Nino. Well, that is not entirely true. El Nino has always been here, man has just created the environment for the big one to enter. For now change is eminent, without it we will perish, and so will the planet. El Nino is the breath of creator, changing all that is in its path. *The Winds of Change*, which bring us the 16th *Insight*, is when we shift from teachings of words to realize experiential realities. This is a path where we learn cause and effect on a very personal level. Where we have the opportunity to become causal beings, walking upright. Owning our spiritual powers and the right to take our place once again as co-creators of life in the universe. It is the prelude to our joining the galactic universe, as the Pathal, the Children of the Sun.

"In the time of the Phoenix the People of the Condor shall once again unite with the People of the Eagle. When this happens, we will hear a great sound in the heavens as the Thunderbird returns, and the flap of its wings shall be felt throughout the universe. It will mark the time of completion, the Emergence of the Fifth World..."

Ghost Wolf - 1993

The Armageddon Within

here will be a splitting of realities as consciousness polarizes to reflect the paradoxes that man has created within the energy fields that surround the Earth. Things will become grey for awhile during the transition period as these different paths begin to take a more substantial form. Remember, as the Hopi Elders have warned us in *Last Cry,* mankind will have several paths that they can choose to walk down as they enter the time of purification. The substance of the inner nature developed while living our Earth experience will determine which path each one of us embraces. How we reacted to situations, how we conducted our relationships with our fellow humans, and interacted with the Earth Mother. How we think regarding our relationship with all Earth's creatures, and the heavens. Our personal attributes to the degree of impeccability and integrity that we have exercised in relation to our contracts, and intent of our actions will all be tested.

We will experience great polarity shifts, and there will be the flip-flopping back and forth between schools of thought. The El Nino is the wind spirit, *Tete Wakan* (Lakota for Wind Spirit.) This is a living spirit that initiates the shifting of all things upon the Earth. *Tete Wakan* will cause a realigning of our inner visions. Our values and our perceptions will alter radically. These are the *Winds of Change*. As the infrastructure of what held our consciousness together for so long begins to churn through the effects of the Emotional Storms, there will be the fracturing, or splitting of the dimensions which results in our taking different paths in accordance to the vibrations we can hold.

Author's Note

In the stories of the indigenous People's there exist many that tell of the coming to this land of the Pale Prophet, the Healer. He traveled to the land of this turtle, as well as the Southern lands of South America. In his sojourn to this land, he instructed the People to hide most of the records of their ancient knowledge in foresight of the destruction, which was coming. Those records which told of the legacy of mankind, from his beginnings to his future destiny when time would end, was stowed away in secret locations, which have remained hidden even unto this day. The records telling of the prophet and the prophecies that remained in the temples have, for the most part, been either stolen or destroyed. The Church in Rome, which is under control of the secret society recognized as the Illuminati, the followers of the black sun, made it their obligation to eradicate all of the ancient records which told the Prophecies. The fear, you see, was that through access to these Prophecies, mankind might find the truth to their heritage and true nature of their being.

Under the guise of bringing the Christ to the New World, the Jesuits or Black Robes, acting as a front for the Illuminati, searched the New World for these records. They knew that there existed twelve locations, or sacred cities. It was known to them that the one known as the Prophet, the Healer, the *Lord of the Wind* to the Peoples here in what is now North and South America, was the same who was known as Jesus the Nazarene in Europe. These prophecies were what he had taught his apostles before he continued upon his journeys, which eventually led him to the land of the Toltec and Mayan Peoples.

Hundreds of these temples were leveled, and cities were then literally built over with new structures in order to hide any possible trace of the prophecies, or the teachings connected to them. Any one who had any knowledge of these temples or the knowledge therein was ordered executed. So extreme was the death order that was issued by the Jesuits that within less than a decade the indigenous population of Central America went from over six million to little less than two million. Thus the Conquistadors left behind them their legacy of blood.

They were not entirely successful, however. Today, the ancient information that survives is being spread throughout the lands of North and South America. The age of the secret societies is in its final hours as we experience the *Last Waltz of the Tyrants*. The Dragon will rear its ugly head, but the choice for freedom and the continued raising of our Spirituality could make the difference in these final days of the dream. We must have the eyes to see and the ears to hear the truth for the window is very, very short. Connections to the occurrences and events of both the Montauk and Monarch Experiments, which continue to this day, are more then coincidental in their consequential effects on the intensity of these final days. Which is why I have elected to release the information that is contained in *Winds of Change*.

May the God of your being lift you from limitation, and may you remember all that you are.

As you have been told in "Last Cry," the Armageddon is within. This is a battle of consciousness between the altered ego and the ego. The ego which is of God, the light, the source of all that is, the Creator. The Mother–Father that is within all that is, *Mitakyue Oyasin, we are all relations*. This is not a metaphor but a hard fact of reality, which we will now experience to the core of our being.

The Ghost Dance

The Whole World is coming

A Nation is coming

The Eagle has brought the Message to the People

The Father says so. The Father Says so

Over the whole Earth they are coming

The Buffalo are coming, the buffalo are coming

The Crow has brought the message to the tribe

The Father Says so, the Father says so

Sioux Ghost Dance Song

The Ghost Dance belongs to no one, least of all myself. I simply follow my calling. It is amazing the ripples that an individual can cause when they choose to walk their talk. I have been shown beyond any self-doubt that it is time to lift our-selves beyond the limitations of third dimensional reality. As long as we keep operating from there we can only hope to perpetuate the downward spiral. It is *the Quickening*; it is the awakening of the human spirit.

The Grandfathers came, and the Grandmothers came, they taught me. They gave me instructions to go somewhere, or to do something ... I did this without question. If I was asked to go and meet them in the desert, 15 miles past the old Cotton wood tree, down by the Red Wash, I went there. Sometimes I had to wait quite awhile for them to arrive, if they did. If they didn't show up, well ... then there was a teaching in that as well. I do not see much of this depth of commitment today.

They gave me a pipe to carry, to use for the People. They gave me maps though the veils. They gave me ceremonies and taught me; to speak to the rocks, to call the cloud People and the Eagles from the Sun. They taught me about the colors I hang in my lodge, and they introduced me to the Star People. .... Know that I have not come this far to lay down my ways. The very ground I walk upon is alive with the essence of my ancestors. Therefore all I walk upon is sacred ground. All that I breathe is the dust of everyone who came before me. For my body is recycled Earth. My body is borrowed, but my spirit is my own, and it is forever. Within me it shines like the Sun.

Tomorrow is someone else's legacy, but today is my moment. It is your moment. Perhaps what we do in this moment can be a guide to someone else who is walking the path just behind. Just as I followed the masters who came before me, and they laid down the footprints that I now follow into forever. In life we choose to follow or chose not to follow our truth. Along the way we learn the pain that comes from following the path that was not our truth. In wisdom, we learn to follow the path with heart. The Crow has come to my vision and told me the path of heart must not be lost to the people of this land, for there is another storm rising that can only be stopped by the faith of the people in the Human Spirit.

In asking for this Ghost Dance, I have chosen to call an end to spiritual silence. In taking this action I am very aware that I have chosen to be a voice in the wilderness. I chose to let my spirit lift its wings and soar upon the thermals of the Grandfather Power. I asked for no safe destination. I simply follow my *heart path*, which I will to the end of this dance that I call my life path. This moment is my dance, my song. Now is the time for us to have our life's review. To initiate change means standing up and walking your own way. It does not mean walking in defiance. It means quietly walking your own walk, walking with grace and poise. To keep on walking though the whole of the world may be against you and say you are mad. You must find the courage to follow the beat of your own heart.

Crazy Horse had light curly hair and green eyes. He was not a Sun Dancer. He never did the Sun Dance. He was a Ghost Dancer.

One of the greatest things I have learned in this life is that we have Choice. Choice to express our own path. Choice whether to participate or not to participate. The strongest power is silent. Like the wind, you can not see it, but nothing can escape it's path. Like the wind, I see many things as I pass through. I see those who think that this is their place. Those who think that this is their special song. I see those who are always trying to lord over another people. They are all crawling around, making this big deal over their short little lives. Ego against ego. Conflict against conflict. Dogma against dogma. Most carrying big signs that say "*hooray for my side.*"

I have danced free upon this Earth. I have no master. I am a warrior, a warrior of the heart. As long as I have danced I have experienced many wonderful people, beings from many densities, and the wonders of a world that most only dream of, or can hope to at best read about in books. I Am that I Am. A light unto myself, for the glory of that which is the Mother Father principle of us all. Lately, a quiet intensity can be felt across the land. I am seeing the Sampacu every where in the eyes of people. This is what happens when the life force leaves a people or a place. Our spirit is dying.

Regardless of what words we choose to define our limited experience, no matter which tribal ritual we cloak ourselves behind to defend our space, we are like so many little clowns dancing. The magic is to not to *have* to defend anything. You need not defend what is true within your heart. But we can not expect every one to see. Like the critics of those who possess the courage to step up and move out of the Beiging of Humanity that is occurring throughout our world. Well, legends are not told about the critics, only about those who stood fast before the spears. (Note: Beiging – as in beige – i.e.: loosing color or, in this case, life force.)

People, can you see it yet? Can you see that the enemy is fear? The formless parasite that is draining this humanity of its life essence is fear. Physically, with the un-awakened eye, you can not see it. You can not hold it in your hands. In essence, it is a state of mind, which you can only be in the emotion of. It can only happen when you allow circumstance to cause you to surrender your spirit to it. There are those who have become very week because of their addictions to fear. They are so addicted to fear that they can not even talk without using the very fear energy that they tell us not to be victimized by.

If only you knew how powerful you truly were. If only you knew from whence you come, and that the wisdom is there for the asking. You are without limitation. You are beyond where fear can even conceive to follow. Fear is the necromancer that is within each of us, the part of us that doubts the very existence of the God Force. The Ghost Dance is the song of the wind, and its call shall be heard across the land. Every tree, every bird that flies, and every scent that fills the air will speak its message. It is time for the Children of the Sun to Arise.

I, Ghost Wolf am merely the messenger. I am the Wolf. It takes a Wolf Teacher to bring the message through in this most decadent of times. This is *the Coyote Moon*, and the trickster is everywhere. Because one has dark skin, or light skin, or wears an Eagle Feather or a Swan Feather … It is all a matter of heart. Where is your heart? To know freedom is to allow freedom, to know the feeling of choice is to allow choice. It takes the courage of a Wolf to stand before the world and say, "Come to the Dance. I have heard the call, and it is time for this Dance."

I do not expect everyone to participate. It takes a great courage to do this thing. To stand before the beast and dance for peace, for unity of the people, for the care of the children whom are now being brought into this world in a time that shows little support for their dreams. It takes courage to stand without anger and say, "My heart shall be my shield. I know that all that is of this world is temporal, and that my spirit will go on from here. I know what I think and feel is what I will manifest as reality when the *great shaking* comes. We shall live again."

It takes courage to stand and say, "Enough corruption. Enough tyranny. Enough destruction. This is the day it stops. It stops here, and it changes with me. For the way it is going there will be no tomorrow to even argue in." Anyone but a fool knows that when one is on a seven-day journey, if there is only enough water for two days, they are going to run into a problem. Do you need permission to lay down and go to sleep, or does someone need to tell you when you are tired? If your spirit is sick, and can no longer express upon this plane, then you are short for this world.

The messengers are coming now. The signs have been placed everywhere from the Stars in the heavens to the fields of the Earth. This is the time of change -- this is *the Quickening*. In our hearts there is a common knowingness, that just has a problem being expressed. The *Ghost Dance* is a vehicle for the releasing of this energy, the Spirit energy that keeps us going in spite of even ourselves. Our spirits can not be burned, or intimidated, they can not foreclose on our spirit, or starve it out.

Words. Words can mean a lot of things. Red. The Red Wagon. The Red Rooster. The Red Tide. The Red Road. The Red Man. The Red Planet. Stop. Sacred. Danger. You've made a mistake. Red Watermelon. Red Bird. Red Blood. Red Rose. Red Sky. I am seeing Red. Red Moon. Red Dog. Land of the Red Sun. The Red Dress. The Red Letter. Code Red...Yes words can mean many thing, can they not? Words are born of the head to try to explain matters of the heart.

My Grandmother's-Grandmother's-Grandmother was told by her Grandmother about the Earth and Spirit, and about what it meant to be human. My Grandmothers died here. They are in the ground. The Sacred ground. Their Dust fills the air, and flows down into my lungs when I take a breath, along with your Grandmothers essence as well. We are all one, there is no other truth to that reality. The serpent energy has humanity within its grip. We are afraid of our own shadows. I have heard this term used a lot by the youth today about the adults. There is a grand truth to this. Perhaps too many of us are afraid of our shadow-self.

The Women need to take their rightful place along side the male in our world society. The Women need to take their rightful place inside their own hearts again. It is the Women who can heal themselves and in that manner they will perhaps be able to heal the men. It is time for the Women to come out from behind the veils and enter the light. If it does not happen by choice, then something will happen to *make* it a reality. Many in South America are already aware of the energy that the Sacred Mother is releasing into the world. The new life forms, they are here -- in the plant kingdom, in the insect kingdom, and in the Fish kingdom. Now you too are changing. Within, in the Silence, where only spirit dares to witness and is capable of understanding.

Globally, children no longer believe in their elders. There is little or no respect rendered, for there is little or no respect they have received. Most children in America have been conceived into a world where there is no room for them. They are destined to live in poverty upon the streets in the urban nightmares we call Cities across America. They feel they are not wanted. Many are left alone by their parents as our economy has dictated that both parents need to work for the family to survive. When the parents return home, they are too tired from running on the Gerbil wheel to spend quality time with their children. We have become a perverted and decadent race. We have gone past the decadence of material worships and denouncing Spirit. The economy of our society has forced us to toil for the sole glory of putting food on the table, a roof over our heads and very little more. Look around you! Walk through your city streets at night, then go back to your heart and review that which you witnessed. Have we not become a Spiritless race?

We are experiencing the ending of cycles, the collapsing of structures; social, religion, financial. It is all written upon the Great Calendar Stone of the Toltecs that was created by the Great Prophet, each event, and each date -- the beginnings and the endings. Right there in Mexico City! You need not listen to just Ghost Wolf, read for yourself... If you still remember... if you can't, then perhaps you should come to the Ghost Dance, there you will remember...

Once again, we are being called to gather at the Ghost Dance ... to " Let our hearts be heard!"

One People § One Vision

A Story of the Great Ghost Dance

by Robert Ghost Wolf

A Story of the Great Ghost Dance

They say that it has been over one hundred years since the last great Ghost Dance was held. Wavoka, a Paiute medicine man led that Ghost Dance in the Nevada desert. Afterwards, the apostle, Porcupine, of the Cheyenne along with Sitting Bull of the Arapaho people, brought the word of the teachings of the Great Prophet, Kanichi-ta-Kanichi-wa. They told of The Great Prophet that had appeared to the people present at the Ghost Dance. They brought his teachings to the other tribes that lived upon the Great Plains.

The last memory associated with the Ghost Dance left to us by contemporary history, is the tragic occurrence of Wounded Knee. Hundreds of Sioux, on a journey to participate in a sacred ceremony to bring about peaceful change to a way of life that seemed to be vanishing before their eyes, were slaughtered. Amongst them was their leader, Chief Big Foot. Those that survived the slaughter were left to the mercy of the Coyotes, vultures and freezing Dakota snows falling that winter. It is a memory of tears that the people of this land will have scared upon their hearts forever.

But, what was the Ghost Dance about? What was the "Messiah Movement" about that still shakes the world when the term Ghost Dance is even uttered? Who was this mysterious Prophet/being who appeared and moved so many? Why was there so much fear surrounding this peaceful ceremony that would spawn such drastic actions to prevent it from happening? Today, there are very few who know who can speak knowledgeably of it. It is an ancient knowledge that is passing from our vision. It is passing with the way of life that flourished here in this once abundant and mysterious land that some call America, that others call ... the Turtle Island.

This is a story about the Ghost Dance. It is not intended to be an accounting of historical events. Written records still exist of what transpired. Those records are in the archives of the Boston Globe and others. They can be found through research in our libraries and on the Internet.

Rather, this is a story of the Spirit of the Ghost Dance. A story that attempts to bring about the higher truths that surround the events leading up to the calling of the Ghost Dance, and of what actually occurred in our mysterious past. A past where many of the truths have been altered to suite the convenience of the times. A past that has been sanitized out of fear, where the true spirituality of this land and its magnificent peoples has been hidden. **It is a story for all peoples, for now we can truly see that it has become a lane of all cultures, all beliefs, and all races.** Yes, perhaps even a galactic land where all beings throughout the cosmos are making their presence known in preparation for the awakening of a new world, a new reality where we might learn to transverse the past and enter a new dimensional expression of Humanity.

We are the eve of a Fifth World - where hu-man-kind will learn to reenter their Galactic community. To regain their rightful place in our Milky Way along side other beings with whom we have shared our evolutionary path through the dream spell of the past few thousand years.

The story of the Ghost Dance transcends time and space. It is a story of a peoples' journey through the spell of Mortality, where we have become prisoners of our limited thoughts. We are being forced to open our minds and expand our consciousness with the passing of each moment. Our lives seem to be moving through accelerated experience, as a moment's experience becomes a week's, and relationships can move through a lifetime of experience in a matter of a few months. It is a story of *the Quickening*. It is where myth and legend merge with reality, and spirit takes on form.

The story of the Ghost Dance begins many generations ago. It begins with the telling of the legend of the Healer - He who has been known by many names and experienced by many peoples. Tah-co-mah, Kate-Zahl, Wa co-ma-tete, Tah-co-pah, Ee-see-co-tl, Wai-co-mah, Hu-ru-kan, Quetzalcòatl, Itza-matul, Kul-kul, Deganaweda … There are so many names by which this mysterious entity, including Kanichi-ta-Kanichi-wa, was called by the many people he met as he traveled the Turtle. Translated into English, we are faced with varying interpretations... such as; Lord of the Wind, the Pale Prophet, the Healer, the Lord of Water and Wind, the silver light that falls from heaven. They go on...

It is said that this being traveled this land and taught the people the ways of love and peaceful co-existence. He taught them to love their enemies. He taught them to transcend the ways of the serpent, to end sacrifice and blood ritual. He instructed them in the building of their great pyramids and guided them to pathways that lead to the development of incredible civilizations from the Toltec to the Mayan, from the Hopi to the Iroquois.

He spoke of his father in heaven and of the wonderment of the gift of life that the Mother gave us with our bodies, through which we might experience the gift of beingness upon this plane. Throughout every corner of North and South America his presence was known. How he was called is for our individual interpretations. Our hearts will know the truth, even when our heads do not allow us to see what is before our eyes.

The story continues with his passing from this plane to continue his work in the Kingdom of the Stars. So that the great reunion between we here upon the Earth and those who come from beyond the Sun would occur, and so we would walk through a great golden age, where hu-mankind would walk upright in his spirit once again. Where we would claim our heritage that was given us so long ago. Longer ago than memory could hold.

He taught them the ways of a Great Peace that held with it a promise. A promise that if the ways of the serpent could be transcended, if we could stop war and killing, we would see his return and the fulfillment of a glorious age of inexplicable achievement for human kind.

This is ancient knowledge. A knowledge that was already legend, already lost in antiquity, when the first conquistadors stepped foot upon this virgin land. But the knowledge lived on, and still lives today. As my friends the Inca in Peru have said, this is the time when the people of the Condor and the People of the Eagle shall reunite. When this happens, the ancient truths of our beginnings and our destiny will be revealed to us. We shall see the Golden age spoken about in our legends. Our legends are our history that has been passed down from one generation to the next. Our history is so old that we only know that when the conquistadors came, they could not believe that these cities were built thousands of years before by a people who lived such a simple way of life.

The Prophet also foretold of the future, of the coming of those from across the great waters of the morning Sun, of the younger brother. The Prophet was fair of skin and had eyes that were the grey-green of the sea. His hair was golden-red like the rising Sun and his beard was of the same coloring. Everywhere he went, whatever he touched took on the properties of his healing powers. Even to this day, to simply think of him, heals the pain within our hearts.

The Prophet was not here without those who were of his kind. They formed a people who lived in Central America, known as the Chigargwins. They were and are tall, pale skinned, with blonde-red hair and blue or green eyes. It is there that the present day Kanichi-ta-Kanichi-wa holds the position of Caretaker of the Ways. There are those amongst the Chigargwin people that those who come from across the sea might call -- Ascended Masters, or the Holy Ones.

With the coming of the younger brother from across the Sunrise waters, the prophecies of the Prophet began to unfold as they have been told and are recorded upon the living stone. There was much devastation, and almost an entire way of life has vanished from this Earth. By the latter part of the nineteenth century it seemed to many of the elder brothers or the First Nations People, that they might vanish entirely from even the memory of hu-man-kind. It was in this time that a simple man named Wavoka had visions of the Prophet. So strong were his visions that he started, as it seemed to him, to be able to communicate with the Prophet Himself. Wavoka was instructed in the ancient knowledge and understandings of the powers of the mind.

He was instructed in the ancient mysteries. For example, if we could focus our intent we could collapse time, and actually recreate the nature of our reality. The effects of the destruction that were upon the land and its people could actually be reversed. That time would collapse, it would never have existed. In essence, we could roll it up like a carpet and what was left would be as it was before the impaired creation process had manifested its effects. Wavoka believed, in other words, that we could renew the energies and it would be as if the younger brother had never been. But the key! The key that we nearly lost was the energy of love, which is the highest vibration in the universe. It, Love, is the force behind all creation.

Having been given this knowledge, Wavoka was then instructed to create the environment where the first Ghost Dance would be held. Where we could dream our ancestors, and actually connect to the great, limitless powers that were our natural heritage. We could, in essence, become them and restore the beauty that existed before the devastation. This ceremony that he spoke of to the many who heard him speak came to be known as the Ghost Dance. It was also called, by the many that did not understand the fullness of his teachings due to cultural boundaries, as the "Indian Messiah Movement."

However, the commonality of the knowledge of the story of the Prophet, the teachings of Wavoka, were quite clear among the different indigenous peoples here on the Turtle Island, each having had their own experience with the Prophet. Enhanced by the desperation of the times, these teachings spread across the land in a very short time. Suddenly, the people were partaking of the Ghost Dance. Many stories of Miracles became common place. Many of the tribes sent representatives to find out what truth there might be to these teachings and ceremonies that were transpiring in Paiute country surrounding Wavoka and the Ghost Dancers.

A resurgence of spiritual strength began to be felt by a disheartened people, who were suffering from the almost total desecration of their way of life and their peoples. The impact of that experience was felt in little more then one generation. It was spoken of in the teachings that Kanichi-ta-Kanichi-wa would appear. People came from all over, including many from what is now South America. The movement was growing. There was a light, a glimmer of hope that the spiritual powers of the people might once again be lit with this new, yet very ancient way. Until then, the more might that was used against the younger brother, the more destruction was met, rendering methods of war futile. Even the mighty Sioux, who could boast at one time of having ten thousand warriors, had fallen in the wake of the flood. The Cherokee, the Iroquois, their way of life was only a memory now. It was for the Native American at the time a bleak moment, to say the least. It seemed that nothing could stop the onslaught of the younger brother and his greed.

The Army was stationed around the Nevada hills. They were watching with absolute awe the amassing of people from the four corners of this land, all with the same message. How could so many have heard without telegraph? Below in the valley over the month prior, hundreds of pilgrims had made their trek from as far away as Alaska. Some even made the journey from as far south as Peru. They came by foot and travois; small groups, a family, a couple, two friends, a single traveler... There were people who held the stories of the Prophet, and those that could only wonder of what they had heard their Grandparents tell. Those that the observers saw before them were amassing into a small village. It was peaceful, but it also had an energy about it that the pony soldiers were not accustomed to feeling in their own personage. Faith, and an inner knowing that what they had come for would occur. The prophet would appear as he had promised.

The Chigargwins brought a large contingency of people with their entourage. They were perceived as a strange lot. Bearded, some having red hair with green or blue eyes, they were often taller than the other Native People whom had assembled were. These were the guardians of the sacred knowledge that had been left behind by the Prophet. One could easily mistake them for Europeans except for their mannerisms and language, which was said to be an ancient tongue no longer spoken except by the Chigargwins.

They camped at the sight for over a week. There were many prayers and they performed the Ghost Dance for days. Purification ceremonies were being performed in the manners specific to each People attending. It was a sight to behold. The newspapers of that day told of an accounting of strange lights in the skies -- a glowing myst that surrounded the dancers. Was this just the dust illuminated by the campfires that were never allowed to go out for the duration of the ceremonies? The strangeness of these ways allowed unfamiliar imaginations to run rampant.

Amongst the People, the accounting has been told like this: Kanichi-ta-Kanichi-wa appeared to the people, stepping forth from a glowing sphere. He told them that he himself was not the Prophet, but one who prepared the path for his arrival. He connected their stories of this Prophet, as told by the different Peoples and their retelling of their experiences of The Prophet. They were told that the purification ceremonies must continue for four more days. They were told not to fear the soldiers in the hills. The soldiers were watching but would not be allowed to interfere. Nor would they see with their eyes what was occurring.

After what amounted to nearly two weeks of ceremony and Ghost Dancing, and the four days of ceremony under the guidance of Kanichi-ta-Kanichi-wa, there appeared a very large glowing sphere in the sky. As if from within the glowing light the Prophet appeared to the people assembled. He walked downward form the great sphere and gave his greetings to the people. He told them that for the most part, they had forgotten the teachings he had originally given them. That the tendency was to participate in war and that many had returned to the ways of the Serpent Power. Blood Sacrifice was once again common place amongst many Peoples, and that there was much separation between Peoples. That there was even more separation between the tribes as a whole and their women were not being honored. His teachings were harsh, but not without compassion.

He told them that their plight was truly one of sorrow, and that they had indeed become lost in the valley of shadows. But, they were always told that they had a choice -- always they were told that they held within their power a choice as to the outcome of the final experience. What they were experiencing was the effects of their abandoning the Sacred Teachings of Love and not maintaining peaceful relationships between each other. They had once again become addicted to the Serpent Power, and had grown fond of killing and war games. They had the taste of blood in their veins, they had dreamed the dream of violence -- so this is what they had sewn, and thus this was what they reaped. If the seed is bad, surely the fruit will be poor.

The Prophet chose a counsel of twelve men and twelve women. Eleven of the men were Chigargwins, the twelfth was an unlikely choice from the warrior tribes of the great plains. Porcupine of the Northern Cheyenne was elected to the counsel. Of the women, eleven were Chigargwins, and the twelfth was a young Mayan girl of exceptional spirit and inner strength.

The Prophet told them that their faith had been strong, however, even if it had been held only by the few, and that their intent had saved them from complete annihilation. And, that because of this they were to be shown great visions of the possible future. That if they who were there would return to their peoples and re-establish the ways of the great peace, the tables could be turned. They would then find their way out of the valley of twisted shadows, which was also part of the prophecies. They had to return to the old ways. The ways that had sustained them, and had fed their peoples with the stories of the greatness that they had achieved. That the achievement was a matter of spirit, that greatness was a matter of deeds. Abundance could only be attracted from the highest vibration of a People, and that vibration was dictated by their behavior and thoughts.

They must return to their Peoples and re-establish the ways of the Great Peace. If they could reunite the male and female energies within their peoples, if they could move beyond their addiction to war, if they could put the killing energy asleep, if they could but move beyond their anger and depression and return to the feeling in their hearts of the love of the Divine Father and Mother that was showered upon them daily without tally, then they would be able to change the energy. That was what was needed to bring back the once pristine abundance that was here – and then would be once again. Then their lives upon this land would be restored to what it was before the coming of the younger brother from across the Sunrise Waters.

He told them many things, and renewed their spirits for their missions were going to be hard and arduous indeed. He also told them that this was not yet the time for his returning that there was still much to be tended to in the preparation of the coming Golden Age. Soon, the end times that were prophesized by your ancestors will be upon the land. You must return and make ready your camps for that moment. Remember that all is choice. You can not stop the Younger Brother but you can rise above the vibration of his energies. You can return to the Ways when you knew how to draw the energy from the Earth, and renew yourselves. They again were told the prophecies of the end times that they might be renewed for their journeys. They were told of two other visitations that would transpire where the Prophet would return to work with the people before his final returning with a host from the stars.

Upon that day there would appear, after many more years of man dwelling in darkness, a great light in their heavens that would block out even the light from the Sun at mid day. There would appear amongst them a great star and from this star would they see those who had promised to return, including the Prophet himself. There would be many signs in the heavens prior to that moment. They were given many accountings of things to be aware of by the Prophet and to give these warnings to their People upon their return that they might know what to be aware of. That they might see the light through the darkness of these days -- that the whole of the Earth was about to walk through. At the end of the walk, they would again be side by side with the Buffalo as they followed the Eagle through the arches of the great bow that would appear in the heavens to lead them to the path of the Golden Age. Then they would once again be connected to their spiritual selves. They would be whole In body, mind and spirit -- the Mer-Ka-Ba. (Mer: light, Ka: Spirit, Ba: body)

There are many stories that followed the Great Ghost Dance. Porcupine, the Cheyenne Medicine Man, went on to spread the Gospel of the Prophet, along with his disciple Sitting Bull of the Arapaho. In 1890 a band of Sioux, led by a Chief named Big Foot, led the fragments of a once great warrior nation through the freezing December snows to do the Ghost Dance. They hoped that the people might be renewed, and their spiritual fires lit once again. That they might return to the ways of the ancient ones, the ways of the Great Peace. That they might be prepared for the coming of the Great Bow in the Heavens, and the Buffalo walk that would lead them to the New World. But they never completed that walk. The US Military slaughtered them all in a senseless display of fear and madness -- at a place of little discernment, called Wounded Knee.

Of the Ghost Dance itself, there are many stories and many legends. Through those who were there, some of the knowledge has been passed down from one generation to the next. There are still in existence several accountings in the archives of newspapers that were prominent in that day. One story in the Boston Globe tells of how the military observers watched as a strange glowing cloud of dust swirled above the natives participating in the Ghost Dance, which was 'Obviously some sort of heat anomaly.' The story continues to tell that there appeared a man 'whose features were undeterminable through the dust cloud.' It appeared that this person spoke to each of the people from the various tribes in their own language. 'Obviously some sort of hoax was afoot!' Ah, yellow journalism in its hay-day! Would there be a more accurate accounting today?

Nine is the Number of completion: With the coming of the ninth generation from the time the great Ghost Dance transpired somewhere in the Nevada Desert, the new humanity is being born. This generation will enter the new world, the Fifth World. This is the ninth generation. They are the Star children that will open the doors.

In my book, *Last Cry*, there are other stories that stem from this great Ghost Dance and the teachings of he whom I call Wa coma-tete, the Lord of the Wind. We can make a difference. We must switch gears **now**. What was past is no more. It will take a new energy, a new humanity. It will require that we ourselves put together the Sacred Hoop once again. It is by our own power that we will pass through this veil of illusion into the next world. The Fifth World is already upon us. We must create an energy that is greater than the one that created the previous energy. It is a matter of creating a new Global Consciousness. One that is made up of me, of you, and those who are drawn to us.

Let us come together to dance the Ghost Dance. "Let your hearts be heard!" as Grandfather would so often say. If you have the courage to participate, you will have the wonderment of opening the gateway. You will have participated in creating the bridge over which perhaps millions will cross into the Nation without borders. I have been told that at each Ghost Dance the presence of those from the other realms observing our conscious choice and intent will be demonstrated at each of the global gatherings. There is no time to waste; we are already falling behind. No one can take you there; this is a self-help program. You make the choices. You create the nature of your own reality. That reality is what your children will inherit from you.

It is time now the great awakening has commenced. Take courage and walk with clarity, and good heart. Perhaps we are the fulfillment of our own final prophecy. What I choose to leave behind me is a bridge the next world. It will be simple and obvious. That way the adults won't see it and take it apart with their fears and judgements. The adults will be all tied up with their doubts and fears -- blinders for the fools! ... But the children, the children will see the gateway and walk over without effort. There, on the other side, I can already hear the voice of Grandmother saying to me ... "Grandson, what took you so long?"

Omanao Patao Hitaka

Robert Ghost Wolf

The Ghost Dance Returns to the People

August 7, 1997 Montana

The day was clear, and the 10 hour ride was magical and not that hot for August. The clouds were dancing and I admit it was unusual to see these many different weather fronts meeting even here in the Rocky Mountains. When we arrived in the small mountain town there was a bikers convention going on. The motels were filled and the streets and parking lots were lined up with Harley Davidsons of every shape and variety. There were many colorful characters walking about so as to make the kids and I appear very normal, even though we were new faces. And I dress like a Tumbleweed Cowboy as part of my everyday normal fashion statement. We were on our way to participate in the first Ghost Dance to be held in over 107 years. The contrast of intent between these two events seemed a little surrealistic, yet from another point of view we were rebels in camaraderie with the cause of Freedom in both our camps. The scenery did make it feel very much like an experience out of a Tom Robin's novel.

We arrived in town in the early evening. I decided to make camp there and ease the kids into being in the wilderness the next morning. Sunset was spectacular, and we had a fun first evening spending our time star watching.

When we awoke it was a Zane Grey kind of morning. The panoramic landscape of the Rocky Mountains is something to be experienced. It is sad to think that most people never get a chance to experience the real West like this first hand. It is a different feeling out here then the rest of the country. Suburban sprawl seems only like a bad dream against the majestic peaks of the Rockies and endless rolling plains of Northern Montana, which along with Alaska is the last of our virgin wilderness in America. It is another reality to experience it than watching old westerns on Sunday afternoon.

The kids got a kick out of a town having real hitching posts! I felt it was good that they should experience that Cowboys were a little more real than what Nashville was offering these days. We ate breakfast and embarked upon the last miles to what would become the site of the Ghost Dance.

Coming round one of the turns we came into view of the Saw Tooth Mountains. It was a definite showstopper. From this point we were escorted most of the rest of the way to the encampment site by two Golden Eagles. I could not help but find myself absorbed in the azure blue of big sky country. The backdrop of the Great Divide against the Western Horizon became a mystical canvas. Ancient Pyramids were easily detectable, as were the ancient trails that led through to very protected destinations that the ancients knew were portals to other dimensions. Oh, the stories that these mountains must hold within their hidden meadows and canyons.

We drove off the main road and followed the trail. Two Red Fawns made their presence known, walking calmly towards our vehicle, chewing on wildflowers. Not the slightest bit of fear in them. We passed through several canyons finally arriving two miles later. It was a pristine meadow that was host to more wild flowers then I had laid eyes upon in one place in a long time. Nestled in the Cotton Woods and Willow growing along the creek bed we would find evidence of many Teepee rings. The stone rings indicated that this had been a favorite encampment for some very ancient campers.

We arrived at our destination and Tim, our host's son-in-law, stepped out of his Landrover. He directed us to the truckload of firewood that was purchased for the camp. We exchanged cordialities and he left to return to town and unite with his wife Mary, and their children. He said he would return to us at the encampment site in two days. Neither one of us could have guessed at that moment, the energy of what was to transpire over the next 10 days building up to the Ghost Dance. The magic that those who participated would experience, the drama, the visions, and the shifting of consciousness would leave all of us changed forever. Many of us who participated are still going through the Dance. It has never stopped, and perhaps never will.

I set up basic camp with my kids while waiting for my wife, Laura Lee. She was *supposed* to show up two days after I, with the rest of our kids, Black Hawk, his family, the Teepee poles and other supplies. There was much spiritual preparation needed and the exploration of the site where we would hold the Ghost Dance itself lay ahead. The evening skies were clear that first night, and the star people were dancing throughout the evening canvas. The Milky Way played its part as a vibrant backdrop.

There have been many stories that had been handed down to me by my Elders. I told the kids stories of the star people, and the Ghost Dances that had happened upon this Turtle Island some one-hundred years ago. While we were sitting by the evening campfire we could hear the sound of a wolf howling in the distance. It is always amazing how far the howling of wolves can travel in the wilderness. It was a welcome sound that we were serenaded with that first evening.

I was to find out later that this was part of the ranch where Charles Russell, the famed Western artist, had spent much of his time `cowboying.' Where so many of his stories had been given birth. We were here experiencing the land as it was in his time. Unspoiled, and unchanged by modern civilization. What a gift this was for the kids. One that perhaps they would not realize until later in their lives.

The second morning we awoke to crystal clear skies, the chill of mountain air, and Mountain Jays greeting us at sunrise. After breakfast the kids went off along the creek and busied themselves fishing. I went hiking along the cliffs. Later, I joined them walking along the creek bed. We began looking for appropriate sites for the ceremony. I was not aware of the history of the place we were gifted with. That history was to unfold over the next ten days.

We were camped along an ancient Travois Trail. The Hopi talk about the Travois Trail in their stories of the beginning times, when the four brothers first ventured from beneath the hollow Earth into the 'Above World.' They spoke about how the brothers traveled in their four directions. This was a trail that was once followed from South America to Alaska. The ancient Toltecs traveled this trail, as did the Mayan after them. It had been a trade route, which lead to a large encampment a few miles west of our location that had come to be known in more recent times as Travois Flats. This fact I was to discover on the third day of our journey. Here I would be welcomed by many Medicine Wheels, over two hundred Teepee rings, and other phenomenon of sacred geometry. Symbols left fashioned in stones thousands of years before. Fashioned by a people who do not even have a name in contemporary history.

We found many stone mounds and markers at different points along the trail. Amazing to me was the thought of how many cowboys and Trappers from the Hudson Bay must have stood where I was standing at different times thought the history of this place. I wondered if they themselves realized the importance of these anthropological remains. To the Blackfoot People the significance of this location must surely have been known. However, to even most of them, it was only a memory one could feel. The living memory was now lost some where in time, lost in amongst the legends.

After lunch I decided to climb up to the top of what appeared to be the highest point in our little valley. Once on top, I discovered what remained of a look-out fire pit. The point itself was now thick in Sweet Pine, which had once long ago been traded by the Blackfoot to the Cherokee for Tobacco from the South. I felt a presence moving into my energy field. As I looked above me and around I was drawn to the cry of a Spotted Eagle flying over my head towards the West. The smell of herbs was everywhere in this pristine landscape that I was to soon to discover held within it qualities of almost every type of terrain. One could find characteristics from desert to woodland, to mountain meadow and grassland in the plant life as well as the rocks.

Here the Buffalo still roamed and the Eagle flew free, dancing with the Hawk in skies that had never surrendered themselves from the hearts of the Blackfoot People. I could hear the songs of dancers, the voices floating seemingly with the cloud people overhead. For a moment, it was as if I were falling into time, or maybe out of time. A herd of Antelope came into view on the eastern horizon as the Eagle screamed above me once again, distracting my daydreaming for a moment. The land of the ranch we were on bordered the Bob Marshall wilderness. Prints from the Grizzlies were prominent along the creeks and wet lands. I was being let know that we were not alone in the air or upon the land.

In those few precious quiet moments before the human drama of the Ghost Dance unfolded, I was as if in a dream. As the afternoon ensued, the presence of the ancestors became more and more evident even to the children. Along the creek where the children played we found Dinosaur bones, mingled with ancient Buffalo bones of extraordinary size and density. The children also found Petroglyphs that told the stories of the people who had come this way before them. That evening they brought their treasures of bones and rocks to the campfire. Until the wee hours of the approaching morning I shared with them stories of the Pale Prophet and the original Ghost Dances. As we sat around the fire that evening, we could almost hear the old ones singing... or did we... I am still left to wonder?

We were not to be without our spirit gifts that night, either. At one point during our stories the entire mountainside seem to light up in a phosphorescent glow. It was as if snow had fallen beneath the swelling light of the moon. Again, the presence of the Star People was prominent in the skies. At another point, it was as if the clouds came in and presented us with an array of pictures from spirit world. We could see dancing wolves, dragons, eagles, squirrels, beaver, and dancers gathering above us. Iridescent mysts floated across the meadow. It was an evening to behold as we surrendered to the comfort of the motor home and nights sleep.

Our peace was to be disturbed at about midnight with my waking up to swirling with lights and the kids, startled and obviously caught up in the stories, yelling **"They're landing! They're landing!"** Headlights from an approaching truck were playing havoc and letting imaginations run wild within our own little turtle. Coming out of the haze of just drifting off to sleep, I was to realize that the first of our guests, War Turtle and his family, had arrived. In a few moments we were all out by the campfire fully awake, wondering what to do as our guest drove off to retrieve his home, a fifth wheel. (Thus his name of Turtle – he who carries his home on his back.) He returned and set up temporary camp with wife and daughter, and his pet wolf, who completed the Montana wilderness setting as he howled us to sleep. The adventure of the human drama had begun.

Those Who Are Called Will Come

J awoke after a night of intense dreaming. I spent most of the morning walking the site, trying to figure out the pictures of them that were replaying in my head. At the same time, trying to figure out where we would hold the ceremonies. I was in the midst's of my confusion, pondering the best ways to go about everything, when a truck pulled into the valley. It came straight towards me. I thought I could discern a woman and children. The woman waved a sign of recognition. It had to be Mary, our host's daughter, and her kids.

She offered to show me to the main lodge for water and to show me Travois Flats, on which she said was a very old encampment site. She felt that perhaps it might be an alternative site for the Ghost Dance, and that we should check it out. My kids had elected to go fishing again, so I took Mary up on her offer. Off we went to view Travois Flats.

As we neared the flats, we drove between some of the Buffalo that her dad, Jack, kept on the ranch. It is always amazing to me whenever I look into the eyes of a Buffalo. It always seems as if they are just about to cry. The flats were located on one of the higher plateaus of the ranch. The site was breath taking as I viewed the panoramic scenes for 360°. It seemed one could see all the way into Canada. John Ford some how had missed this location in choosing sites for his legendary western movies. But there was no doubt that had he seen it would have been used somewhere in one of his movies. I could almost see Jimmy Stewart riding in from the range.

We drove on into the flats and stopped just about mid way. Mary said it would be best to walk from here. She wanted to take me to the top of a hill where there were many mounds to be found. It had once been indicated on the USGS maps as an Indian burial ground. She said that there had been reports of a few diggings but that no remains of humans had ever been found in the history of the ranch, which had been in her family for seven generations. We were to find out later the clearer picture of this legend. The mounds that I saw seemed to indicate some sort of markers not too different then those we found near the site of the encampment. Others, it would turn out, were places where watch fires had been lit, many thousands of years ago.

We walked through what were literally hundreds of Teepee rings and stone mounds covering the actual flats, which lay just below us upon a mesa, which was comprised of perhaps several hundred acres. What ever this place was it was very well known, and obviously of major importance. To those who once gathered here the site would have been considered a city by standards of their times, and probably was host to at least two thousand people or more. Again, many things were to reveal them selves to us later when we would perform ceremony on this site to free the spirits that seemed to be locked here for some reason.

We elected not to hold the ceremony here but to return after we had performed the Ghost Dance to work on freeing the spirits with the pipe carriers that were coming. As we turned to return to the truck I could feel a cold chill run down my back of my neck. Yet, at the same time, I wondered about the other side of that feeling. It was as if I had been here before. I knew this site, as it had been, not as it was now. I got flashes of when it had been teaming with life, and bustling with trading, and the gambling of men. Filled with the laughter and sounds of people traversing back and forth. Yet I knew there was a deeper meaning still to this mystery of Deep Creek that would unfold in its own time.

When Mary and I returned to the encampment people were already starting to arrive. We greeted a few along the road, yet our thoughts were still back at the flats. As seems to be the situation with these type of events, there are people who arrive at the last moment. They do not realize the spiritual preparation that is necessary, nor the physical labor it takes to tame a wilderness setting, and yet leave it as if you were never there. We had about three days until the beginning of the actual events that would lead us into the Ghost Dance.

Moving Stones - Chopping Wood

ary had brought us some supplies on one of her trips back and forth from town. We prepared another campfire meal. I put on the evening of coffee. Funny how it always seems so good to smell that brewing mud when you're out in the wilderness at night. While I was pouring myself a cup of that fresh brew, I saw another truck coming towards my campfire. He Who Barks At Midnight and White Hair had arrived, two very familiar and very welcome 'Wolf Lodge Faces.'

It takes a lot of work to set these "ceremonies" up in the wild, and these two boys, well, we had a few under our belt together you might say. They busied themselves setting up their camps and checking out the Spirits. They were tired from the nine-hour drive and the kids, well, they probably hiked thirty miles through those woods near the creek, and they were bushed. We would need our rest. There was a storm moving in, and we had a few days of hard work.

We slept well that night and rose early. We wasted little time around the morning campfire and He Who Barks At Midnight, White Hair and I went off to plan the building of the Lodge and the Arbor for the Ghost Dance. Moving stones, and moving them again. Gathering willow and firewood. Unseen heroes of the day, still finding time to let our two legs take us to places where our eyes would see the little visions. The signs that tell you of the way of things, and the possible outcomes, silent messages from Spirit.

People would keep wandering into the encampment day and night for the next two days. War Turtle had taken on the job of overlooking the encampment and directing traffic to the designated campsites, in between cutting the firewood for the camp with Tim. We affectionately gave War Turtle's wife the name *She Who Makes Coffee*. As somehow every time we seemed to be running out of steam, she would appear. Standing with a cup of coffee or herb tea.

The funds for the firewood had not stretched as far as we had hoped, so War Turtle assembled a work crew. They located the appropriate dead trees and eventually had about twelve chords stacked at various locations around the camp. I found myself at a truly interesting site atop a rock outcropping above the encampment. I watched the pick-up trucks and little work groups, moving like ants across the meadow below me. In two days we had built a little village that would have been a fine place in the Blackfoot wilderness or in Sherwood Forrest.

Coyote Reveals - We Learn to Trust in Spirit

No party is complete without its Coyote. One could have little doubt that we had our own *Coyote Medicine Camp*. As a matter of a fact, you could say that we were about to have almost every kind of experience you could imagine at this gathering. I mean, this really was right out of a Tom Robins Novel.... *Another Fireside Attraction*. We had Coyote Man and White Coyote Woman. Then there was Eagle Man Biker and a Neil Young wannabe. We had assembled quite a cast of characters.

It is always a wonderment to me how these kind of events always have their contrasts of polarities. On the other side, we had our representatives from *the Masters* and the Above People. They were spreading their wondrous violet auras, touching everything they passed. Whether one was consciously aware of it or not was immaterial. They were there to rain enlightenment upon the people and to uplift Earth's little creatures, and no thing *of Spirit or flesh* would deter them from their mission.

Grandmother Turtle, Grandfather Warren, Travels in the Dark, Riding Buffalo Woman, Dancing Flower, Strong Fire, Francis Rainbow Heart (one fine Irishman,) Black Hawk, White Wolf, Running Wolf, Golden Eagle, Dancing Grizzly, Raven White Dove, Lilly Rivertree, Grandfather Richard, Bobcat Who Dances, He Who Barks At Midnight, White Hair, Bold Wind, Flute Carrier, Star Dancer, War Turtle, She Who Makes Coffee, Peace Bird, Night Hawk, Falcon, Ghost Wolf, Mary Owl Dreaming, Morning Star, Spider Hawk, She Who Fights With Wolf Medicine. Not everyone can be named in this chapter, it would take an entire page, for that you will have to wait for the book. Also, there were many who came through the veils to participate in the ceremony. Those who had no Earthly name. Yet we could feel their hearts, their energy presence. Some could even hear them talking throughout the dancing and drumming. We would hear their songs in the wind, which they gave us to sing. Then there were those who actually saw them, walking, watching, dancing.

This was a melting pot of many cultures. Apache, Blackfoot, Cherokee, Lakota, Mohegan, Cree, German, French, Welsh, Canadian, Aztec, Mexican, English, Italian, Oriental, Irish, Sioux, Iroquois, Cheyenne. We came from Washington, California, Oregon, Canada, Alaska, Michigan, Montana, Colorado, and many other areas. Perhaps an experience one could say was uniquely the American West. But the deeper message was still to be found in our sojourn here in the Montana Wilderness. One that perhaps most were not aware of upon their original decision to undertake the pilgrimage and participate in the Ghost Dance. But all things in their time, and to be sure, Coyote would have his dance first. Only with those who would accept his gifts with open heart, and good humor would Coyote share his wisdom. With those few brave and non-judgmental souls who could learn to laugh through the tour of their own limitations, and self created human dilemmas, would he reveal his magic.

Coyotes magic was there to reveal our truth, so there would be no barriers between each other or our hearts. Coyote was there so that for one moment in time, we might know what it felt like to be in the presence of divine levels of reality. To return for those brief moments in the unfolding of our lives to the world of magic, spirits, and to walk through the dimensions, which for some occurred quite easily. For us to realize that the magic was achieved through the unity of the group.

Learning that one who stands alone without camaraderie is, in fact, he who would follow dogma without question, which had been the way of the herd. Here in the energy of the dance, it was clear that there was no wrong or right, only sacred and not sacred. There is no good or bad, only aware and not aware. This was to be a Dance for the People. It was their spirits that would need to shake loose of the petrified rock, they knew as flesh that now encapsulated their spirit. This could only be achieved experientially in the state of absolute freedom. There could be no priests, no dogmas. We would all have to develop the ability to trust in Spirit. Spirit is a personal matter. Each one's experience of the creator is their sovereign right. It is their story, not *his-story*.

Spirit directed that there would be no people telling you how and when to move, what was sacred and what was not sacred. That was not going to work any longer. There would be no priests at the Ghost Dance. Everyone had to own the experiencing of the Creator in his or her own way. So that it would be theirs and they would own it. So that it would not be someone else's story. It had been someone else's story for far too long. Which is perhaps why, in this contemporary society, we as individuals seem to feel so personally dis-empowered. We are it would seem, groomed to give our power up at some point in our early childhood. Maybe it begins right from the moment we enter the public school system, and are taught to accept the benefits of fitting into the norm. We are taught, by the belittling of elders and piers, that being different and individual is abnormal. What the group feels is good for us. They hate you if you're clever and they despise a fool.

The Stone Peoples' House

The days were beginning to fly by now. You had to pay attention or you just might loose one. He Who Barks At Midnight, White Hair and I decided to have Mary and Tim help build the *Inipi* with us, so that they would become a living part of the lodge. Later they would be able to enjoy it for their family lodge. The prayers were said at the chosen sight asking permission and giving our blessings to the site. The willow was located, the offerings were made, and then the willow was cut. We brought the firewood, and the Stone People we had invited from the Spokane River in Washington. (One does not just 'gather' a bunch of stones for the lodge. One *invites* the Stone People.)

The Lakota said they were coming, so we elected to built a Chippewa / Ojibwa lodge, a Turtle Head lodge, facing East. This would allow for the Lakota to build their own lodge down river from our lodge. Ours would be a universal lodge and a teaching lodge. I felt strongly that there had to be a place where people could just learn, perhaps there were those coming who had never even done a *Inipi* Lodge. We had to be prepared for all things. The Women could use the Turtle

Lodge for their Moon Lodge. No one was going to be turned away. Grandmother had invited everyone to her dance. It was going to be for "we the people."

I have experienced and poured water in hundreds of lodges. There have been hundreds of people along that path, each with stories of their many experiences. I also have been asked by the Grandmothers to clean up and close the bad ones. I knew first hand how difficult it was for most people to come to a totally pure environment and experience *pure sacred*. No dogma, no discrimination, just pure Sacred.

A storm was moving in. It looked as though it would rain. The Coyote dancers said they wanted to do *Inipi* lodge to help bring in the people who were still on the road trying to get there. To we who built the site, the move seemed a little hasty. We had blessed the sight, and this was all a matter of giving up control over to Spirit. So we relented and elected to let it happen.

There were several amongst the group who chose to wait until I held *Inipi* lodge the following night. Everyone had to do *Inipi* to be purified before they could come to the dance arbor and dance the Ghost Dance. Plus, there were still people arriving and the storm was looking like it was going to get thick given half a chance. By the time they got the lodge started, after fighting the wind and the rain, the camp itself was in total chaos. There were vehicles stuck on the roads. Someone even got their motorcycle stuck in the mud. Another had to camp out at the main road with a party of five, in their fifth wheel.

The rain was more like a southwest monsoon at times. Did they have bigger drops of water in Montana? I wondered to myself. The wind was howling. Runners came up to my campfire to tell me of the arrival of Laura Lee and Black Hawk and his family. They were back on the main road, with two vehicles and the Teepee Poles they had brought from home, along with enough food for a small army! The runners also informed me that representatives from AIM were there. I hopped in War Turtles pickup and was down the road in a minute to lead them into camp, and to see what kind of mood AIM was in.

I was familiar with AIM in the days of its conception. But things had changed since 1973 and the stand at Wounded Knee. That was the Ghost Dance that never happened. This was the 90's, and heroes can become villains, and black hats, well, these are vague times, are they not? I was taking no chances with my wife, and kid out there -- even if Black Hawk was with them. Things have been known to happen in the West from time to time. Spirituality does not mean that one gives up the ability to stand up against adversity, only that we have a choice in dealing with it, and a chance to direct the terms and conditions. Hopefully by resolving things peacefully, and with honored diplomacy.

The pickup was four wheel drive but this mud was thick and slippery. The rain was highly unusual. We estimated that perhaps three inches had fallen in less than a few hours. We met Black Hawk along the way, and directed him to our campsite. He was already out of the Suburban and setting up his tent with a work crew by the time War Turtle and I returned. Down the road the ruts had become a good 6 to 8 inches deep, and getting wetter by the minute. I believe peanut-butter soup would have be a good term for it. Then, as it would, the rain would suddenly stop for a moment, and a strange warm wind would move in.

When I got to where Laura Lee was it was one of those moments. There was no way of predicting when or whether the rain would pick up again. She was with some people from Missoula in their trailer. They elected to wait out the rain there rather than trying to make it to the camp. I passed the boys from AIM. It appeared there were three of them. It was going to be awhile before they got out of the hole they had dug with their sedan.

When I got back to the camp with Laura Lee, it was a sight to behold. People were coming out of the *Inipi*, People were setting up tents and trying to move to higher and dryer land from some of the low spots. It would have made a great movie! But then this whole event was going to be that kind of event in our lives. This was a definite human drama. The *Inipi* had released a lot of energy and by the looks of things around me the Coyotes were lose and dancing. There were Medicine Men who showed up at my campfire that night that I never did see again. Drummers were in their tents and campers were drumming. I could hear Robbie Robertson's *Red Road Ensemble* playing from yet another site.

One of the Medicine Men boasted that it was in fact he who brought this weather to test the People's intent. I blessed him and invited him to the ceremony that we were holding to remove the storm. I told him I hoped he was mistaken because when we got finished with our pipe, if he was attached to this weather, well, he would probably blow out of the valley with the storm. We went in ceremony and I lost rack of time. Strange, I don't recall seeing him again.

Somehow we got everyone's tents up, their campers situated, etc... There were six of us standing by my campfire some time in the early morning hours. We were too wired to sleep, and we sat there watching the campfires that illuminated the encampment turning the sky a fiery pink over our heads. I remember walking into my motor home at some point. The kids were all in tents now. Laura Lee, who was already asleep, awoke for a moment and asked if I was OK. I acknowledged that I was and the next thing I knew, it was morning. The sound of children playing outside my window became my new alarm clock.

This new day was the day we had to get everyone ready for the dance. There was a lot of work to do and it looked like Spirit was still undecided as to what it was going to do with the weather. Most of the morning people tried to dry out, and get acclimatized to the camp. We decided at one point to put up a double Teepee with the poles. We had plenty of visquine and canvas tarps. The materials were of so many colors that we unintentionally built a rainbow Teepee. We set up a pretty good shelter for the people to gather in, although it was a fun experience setting it up! We had limited supplies and no one was getting out of the encampment today. The storm had made the roads impassable in or out.

The Eagle dancer? Well, he and his people graciously set up kitchen at their camp so meals were going on there. And oh yes, Coyote was still at large. The games people play were going on, and the rain had driven out the weasels, blue eyed crows, and snakes. The camp was alive with them. That evening it was decided that after dinner, we would have 'dance class' so that people who did not know at all would have some Idea of how things should go at the Dance. I was going to pour water at a lodge that evening. Remember. Coyote was still at large. There was a split coming to the camp that most were not understanding just yet. It was still just an energy form.

Most were at peace, and the lodge that night held 40 or more. The energy flow was incredible. But there were still people coming into camp throughout the day. Not everyone had done *Inipi*. There wasn't a Woman to pour water for the Moon Lodge, so we would have to wait one more day for situation to finish turning. All in all the camp seemed to begin to be settling down and trying to make a good camp through the twisting and weaving of energies. Both of the dark as well as light.

Between the rain and the people still dribbling into camp at the last moment. It put a damper on a scheduled start. Welcome to *Indian time*.... These events can be truly funny if you maintain an open and good heart. People expect so much from the ceremonial leaders, not realizing that in fact that the outcome is based upon what the people themselves bring to the circle. My sister once said that we are a planet of the mortally wounded. We need to keep big hearts at all times. And along this road we must learn to allow a lot, and expect people to fall down along the path. Perhaps it is all a matter of allowing.

There were many who walked around that day getting in contact with the land, with their feelings, their inner desires. There were so many feelings that were flying around. So many emotions. Some of which we could have no Idea of their true origin or nature. There were new feelings, and we were not alone. The spirits were moving about restless and unsure as well. Who were all these two leggeds who had come to their quiet mountain meadow. The place time had forgotten. There were so many from varied ethnic backgrounds. So many questions about what had driven each one to come here, and some from so far away. So many who had brought their expectations and agendas. Yes, the Spirits were asking questions also and feeling their way through this Ghost Dance experience.

School

I sat for a long time with my friend the dancer and his little band. We shared coffee and smokes and jokes. We talked about what should be done, and how we could share the responsibility of working wit all these people in the camp. They would need to have a chance to learn and ask questions. We decided to set up a little school in the Teepee we had constructed the day before in the storm.

"The People are like children. They need some guidance. Some of them have never danced for real before. We are a broken People, it is not like the old days when we did this all the time. Today they come to *Pauwau* and most sit on the side and eat hot dogs, and watch the show. And no one knows the songs any more. We must be big and let them come past their fears of not knowing." I said.

"Yes that would be good. We could set something up and my wife could show them how to make shirts, and dresses out of blankets." He replied.

It had been a long time for them, too, since so many had gathered here for the intent of ceremony. Too long since the pipe was shared in circle upon this land. It was wake up time in the Montana Wilderness in more ways than one. The day brought memories to some that they were unfamiliar with in this life. Others who had been locked up emotionally were releasing. The children were something to behold as well, and there was a great learning in the watching of them for those who had eyes. A lesson in coming together, and breaking down invisible barriers that keep us separated and thinking we are alone in this life.

Everything was moving along smoothly on the surface. Yet I could not shake the feeling that all the hidden agendas and discord would erupt before the night was through. The cleansing of everyone's intent was far from over. The day would bring many personal experiences, and the night would bring visions. It had begun and we were at the beck and whim of the Spirit world. In the end, all agendas would have to be abandoned, all expectations released. Only those with open hearts that had no judgement and minds that were free of personal agendas would make it to the Ghost Dance. This was Spirits party, which the Grandmother of Grandmothers had called. When the Full moon came she would be watching from her grand arena. We were the dancers, *Makaakan* was the watcher of the turning of events.

The Women's Circle

The women gathered and set up some logs for the older ones to sit on, others brought chairs, and they started to drift in from around the encampment. I was asked to sit in, as was Grandfather Warren, to sort of moderate things. I should have realized that something was up then. Owl Dreamer walked over to where I was sitting and she was nervous as a cat in a wolf den.

"Can I talk to you?" She asked.

I nodded my acceptance.

"She told me that we had to wear dresses. I told her I did not have a dress. No one said I had to bring a dress." She began.

"Well, traditionally the women wear dresses, but one can make a shawl out of a towel or there are plenty of blankets." I replied. However, she was a little more agitated then her actions would give away. Something else must have gone on, no doubt it would reveal itself shortly.

"Listen" I replied, "this is your party, this is your place and you invited us all here. I called you sister earlier today, and I do not say that lightly. I will support you what ever you decide as long as it is in integrity and honor." I looked up and a large flock of crows flew overhead from the west , the direction of Travois Flats. They circled the encampment and then headed South. Just then some of the kids came up from the river carrying bones.

They ran up to Owl Dreamer and myself "What kind of bones are these Mommy?"

"Those are Buffalo Bones." She replied.

I extended my hand to one of them. They placed one of the bones in it, and I looked real hard at the bone. It was fossilized, and really large.

" These are ancient." I said.

"The creek is full of them. Grandpa said that the Blackfoot told them that this valley used to be filled with herds of Buffalo. The big ones!" Her expression broke into a smile, which eased the tension building up.

"Well, big is the word! These guys were gigantic by the size of this one." I got the eeries. For just a second I could see them in front of us, a whole herd of them grazing around us. I looked at Owl Dreamer and for an instant she was not in jeans but in buckskins, then the time rip closed, and we were standing there as I heard the voice of another woman calling us to circle. "We'd better go -- the day's burning up."

I was instructed by my sister, Moondance, to always have a witness to stand by me at ceremony, so that no matter what transpired, there would always be some one to say, "This is what I observed." So when I saw He Who Barks At Midnight walking near by... well, he was my usual and most likely candidate.

"He Who Barks At Midnight," I yelled across the field, "you might just as well join in with us."

We all three walked over to where the women were gathering, and it was not long after that Grandfather Warren sat down with us. Grandfather Warren had acquired a camp nick name 'Older Than Dirt!' The man was ancient -- yet ageless.

Crossing Lines and Breaking Down Walls

It was the day before the full moon. We held a noon meeting to gather the people into circle. I gave the talk about why Grandmother had gathered us here. A talk about the lessons behind our coming together, the ones that were evident and the ones not so evident. We finished building the Ghost Dance arbor, and rebuilt an old medicine wheel that had revealed itself near the dance site. The People finished making their Ghost Dance shirts, and shawls. And Coyote came to give his grand lesson to us all. This one would take us to the threshold of our fears, and into direct contact with our self-doubt.

We would become our own mirrors for this dance with truth. It was the revealing time, and no one would be excluded from Coyote's dance, **no one**. We were to gather again after dinner and do a sort of pre-dance. This was to be after the Eagle Dancer danced at Sundown to welcome the Eagle Spirit. After he danced I would go down to the *Inipi* Lodge and offer two Lodges, one for the Women who had not Sweated and another following for the Men who had not sweated. Travels in the Dark, our Blackfoot brother from Canada was giving a *Inipi* for the children that afternoon. He would join me later that evening in the Men's Lodge. Everyone would go through purification before they danced.

Another Fireside Attraction

Well, the dance started off with truly strange energy. First the Eagle dancer showed up wearing a Coyote Costume. Which under the circumstance was to be expected. Then we began the dance, I was drumming and singing with some of the people the Dancer had brought up from Oregon. There was also an uninvited guest that somehow wound up at the drum, who sat down right across from me. Another Coyote trick. I chose to pay little notice to the tricks, and proceeded with my job, which was simple. To steer the people in the manner they choose to get to sacred ground.

It was my job also to be the Peacemaker. Grandmother would give us the law, we were to do as she instructed. If we could come to the circle free of our personal agendas, with open hearts she would instruct us. It was also a universal realization by everyone there including the Coyote Dancer that we had all been on the road to the Ghost Dance before. Some had danced with Wavoka. Others there had been on their way to Ghost Dance when the slaughter at Wounded Knee happened. Through Pipes and Lodges it was a universal awakening to these facts we had in commonality, and it certainly was no accident that we were all here again.

My fire keepers were down at the *Inipi* Lodge, having left after the initial dance ceremony to prepare for what needed to be done. The dance of the people began with a lot of emotion. People were overcome with emotion. Several times I had to stop drumming to aid the girls sitting next to us. It was as if floodgates had opened and visions of the past times were filling our eyes and overflowing through the tears that fell.

I broke into a Hopi song at one point to lift the energy to another level. There was a fire that rushed forth from the drums and the People were truly lit aflame. Everyone was renewed and beyond the first wave of visions.

When I finished the song I had to go down to the *Inipi* Lodge to do my job. The Coyote Dancer walked over to me and voiced his first fear. "We will not have enough songs if you leave."

I turned to him and replied, "I must do what I must do, and the People must be given the opportunity to learn about ceremony, they are children who have simply forgotten, you know that... Spirit will give us the songs, have courage and the assistance will come." He looked at me. I could feel a queerness to his energy and I hesitated for a moment. Then the wind caught me and I was off to the *Inipi* Lodge.

The singers looked at me as I moved from the drum area and left to go down to the *Inipi* Lodge. Their eyes had that look that said "Please don't go." But I could not stay. The *Inipi Lodge* had to be done so every one could join in the dance. There was something else afoot here, best to have Spirit take its own course, then the nature of a thing will reveal itself. I walked through the cloud of swirling energies and down the hill towards the creek where the *Inipi* Lodge was being prepared. Behind me I left children, Elders and adults, dancing and singing. But I was aware of the twisting energy that surrounded the singers and the Dancer as I left the circle.

I heard Grandmother's voice say to me along my walk. "Keep walking through the grass, and trust Grandson, keep walking through the grass."

This seems like such a hard thing when the monkey mind is screaming in your ear. Especially when one is in the position of listening to everyone's fears, and taking the blows from the Coyote Spirit for everyone directly. I was the Ceremonial Chief but what does one do with something that has been totally called by Spirit and never done before. What is one to do when there are no rules, just the Sacred to follow. Would they all hear? Would they hear in time?

The Women arrived, and their *Inipi* was very powerful. I have been trained by the Grandmothers in the ways of several of the Women's ceremonies. Often I have been assigned the role of a guardian having to employ my positions at times inside and on other occasions outside their ceremonial camps. Blindfolded, I stayed and poured water for four doors, and turned the Lodge over to them for the fifth round. As I went outside to prepare for the Men's Lodge, I sent the head Fire Keeper, He Who Barks At Midnight, up the hill the call the men down who had not yet sweated. As he went up the hill I looked up over the cliffs that were in front of our site at the almost full moon. Tomorrow would be the real test. Tomorrow would be Grandmother's night. What magic was she weaving? And what about this strange Coyote Medicine that was spreading through the camp? What was the meaning to the method behind Coyote's games this night?

The moon, which was not quite full, already was intensely bright. Her glow seemed to pull at your skin. It was like cool sunlight and there was this irresistible desire to look directly into her glow. I thought, to myself, it must be the fact that we were in this wilderness, there was so little to filter out her radiance. The sound of the creek outside the Lodge and the smell of the Sage, Cedar, and Sweetgrass filled the night. Although there was apprehension, the knowing of the presence of Spirit and magic was also undeniable.

I heard a noise across the creek. So quick was it, and so altered was I from having just done two *Inipi*, that I had to think for a moment if I had actually heard it, and what dimension did it come from? My eyes drifted up to the cliff to my left, and there he was, Coyote himself large and bold, so large he almost could be taken for a wolf. Looking down at me our eyes met and then locked. We exchanged direct recognition of each other's spiritual continence. OK, I thought, this could be confrontation time. He has a lot of courage to send his runner to meet me face to face. This is when the gears must be going to shift. Hang on its going to be a ride. Then in a second he was gone. I was again left with one of those little feelings ...was it a Spirit or was it flesh that I saw?

Some time had gone by since I sent He Who Barks At Midnight up the hill. A little longer than I thought it should have taken for him to get back with the men for their *Inipi*. It is hard to have a clear sense of time when in ceremony everything takes on a ultra real sense about it. And time, well time is an illusion and it does not fit into *ultra reality*. Minutes can be hours, and hours can be minutes in *ultra reality*. But feelings are very clear, even if the mind that interprets them is not. Which is why we are taught in ceremony to follow the heart rather than the mind. For the heart is always the better interpreter of the two.

I could sense agitation up on top of the hill where the dancers were. At the same time I could feel a cold wind blow behind me around the lodge fire. It wasn't yet clear, but something... Old Man Coyote was really intense with his presence. But what was it? What was it I was supposed to do? Should I do any thing outside of making sure that everyone was safe and continuing to prepare for Grandmother's appearance in the best way I knew how? I got a grip on my intent, and pulled back into myself. Then I caught my humor again. My thoughts brought up the humorous side of Coyote medicine. Good Joke Grandfather..... OK, I see the sign.... but what does it mean?

Never the less, something was awry up the hill. Old Man Coyote, whether Spirit or flesh, had shown me his face as well as his Spirit. I'd best be awake and be prepared for any twist of events this night, I thought. From any direction, and in any form. What ever it was it was coming, and coming quickly by the feel of it..... I finally saw He Who Barks At Midnight walking through the trees along the creek making his way back to the lodge.

"Well, looks like Coyote and I had a little run it up there." He said.

"What do you mean?" I asked.

"Well, I went up there and was looking for the men, not seeing them right away I felt that I should leave an offering for the fire circle so I went into the arbor, and up to the fire pit to leave it. Well, it seems that I crossed some sacred line they had called on the ground. Any way they stopped the dance. Coyote yelled at me and I looked at Coyote and said 'well it looks like you caught me red handed.'" He hesitated. He Who Barks At Midnight always likes to be perfect. "anyway, I think they were upset." He added.

In truth, I sort of only half heard He Who Barks At Midnight talking to me as I was in an altered state from the first two *Inipi's* and preparing for the third. Sometimes our mind can seem to move so fast that we loose track of where we are going and at what speed and in what direction. Our instincts take over and seem to compensate for our moving in and out of the body. My instincts were telling me that I had to get the women out of that *Inipi*, **now**.

....And the Ladies were not taking to my subtle suggestions. I could sense we were running out of time. It was good that they were enjoying themselves and that they were moving through the energy. However, I knew they most likely were so into the Spirit of their lodge, that they had no idea about what was occurring up at the dance circle.

The men arrived and I instructed them to "go and sit by the creek, and to look deep into your hearts. Let spirit be your guide. We must soon choose a course of action. And look away from the lodge!" I walked over to the *Inipi* and trough open the flab and said "ladies we have to close this Lodge the men must have their turn." I knew I would get flack but sometimes you are damned if you do and damned if you don't. Either way I had to move some energy and move it quickly as I knew that Coyote Dancer was up to some form of grand mischief.

After receiving my verbal lashes, I quickly closed the flap and went down to the creek side with the men. We waited. It must have been about twenty minutes later the women began to come out. I just had to move the Women along, and yet they did not leave until they were finished. Time is such a ridiculous thing. Contrived lunacy.

The women finished and we could no longer hear them. They had walked around the bend away from us. It is funny how much you can understand by paying attention to your hearing. Second attention is something else. I cried out, out of courtesy, "Any body still here besides us buzzards?" There was no response. It was our turn. This had to be quick, though one should not rush ceremony. But we had to meet what was ahead of us up the hill. How does one direct time in a place where there was no time?

The Inipi was still hot when I entered it. We had used 63 stones in the Woman's lodge. The men entered, and I turned to the Fire Keeper, "bring 16 stones." The Inipi just seemed to move of its own force. We cried, we sang, and Spirit came. We were given songs for the ceremony, and visions of what we were to guide the People, and Grandfather made it very clear to us that we should not smoke our *Chanupa* there in the lodge. Rather we were to go and bring the *Chanupa* up the hill to the arbor.

We were to take the energy of the *Inipi* to the arbor, and release it there. It was needed there. The final songs were needed there. We all received this message. We closed the *Inipi* and the circle after perhaps two hours and walked the long walk up the hill. The night sky was filled with cloud paintings. But the air was cold. There was a strange silence. We knew that the dancing had stopped. There was a myst that covered the ground like little serpents slithering across the grass. In some spots it was warm. And in other spots it was very cold.

Grandfather's Dream Walk

I could see a few people up by the fires where the arbor was. I could make out others walking up behind the arbor upon the cliffs. I remember the feeling very clearly as I approached the arbor carrying the *Chanupa*. It was as if I was walking through time and walking at Wounded Knee a hundred and seven years ago. I was walking through Spirits. I could feel them, and once more I could see them all around us. Some in blankets, some in torn clothing. It was freezing, and the cold chilled the bone to the marrow.

I could hear screams and wailing from those Spirits, and the men who walked up with me form the lodge could feel it as well. There was this malaise that seemed to hang over the arbor, like a spiders web. Time was no more than a torn disintegrating fabric before us.

We were experiencing their fears. It was the fears of that ill-fated Ghost Dance at Wounded Knee as well as the fears of their souls as they returned to finish at this one. I could hear the voices of the old ones as they mingled with the feelings of today. Dimensions were awakened, and reality was cracked wide open. As we walked to the arbor, we were serenaded by the sound of not just one Wolf singing, but two. Apparently there was another Wolf accompanying War Turtle's wolf, or was it a Spirit Wolf?

The smoke was joining in with the myst, and creating little whirlwinds across the phosphorescent grass, lit by the emerging face of Grandmother Moon. People stared to run up to us, I could not yet determine what they were saying. Nor could I determine which reality they or I were in. It was as if we were walking through realities. The *Chanupa* seemed to be my only reference point. I found I had reached a place where although I could comprehend everything, I could not differentiate between the spaces of events. "We have ripped time open," I thought to myself. We are walking through the void.

As we entered the arbor people seemed everywhere around me, and the others from the lodge. There was a ghostly silence to the arbor. They started to tell me what had happened. I was coming back into cognizant reality. But I could not yet engage with that which I was hearing. When I moved, it was as if I cut through the atmosphere. I could detect little sounds like obsidian chard's clinking in the winter wind. I kept thinking "we have ripped time open." I looked into the eyes of those now surrounding me and knew they were not aware of the severity of our impending reality.

All I could hear were their voices. In a flurry of panic they came at me. At first I could not distinguish not the personalities connected to the voices.

"They said that we would be cursed with a years bad luck because someone crossed the line... The second time, they said "that's it we can do this no longer."" One cried.

" .....they packed their things and went down to their camp and we waited here for a while then everyone started to break up." Another added.

"Others went up the mesa and are doing pipe ceremony up there...... They said they saw the Grandfathers walking up there."

"We could hear voices.... Like singing coming from that area over there." someone said, and pointed.

The chaos was complete. I guess that it was Travel's voice which brought me back to the here and now.

"They have no courage." he cried out, raising his hands to the stars. " We have come back with the words of Grandfather, and they run! They fight like dogs over scraps of food. Who side, who is right, who is wrong."

I found myself reaching out to grab his arm. "It is all right. It will be all right" I found myself saying.

Travels looked at me and I could see there was fury in his eyes. It was a look I have seen over many lifetimes in the eyes of men on the battlefield -- fear and rage mixed together.

I saw the face of a woman come into focus. She was standing not too far from me. Her silver hair was blowing gently against her face. There was a serenity in here eyes, yet they were watering.

"Can you tell me what you saw, and think happened up here?" I asked her.

"Well, the one in the Coyote cape, I forget his name, said that someone had dishonored the sacredness of the arbor. He said that they had crossed the line too many times. It was being disrespectful."

"Who crossed this line?" I asked her.

"I am not sure." she replied. "I didn't even know there was a line, until they said they were leaving and why."

I looked into her eyes as she was speaking, and there was actually very little to say, for I was watching her entire experience which was there for the viewing. "What did they say, exactly? Now think, it is important. You see it does not matter so much what happened, as much as it does what everyone thinks happened."

I realized the confusing context of my worlds, but things that make sense to Spirit do not always make sense to ordinary mind. She looked confused. "Listen just tell me what the words were they used when they stopped and picked up their things and went back to camp."

"They said, I mean actually, it was his wife who said that we would endure a years bad luck for dishonoring the circle. That they could no longer participate because we were being disrespectful..... I mean, we didn't know we were being disrespectful, and we did not mean to be..."

"Yes, Yes I know ," and I reached out to hold her as she was starting to shake. The others took their turn telling of what had transpired. At the same time, I was having to deal with my own rage. I was beginning to see the game, and it was nasty. But Coyote can get this way. It is a matter of overcoming and rerouting our emotions, not in the denying of them that we draw energy and wisdom to us from an experience like this.

We began to gather around the fire that had been built for the drums, and the crowd slowly but surely began to grow. They told their tales and at one point a small group came into the circle and I could see it was Running Wolf and those who had gone up the mesa to do Pipe ceremony.

"Ghost Wolf, this is going to happen. We are going to have this Ghost Dance." Running Wolf proclaimed. His voice shaking -- half from cold and half from emotion.

I offered him a place by the fire between myself and Travels. Some one was making coffee. I remember smelling it, and I noticed that Travels had apparently left my side and gone over to the arbor fire and was putting more logs on it. That is the last thing I remember of this world until I walked down to my camp as dawn was approaching. Travels remained by the Fire, holding vigil till dawn. I knew the People could count on him. Someday, he will be a strong Medicine Man for the People.

J could sense the fear in their eyes and their hearts. Like children of innocence they were easy to read. We smoked the pipe and talked around the fire till the dawn star appeared. I was told that Spirit took me over and they say I spoke non-stop for hours about creation, and lines that we draw, real and unreal. The pitfalls of judgement to the human spirit -- superstition verses moving into the unknown -- trusting in the Source that is within us all. Funny how it is seldom Creator who sends his wrath upon mankind, but how freely in our own fear we try to make someone else feel smaller and inadequate. I vaguely remember hearing Grandfather's voice ...

"So someone appointed themselves high priest and you were told that you did not comply with their self manufactured rules. We have some one who did not have sufficient belief in their own ways so they adopted someone else's. They do what they do without explanation, or reason. They follow blindly someone else's dictate. They never question why, nor when. They would judge you when they do not even posses the ability to comprehend the depth of their own actions. They are merely slaves to dogma. They will try any manipulation they feel necessary to force you into their little sandbox where they have control. Fear Mongers, do you know the term?

"What will we ever do with those that would be troublesome priests? Intimidation based upon what little they know, is placed upon you and your fear of offending Spirit. Spirit does not care about your carefully chosen words, or calculated actions. Spirit reads clearly the intent of your true desires, and responds to the emotion of the moment.

"I release you from your fear. Now, if you want my declaration to work you must release yourself. Now, forgive your accusers. Bless them and send them truth and love. For when the seed of truth is placed amongst lies it will corrupt to the fullest, and love will heal them and encourage the truth to grow. Thus you are free from the consequence of engaging in anger. The lowering of your vibrations to access anger is not worth it to your glorious continence. Leave them to play in their sandbox.

"We can create our little games as we play in our sandbox. We can make mountains, and castles, and rivers and the end of the world if we so choose. But it is when we start to effect others with our games that we need to be conscious of crossing borders, and entering someone else's space. When we play games that manipulate reality, and cause other's to feel guilt, or unworthiness for their beliefs, that is when we go over the edge and become the tyrant.

"We forget that everyone around us, for the most part, has their own sandbox as well. They are living their own truth. You have your sandbox and I have my own. Gandhi had his sandbox. His sandbox was India. Hitler had his sandbox, his was the world and perhaps the universe. He desired to control consciousness. Hitler was the last of the Dark Lords, and much of what you are feeling today is the result of his reign as the ninth lord of darkness. We have now entered the Cycles of Truth wherein the pathway to mankind's enlightenment, their true enlightenment, shall be realized and the dream of the Old World will be completed. Tomorrow at sundown you dance the Ghost Dance...."

This is all that I can remember of when Grandfather spoke through me that evening.

Coyote's Game Plan

Coyote's game plan was becoming clear to me now. We learn who we are when we learn what we are not. We see what others are when we see what they lack. The actions between words are important to observe. They tell us the true intent behind the veil. If we are to attempt to cross into the new dimensional reality, the Fifth World, there are certain conceptions of reality which must transcend in the process of our own hatching from the cosmic egg. We are, at this time in our experience, indeed very like the caterpillar, about to start spinning our cocoons. We are about to emerge as the butterfly birthed into another world.

There is no ending to life, there is no death to life, life is of its own nature -- a forever road. When we leave this world, we go to a place where we decide whether or not we choose to be reborn into the next world or to return to this one. In essence we are born into each reality, we simply change our resident vehicle. There is no death, only the changing of worlds. It is the Soul that travels while time itself stands still.

The Ghost Dance has no agendas, nor is it a Ceremony of any particular People. I would refer you to the story of the Ghost Dance and the Pale Prophet, the one I call *Wacoma Tete, Lord of the Wind*. The Ghost Dance is about the transformation and manifestation of Spirit, where we move beyond space and time. It is a ceremony where we integrate time and space, and moving beyond limitation, hopefully, we release our spirit. Our spirits have been captured by the spell of limitation. We have forgotten who we are, and what we are. We can not go forward if we have no remembrance of our past. For without that element we do not understand why we are here in present circumstance.

The purpose of the Ghost Dance ceremony is to free our Spirits that we might join in the freeing of Mother, *Maka*, and *Makaakan* (The Goddess) that is within and around us. Thus we are lifted from the limitation of the Body-Mind-Consciousness via the spiraling currents of our *Mer-Ka-Ba*. In the Ghost Dance ceremony we access ascended thought, thus we reconnect with Source It is a process of our surrendering to that Source, and through natural process we allow our spirits ascend to the higher octaves of our consciousness.

The Ghost Dance is all about freeing the spirit, not creating new ways to contain it. It is about freeing the Feminine, it is about feeling the dream of *Makaakan*. It is about removing limitations, and opening ourselves to new points of reference. We can only hope to expand consciousness when we allow for new points of reference . Otherwise we will continue to recreate the same energy we have fallen into over and over. We must create a greater energy then that which created the circumstance in order to change the circumstance.

There are Ceremonies that reflect the one we know as the Ghost Dance. They are known to each Indigenous Society. The principle desire in each is correct and in commonality. We are more than flesh and bone, and with pure intent, connection to Source and the understanding Universal Law, all things are possible.

Love is the force which sanctions all realities it is our connection to the life Source. Love is untamed, and knows not the state of fear. Although fear within us will shut us out of the state of love instantly. It is a free essence. A part of Creator. A part of all that is, and it can never be absent lest all that is -- is no longer.

Love in the purest sense has no restrictions. It is lawless like the Creator from which it emanates. Love is a force that knows no logic or reason, it creates its own set of values as it evolves for as long as it desires to be felt. It is the cosmic glue that holds all of the all in relationship. The only reality that exists is no reality. Love is the Peacemaker and the lawgiver. It allows us to option to exercise all realities in whatever illusion we chose to manifest. The Ghost Dance is Grandmother's, *Makaakan's* gift of love for the People. It is inspired by the flight of their own spirits. It is restricted only by the limitations of our own hearts.

The Ghost Dance is about the Grandmother Energy. It is about dreaming the new reality, dreaming the new dimension. When we explore the science of dreaming we unleash our true spiritual power. It is about the birthing of our spirits. It is about crossing the barriers of time. It is about time travel itself. In this Grand Purification Ceremony we move through many dimensions and experience many realities. Some happening in different time zones, both past and future We learn to hold onto that which we love by giving our hold up. For in the surrendering we realize we are a apart of everything and that is our touching stone to eternity. To surrender is the act of allowing for manifestation to occur. We simply get out of the way of our own desires by becoming the whole.

In order for the Spirit to fly it must be free. In order for you to ascend you must free yourself from Dogma and limited perception, and allow yourself to be that freedom. One can not keep the Hawk in a gilded cage. Oh, yes, we can capture the Hawk, and confine it and slowly watch as its Spirit dies. The Human Spirit is of God, and God can not be confined. We have allowed our spirit to become so stifled for so many life times of perpetuating the lie, that we no longer remember our true self. So we need now to allow for new points of reference to occur, to allow our perception of who and what we are and for the nature of reality to expand.

Emotion is the stuff that the next kingdom (reality) is made of. The whole of it pulsates with passion. Respect and Sacred is what is required of our actions, and intent to enter the realm of higher truth. We must allow ourselves to feel deep profound feelings. We must allow them to come forth. We learn to do this by entering a state of neutrality. Not charging the circumstance of the dream. Thus we come to know feelings of self-joy, and fulfillment. It is one of the steps to ascension. These feelings elevate us, and give us purposeful values and perceptions of self.

No one enters the gates of the Fifth World unless they have love within their being, and know joy within their being, thus becoming the living expression of it. For if the *Golden Age* is perceived as heaven, then surely heaven world be the *Isness* of life. *Isness* perpetually is creating the state of itself, perpetually in the state of Joy. The body will continue to evolve and refine its nature to accommodate the greatness of the creative mind that occupies it. Spirit creates ... the body accommodates the will of Spirit.

The E-mergence

We are light visitors merely wearing borrowed robes, which are gifts from Mother Earth, *Makaakan*. We have arrived at cross roads in life. From here we watch the ending of one dream and the birthing of a new on. Our birthing into this new reality will never be attained by intellectual process, nor will the doorways be pried open by the mastery of technology over natural forces, there is no competition. Nature will win. The keys here are simple, although the observation of events in the game and our part time participation in them can seem painful, it is a matter of heart. But many of us have lost contact with that element we call heart.

There is a road that leads to the path of heart. It is a twisting path with unlimited doorways, some giving accesses to other trails, some leading us nowhere. Even in that there is a learning. The mysteries of that path are intriguing and different for each journeyman that desires to travel upon it. For some, it is a road that leads us back across the abyss to the place of forgotten dreams. For others, it is an action packed journey through brave new worlds that lead to the future. There are as many experiences as there are clouds, all of them changing continuously.

The secrets of making *the path with heart* clear for passage can only be realized through our deepest emotions, our passion for life and our becoming more *in the moment.* We must learn the secret of being the *Isness.* That *Isness* is the All, from which the Source manifests all that is and will ever be ... the Great Mystery. The pain we feel along the pathway is our separation from life and the life force. Most have fallen out of rhythm with life and can no longer touch the life force at will, which is why we walk through this *Hall of Mirrors* that we might see again.

All we come to feel as life force in our brief experience upon this plane is Creator. The ability for us to feel this wonderment is a gift of love. We experience the heartbeat -- the pulsing of life as feelings. It is these feelings with which we weave our illusions, upon our dream board like dream spiders dreaming reality. We create the game board, which we then overlay upon the unified field. Love allows it to exist. For when we have an absence of love the illusion dies. The result is life experience literally a virtual reality. We are here for the purpose of experience. We are creating the nature of the game as we go along. It is a creation game, for *mankind the species* is a compulsive creator. We will create for the sake of creating. That part of the Source is intrinsic within us.

We need now to complete the process of *the grand initiation.* To accomplish this, we need to understand the process of our beingness through every feeling, every emotion. We need to understand ourselves in our completeness. We are having our emotions or lack of emotions intensified to accomplish this task. Emotion is eternal memory recorded by the Soul. Every inadequacy must be realized so that we are free to expand without limitation. It is a grand plan, this *Hall of Mirrors* we are entering. For in love all that we are will be revealed to us. This time is about feeling and freeing ourselves, it is about merging, the merging of reality, merging of feelings, merging of dimensions, merging of cultures, merging of spirituality, merging of consciousness, merging of relationships and the merging of male/female roles. We are experiencing the 'E-,' which is being made possible by love.

The purpose of our feeling these things is Source's way of guiding us to a point of realization. Whereby we move intuitively towards an invisible point of balance. The term *walking in balance* is often embraced and tied to Native American wisdom. It is a phrase I have seen hanging upon many walls and woven into dream catchers. The intent behind the statement to me translates into our allowing the merging of our parts through natural process. Understanding that *Makaakan,* the Spirit of the Divine Mother, will make us whole. That it is not a matter of resisting, rather it is a matter of allowing. For in our softness we allow the feminine energy of the *Makaakan* to enter our being and open our heart. We could call this mystery ... a matter of love.

The Nature of Armageddon

By being the wholeness of ourselves, we are then governed by the light which is the Source of all that is. We no longer suffer from the friction within ourselves. We stop fighting ourselves. We are free from polarity. The condition of polarity is the underlying cause of the internal strife. The battling within our being of polarity and contradiction is the Armageddon. One could say that the term Armageddon is merely another word trying to describe the suffering we feel as a result of the tearing of ourselves apart, while under the illusion of separation. Our pain that we feel while playing out the role we have chosen, is the awareness of our separation from the whole realized. Our separation from Spirit, from our selves, from each other, from our society, from nature, from the Earth, from our souls, and from the Source itself.

How are we to ever understand that the ancient Toltec People believed in the one God of all if we remain locked in our separation? How are we ever to open the Keys to Enoch if we deny the Emerald Tablets of Thoth the Atlantean? How are we ever to open the doorway to unlimitedness if we keep the heart locked in a gilded cage? If we deny our awakenings, if we deny our darkness or our divinity we deny the wholeness of our being. It is in the dance of the darkness and the light which allows us our experience. The dark and the light in life is but the reflection of that which is within us.

I am certain we have all heard the saying *"the truth shall set you free,"* but more than often it takes courage to stand in our truth before we can see it as such. We have come through social consciousness which values its corruption more than it does its divinity. It encourages lies and admonishes the honor and integrity. It demeans individual thought and praises mindless obedience to materialistic values. As the spirituality of the thing dies the legalities seem to rise and devour our personal liberties. It is *the Last Waltz of the Tyrants.*

Tyranny is the serpent that always wears the easy smile while silently plotting to take everything that insures your freedom away, while undermining your sanction to create, thus creating within you the illusion of separation. *Divide and Conquer.* If we loose our freedom we loose our creativity. If we loose our creativity we die as a species. Thus the serpent devours its own tail. It is the cycle of self-destruction.

It is the tenacious few that have the resilience to come back again and again, to stand up to centuries of dogmatic hypnosis of the populous that will create the New World. We are going to a place and a state of mind that has never been before. It is the mothers, fathers and children, the lovers, those who refuse to give up the dream of beauty who in the end will inherit the Fifth World and create the *Golden Age*, which is our destiny.

Let no one judge you, and judge no one. Surrender your judgements and you shall pass through the gateways of darkness unscathed. For yours shall be the light of the Father/Mother eternal and *Makaakan* shall lead you by the hand through the darkness. You are the children of one mother and one father who have come to awaken, come to be renewed, come to renew *Maka* in a sacred way. The freedom in a thing is found in its Spirit, for Spirit is not dictate to the laws of mankind.

Where we are going we are going to have to develop the ability to access unlimited consciousness. We are going to experience many things in the next decade which were unfathomable in our Grandparents time. We are going to experience life forms from other dimensions and other planets. We are about to rejoin the galactic community, if only by our own will and desires. We have decreed it.

We are already experiencing the wonder of children being born upon this plane who are advanced beyond what we would call normal intelligence. They are the new *Manu*. The new race. The race of the future. They are different. There are hybrids amongst them. We are dealing with walk-ins and walk outs, are we not? We deal daily with channels, and angels delivering information that holds claims of altering our consciousness, or guiding our global transition into the Fourth Dimension, and perhaps the Fifth. We are dealing with every aspect of our perception of time being dismantled on a daily basis. Why? I would ask you, "Are *we being prepared for contact?"* Are we being prepared to deal with the manifestation of shifting realities? ... Only you can prepare for the inevitable experience of *the time rip*.

Morning of the Dance

he rays of morning came, Travels in the Dark surrendered his vigil in keeping the sacred fire that would have been abandoned had Coyote been allowed his treachery. That fire was later that day to be reborn within Travels, as he claimed his spirit upon the land that was, by heritage, the home of his people the Blackfoot.

Blackfoot country is the last hold out of American wilderness. All the other land upon the turtle has been devastated by the encroachment of modern civilization. Pollution precedes the annihilation of the wild creatures, and the Grandfather trees. These acts of mindless debauchery of the land leave us with a dying reality, which then leads to nightmarish creatures walking in human bodies without the slightest essence of human spirit. Society's children are dreamless and honorless, and Spirit is a forgotten word. *Sacred* has become a forgotten virtue, and the women do not sing, and children no longer laugh. Our Elders are mocked and ridiculed as we walk through once great and proud cities, observing what has become the *graveyard of humanity*.

But here in Blackfoot country, although we do not know for how long, the Buffalo still roam, the Eagle still flies, and the Grizzly plays with its young listening to the evening serenade of the Wolf under the full moon as it has for thousands of years. You can still drink from the creek, and Brook Trout taste sweet. The smell of wild flowers even color you sleeping dreams.

Breakfast was served late, to which I did not attend. I spent most of my morning up on the mesa with a thermos of coffee getting another perspective of the little encampment. The weather was clear, the storms had passed. I realized that we were given almost every test to our intent that could be imaginable. Spirit was not going to let just anyone in on this special event.

This had to be a story where we followed the lead of Great Spirit, no matter what the external circumstances appeared to be. Old Man Coyote was playing a very clever game. I could not tell anyone what I saw, but I had to cause events and mal-intent to reveal itself by its own accord. Already the sacred geometry of the field below could be observed from the heights of the mesa. I clung to the jack pine, feeling like a hapless boy, wondering what the outcome would be. I danced on the clouds trying to move beyond my own disillusionment. Harder still, I tried to go beyond judgement of foolish actions. Hearing constantly in my head the words of Grandmother when she was here by my side, instructing me for this very day.

"They are going to be hard on you for doing this. They are going to say at first this was only a fad, a whim. They are going to say that you had no right to do this thing, but you and I know that only *Wakan Tanka* can give consent for such a ceremony, and the instructions for such a ceremony can only come from Spirit. No one is left that remembers the whole story. The People are like children. They have forgotten how to be Sacred. They have forgotten the ways of Spirit. Let no one be a priest that rules over the People. It must be their own Spirits that call forth such a thing. The Ghost Dance will continue long after the critics vanish from the scene. You will have to live with that not their words of fear. The Lord of the Wind, *Wacoma Tete* himself shall preside over the ceremony.

"It is the Spirit of the People that will let them know they were observed by those from beyond time. They will send their signs and they will come to dance with you. Only the humblest of you will last long enough to see this occur. Only after great fire will you hear the songs of the grandmothers upon the wind, and the tears of awakening will flow from your eyes. They will be tears of joy. People will turn every which way, and so will the manner of their talk, and their heads will be on backwards. You must focus on your intent. You must remember why you were chosen and taught these things.

"Do not look into their eyes. Look deep into their hearts. Talk to the Spirit of them, not the ego. The Spirit will hear, and the way for harmony will open. When you are criticized by them look into their Spirit and love them. They are children. They have all forgotten. Especially those who will desire to become priests, for theirs will be the biggest fear. They have lost their ability to trust. When we have lost all connection to our Spirit we can no longer trust that *Mystery* knows what is best and would not lead us upon a path of knowledge to our destruction. Spirit will deliver, you must trust in who you are. Remember who you are.

"Give them your Spirit. Forget your everyday self. Do not teach the People. They will not hear that. Just be the heart for the People. They will feel that as will their Spirits. They will rally in the end. They will know that this was no fad. They must be respectful to each other, to the land and even to their enemies. The world will be watching them, and Grandfather will know their hearts. Spirit doesn't come until we offer Spirit our heart, that's just the way it is. Some things just are..."

Coyote Dance

We had faced every kind of occurrence one could expect to try and break up this gathering. The Coyote Priest had done his best to disrupt the energy. But something had occurred that Coyote was not anticipating. Spirit had come and the Grandmothers had made their declaration. The old ones had shown their faces and embraced the Gathering and the People.

Grandfather had come and spoke to the People. We had crossed over the line. Sometimes the Spirit of a person can, with pure intent on their part, lead them through a maze of obstacles so that they may stand in the clarity of the light. The intent of the People has become clear, some had come for Spirit, some had come for themselves. There were two camps now. From up on the mesa one could observe that. One could easily see the intent of beings by their body language. For the tonal of a being, or a People, is obvious when viewed from a place of objectivity.

The storms, the strange weather, floods, high winds, I saw everything through the Shaman's Eye. We could not please everyone. Like Grandmother said "some things just are." The events of the previous night were clear to me. Old Man Coyote had revealed the tricksters, and the last energy from the dark had been released. Now there had to be a clearing. The initiation was close to its ending. The People had to make their own choices. They had to reveal their intent to Spirit in circle, and I had to offer the tricksters an honorable way out. I came down off the mesa and was headed for camp. Coyote Dancer must have seen me coming, for he was there. We met in the field under the full light of the Sun.

I looked into his eyes and he into mine, but there was no conflict there. Just two souls touching each other. He could not hold the stare, and it was time for me to offer him the chance to choose an honorable way out.

"Aho my friend you had a rough night." I said.

"Good morning," he hesitated looking down at the ground stumbling for the next word.

"I think it would be best if you go" I told him, trying to not put the tone of challenge in my voice. "If one does not feel good about being a part of this Ceremony, then it is best that they honor that feeling and go. There are no bad feelings here towards you...go with our grace and our love."

"We ran out of songs like I told you. And ...."

"Say no more. Your job here is complete, but look deeply in your own heart for what you send will come back to you ten fold for each person you sent it to. You and I both know the rules of the game. This was Spirits game. The People were as children they needed your guidance, not your judgement. But like children they hold no malice. Go in peace." I told him.

"We meant no harm. I have the ways that I know, I tried to honor everyone." he offered.

"But did you hear the words of the Grandmothers? No agendas. Come to the arbor with no agendas, and *Makaakan* will guide you through each step. We are supposed to be here for the Mother, not our own desires. Tonight, I will lead the People in the dance." I stated.

"I wish you well then my brother, let there not be bad feelings between us. Perhaps we can work together again." he responded.

"We will both see what Spirit has to offer us. These are strange times We are all walking into the unknown. And there is much to learn before one accepts the role of leading the People. This I have learned here. I thank you for that opportunity." I extended my hand, he accepted and we shook.

"By the way, stop by my camp I will give you something so you get back home. But it would be best if you leave soon. There is no point in dragging it out. We both know who we are."

We looked into each others eyes one last time. There was no veil between us. Coyote had his out, and I had to gather the People so they could come together. I sent People over to Coyotes camp to gather our food stuffs and to prepare a new kitchen in the Rainbow Teepee. It would prove to be a good place for the new kitchen.

I walked towards some of those gathered nearby in the field who watching the meeting between Coyote and myself. "Get some help. Our friends will be leaving. Those that choose to go with them should go now, also. We need to set up the new kitchen. Tell those who are staying we will gather in two hours for circle."

I felt my body jerk as I was walking away, always a sign to me that Spirit was saying "Pay attention to what is going on.", or an affirmation that what was going on was truth. It wasn't over yet, I knew that. I still had to meet one more time with Coyote at my camp. Now that the split was made clear and placed out in the sunlight, there would be waves of energy resulting. I was about as scared as I had ever been, for now I had also made my choices. I had accepted leadership of this Ghost Dance. It was in my hands now. That was a lot of responsibility.

I walked over to my camp. The kids were playing down by the river. They were having a ball playing in the creek – oblivious to the goings on of the adults. It gave me a much needed light-thought frequency. I got myself a cup of coffee, and noticed some of the women walking over towards me. It was one of those moments when you know it is time to light up an American Spirit. Slowly, they approached me by the fire as I sat down on a stump.

"Morning ladies." I greeted. They all responded, greeting me in unison.

Owl Dreamer spoke to me ...

"We have seen and honor what you did. But perhaps we should let them know we have no bad feelings. It is just that we could not accept their decrees. Everything about what they said was fear based. We have all come here following our heart path. We have seen everyone gather and talk around the campfire. We all spoke of how everyone that was here had experiences with Ghost Dances in the past. How many of us were on our way when we met our end at Wounded Knee, with Chief Bigfoot. The rules were uncalled for and the delivery was one filled with fear based declarations."

There were a few seconds where the space between her delivery and the next spoken word was as big as the Montana Sky. A space where you could hear the next word and read each others faces without speaking. The next word was obviously mine.

"I support what ever you all decided, and I feel compassion for your reasons for your choices. Understand though that each action we choose will have its reaction. We can not think about our decision now, we have to move forward with love. Spirit is running the show and weeding out the camp. I think right now we have to pull this camp together, and pull it together fast. We have to go to ceremony soon, and the Children have to eat. This is obviously how this event is supposed to unfold. *So Be IT!*"

Grandfather Warren spoke out. " I have something to say! I suppose why I am here in this circle is because I have awakened to my feminine side, and find that I continue to embrace it everyday... Last night I stood and watched as we danced. While I watched the Masters gathered while we were dancing under the stars. I saw the Grandmothers and Grandfathers standing and dancing amongst us. Then I saw them stand back and watch as we stopped our ceremony and gave into the fear of one person. I saw them throw their hands up and wonder what had happened, after we had put out such energy that we (had) pierced the heavens. They watched in amazement as we just walked away. They wondered why we could not realize who and what we were. We came here to dance. Tonight we have a chance to follow our hearts and spirit without remorse or ridicule. We should do so."

Tears filled his eyes and he was shaking. His emotions overflowed into everyone present and we all found our eyes watering. Grandfather Warren got up from the log he was perched upon and walked towards the arbor. There was little left to say.... Grandmother had entered the hearts of everyone. It was one of those moments in a circle where everyone looks around and acknowledges one another and there is simply too much going on for verbal communication.

The kids all helped and we reestablished the kitchen and with a precise quickness and ease. The camp shifted into its adjusted mode and embraced the new reality. It was like after a sudden rain storm in the summer that disperses the heat and stale air as the sunlight breaks out and all of life seems refreshed and new.

In summation, to make this long story short, we did the Ghost Dance for two nights. For some there it was the completion of a long journey through dreams and lifetimes. For others it was a reawakening to the reality that indeed they had come from the last Ghost Dance to be awakened in this time. At a future date I will publish a book that tells the story of this Ghost Dance in detail, from both my perspective and that of the People, along with their letters. It is, after all, their story and their dream. I will leave you with an excerpt from a letter by one Ghost Dancer as an example of the depth of each persons human drama. This letter tells one of the stories of what happened one day in Montana, when we set our intentions to dream a new global vision and we reawakened the Ghost Dance...

August 26, 1997 - A Letter from Flute Carrier

Hi,

How can I talk about my experiences at the Ghost Dance? It is like doing a life review. So much has come up or was released with my participation at the Ghost Dance. Some one asked me what happened at the Dance, and I said after a moments thought, I don't know for sure, but there were five rainbows interconnected day and night the last five days of the ceremony.

As each day has gone by I have been so busy. It is like so many events in my leading up to this point. So much went on, I saw and experienced so many things that I do not have the words to explain them all.

My life has been to say the least, very full. I was born May 19, 1961 at Shepherd Air Force base, Wichita Falls, Texas. My first year, I lived with my grandparents. My older brother had a Medical difficulty that required my Mothers consistent attention.

Like I said, from the beginning it was rather full. My Mom and Dad moved just North of Reno, about 1965-1966. All I remember of Texas was bowls of cotton, wild strawberries, snowmen, and my best dog, he doubled as a horse.

The first Dream I can remember to this day. I was walking in the snow carrying a baby. I was a child also. We had black hair and wore buckskins. I had been wandering in the snow for four days. We died. The dream first came when I was around 8 or 9 years old.

About the same time, I had a nightmare about the spider people. They would come into my room and carry me out of the house to a beam of light. That is all I remember of that dream, except I still have it, but not as often though.

The "dying in the snow" dream was connected at the Ghost Dance.

Anyway my childhood did set the stage of my life. The middle child, and first, last, and only. I had plenty of battles, both physical and mental. I had courage and dared the face of danger. I had my ups and downs, like every one else. The difference was, mine were and still seem to be extreme.

In 1981, after being gone for 5 years, my father, returned to tell me he was dying. He also told me I am ¼ Native American. He said not to tell anyone, but one day I would need to know -- part Mohegan and Cree. He said not to tell anyone, because when he was small it was unsafe to be anything but a W. A. S. P. white man.

I hope he isn't turning over in his grave now. I remember hearing around the house as I was growing up, how my family has been involved on both sides of every war since the beginning of America.

In 1992, I met a fellow by the name of Jack, a full blood Choctaw from Oklahoma. He said he wasn't Shaman, but I didn't believe him. He said I had an "Indian heart". I didn't really know what that meant. Although, I had been interested in metaphysics since I was about ten, and still to this day believe in miracles. I did not know what being Indian really meant never mind Metis, or mixed blood.

Jack taught me about the 'Medicine Wheel", some basics in how to read what I already knew. He taught me about smudging etc.

I had gone to a gathering in Sandpoint, ID, around 1987, but Jack is the major factor in how I got to where I am now. All my life I have done my best to live with my heart, to be myself.

My way of life, as Jack said, is what he called the Indian way. I have for the most part been extremely alone in my studies and experiences. One particular night, Jack was driving me home from a small ceremony. It was late and very cold. At the exit ramp just before mine there was a coyote under the street light. I took pity on the poor thing, and bought some food at the near by grocers. He the coyote waited until we got back.

Jack looked at me as we watched the coyote eat. He said, "You are truly powerful and blessed. I am not the teacher for you, but I will get you on the right path." I miss him with all my heart. Our lives got busy and for a while I weakened, and Jack disappeared.

Just about the same time I met Jack, I had the weirdest experience ever. I had dreamed of a choker. So as I sat at my desk with my beads, surrounded by all my Pegasus posters and Unicorns [the druid in me] to begin the piece that I had dreamed. As I began the piece, the room disappeared, I was in a semi-arid mesa valley with some other children, and we were around 10 summers.

My dad and brother rode into camp; their hunt was successful. My dad was an important person in the tribe, so I wasn't able to get close enough to get a hug, with all the excitement. As he looked at me with that all knowing eye of his, I smiled shyly and he tossed me a crystal. The world was grand, so beautiful.

One day as I was getting the food and night came, the shouts of the camp changed, from joyful hunting tales, to screams of horror. There was dust and noise and horses every where, I went to find my dad, "Run little one," he shouted "Run as fast as you can, don't look back. I will come for you when I can."

So I ran. I grabbed the baby on my way out. Her mother was dead. I ran and ran all through the night and all the next day, with the sounds ringing in my ears. Then, it started to snow and the snow became a blizzard. I walked then and I saw the baby was dead. I lay down to cry, then I was back at my desk and the choker was done. The crystal I had was the same one that my "dad" had given me. Well, I did not know what to think.

I told Jack all about it. He was not sure what it meant either, until after the coyote feeding thing. The last thing Jack said was "He is still looking for you. He is keeping his promise."

The eyes of the father in the time transport, are the same eyes as Ghost Wolf's. At the last circle, when he looked at me with those wolf eyes of his, and said "Hi, Little One", the flash back hit like a ton of bricks and a thousand walls came down. Owl Dreamer is-was my aunt and was studying medicine woman stuff, Running Wolf was the oldest brother, and I was the littlest one, hence the name "Little One." And how could have Ghost Wolf known, it was all too much for mere circumstance.

Since Jack, my dear friend, I spent a lot of time growing. In August 1993, I did my first medicine wheel mostly alone. I told two friends where I was going, and if they wanted to come with us, Sara & I, they had to respect my wishes. We went to Mt. Shasta, the wheel was Basic. I made it out of a cornmeal and tobacco mixture, with a crystal at each point. Then we sat quiet for a moment or two, then I sang (something from very long ago.) Next there was a very loud noise, one I had never heard before. I had called the Big Foot or Sasquatch. My friends were stunned and so was I.

I stayed on the path Jack put me on, only a bit quieter. Bill, my husband, was there the night I called the big foot. After that things got strange again.

Actually life has been very different since the time transfer thing. In a strange sense of things, one could say I did my first Ghost Dance alone. I have the crystal, a flute much like the old one, and most of the stones are back.

In August 1994, Bill took me kicking and screaming to Las Vegas. We lived mostly in the campgrounds and ate chicken wings. While we were there, I saw condors at Lake Mead. I see lots of stuff that isn't there or isn't supposed to be there.

In April 1995, I dreamed of a red and a white wolf. In the beginning of my dream, I was on a bicycle and with another person. We were going up an alpine type trail. We were just past the last farm and into the meadows when I saw the wolves. The person I was with said it was my imagination. We discussed it some. I finally let it go, but not for long. The wolves were following us.

The person driving the bike said, "I was nuts." After some time we reached a very high mountaintop. There was a stream that fed a small pond. I was thirsty, when the bike stooped; I headed for the crystal clear water. "Where are you going?" the person said. "To get a drink," I said. "But it is poison" the person said. I thought about it for a minute, and went to drink anyway. Gosh the water was so good.

Just then the red wolf jumped out of nowhere and bit the person on the throat; they tumbled down the other side. I was frightened, my back against the wall. Frightened I looked around thinking, where is the white one? She was right across the pond, with a silver and metallic red fish in her mouth. I didn't know what she wanted, at that second I thought I was next. Then the red wolf was standing next to her, she came around to me and dropped the fish at my feet and turned and went back to here mate. Whispered on the wind they said, "Your family is coming. You are protected. You dared to follow your Heart."

That dream has been & was very shocking. I am still not sure what it all meant. Except the eyes, Ghost Wolf's eyes are the same as the Red wolfs. Which sometimes seemed to be Yellow and other times Blue. Anyway, what was so special about that water? I was just thirsty. And Why were there red and white wolves. Why was the person with me, the one that the red wolf killed? I had trust in that person.

That May we came to Idaho. Bill loved it at first, because of Randy Weaver. I hated it for some reason. Until Sara and I walked up to the magic nine alone. We stuffed ourselves on berries, this hill has a power all its own, a simple magic.

The "magic 9" as I like to call it sits directly over an underground river, at a spot where two rivers join creating one. I felt the power (love) the first moment I ever stopped here three years ago. I want to put the medicine wheel back (mend it), right where it was, on what is now the pipe line. As you may say, I have answered my own question. However, there were those of my family, who did not believe that I had the star stones, even after I showed the stones to them.

Why do people only allow their own truth, and reverse the truth of others? They look at me as a weak person, for I have always followed my heart, even when in conventional ways it was wrong.

The growing since the Ghost Dance, is astronomical. I have never really had what the old world called a best friend. I thought my husband was, as I watched the two eagles on our marriage day flying. Now for two years the she eagle has flown alone.

I realized that I am my own best friend. Today I am complete. My soul mate is me. My twin soul is me. Over the years, in prayer - mediation, when I ask where my twin soul or soul mate is, the answer has always been; Why do you ask for what you already have. On the coldest loneliest days, the voice would wipe away my tears, a hug, as real as this letter. Then the voice, your voice, always said you are never alone, I am always with you. In the old world when people would say "You can't do it alone." They would say I was crazy when I would reply that I am not alone.

You, Ghost Wolf, are so... well, thank you, you didn't put on airs of "I am so powerful, or bigger than, or better than." Your humanness and simpleness are wonderful. Now, I totally comprehend the understanding, knowing, a gentle strength, true power -love that you are.

Oh, I almost forgot, I received my flute for my birthday that year. Again the message they/he is looking for you, came to me from the flute transporter.

Since I first came to Idaho, those closest to me, except Sara, tell me I did not see what I know I saw. Even when there is a witness. At first I was afraid to write this letter, especially the important parts. Partly because of, well, it is almost to odd to be true. However each time I go over what brought me to the Ghost Dance, there is nothing else that comes to mind.

Is it fantasy and make believe in a desperate world? Like a few self-proclaimed teachers might say? Well, they were not there when I called the Sasquatch and he came. Nor were they there in Alaska last year, when the eagle gave me, me of all people, a feather, not one but six. They did not even want to hear about the transport through time and space or the crystal that wasn't there.

Funny of all the stuff, I have heard stories of and discussions about. I can remember doing in this lifetime.

I am still a little afraid. I do not have great power, except perhaps love, if that is considered power. I have no great education. I was left on my own for most of that. Before the Ghost Dance I was confused as to the meaning of the signs and symbols I would see in dreams or in my life. Now somehow I can understand them, but I still do not have the words down.

The star stones (Aulmauracite) are alive. How they came to me is a story I want to share. One I got at the Ghost Dance from Laura Lee, and I have had two more. The Others my birth father in this world left me. The one your Son Grizzly Bear Dancing gave me is three. The third one I somehow remember loosing very long ago. It was a gift given in love, lost in fearful confusion, returned in the innocent love of a child.

I don't know a lot, I am bendable, I might be crazier than I thought, or like my heart says, "It is so." "It is truth."

As Ghost Wolf kept saying, only 10% of my heart grew heavy. Ten percent, that isn't very much at all. He also said the hardest words of all at the Ghost Dance. When he told me I have to learn to say "No" and draw lines for my boundaries of what I can except from people and abuse for any sort.

I first heard of Ghost Wolf about a year ago while playing on a friend's computer. So much has happened since them, and the magic of the Ghost Dance, although now a lot of it seems like a dream, it changed my life forever.

Life changes always, constant. I have been mildly surprised each day since the Ghost Dance, and it has all been good. I don't feel trapped by guilt any more, or blame. With joy I look forward to the new millenium and the transference.

We are strong, only together. The feeling of loneliness is gone, and I know who my Mother is, I danced for her and with her. I now embrace my native heritage, the missing piece of what I am is back.

I am in a new school now. Remember when you said, "We have to learn to say no to others out side of Spirit?" Do you have a clue how hard that will be for me. It is the hardest of all lessons to learn. To say no, openly to another person, seems to me to be openly rejecting them and hurt their feelings. Gosh, I really try hard to watch my step in the field so that I don't hurt a flower or step on a bee or snake, in fear I might hurt them. If any one can understand the dilemma of being human you can, as I watched you and learned. I saw you struggle with the right words so how not to offend any one person. I wanted to cry, when the eagle dancers left. When your soft voice said it was OK to cry, and reminded me of the 10%. Like the mother I am, I realized that we had to love them enough to let them go.

Flute Carrier

The Eagle's Gifts

There are many visions about these end times. People are talking. Opportunists are trying to create a cash cow by creating fiction that they can sell to the people in Los Angeles, who will make movies about it. But it is a great hardship to see these things that are coming. Such visions are not matters, which gives seers great Joy. It is even harder to talk of these things for the visions are felt very close to the heart. Not all we see is good. Not all we see applies to everyone. Most people prefer to be told what they want to hear, not what they need to hear.

I wish often that there was a magical way through this time, and that this time was behind us. The stress of knowing and seeing can be overbearing and make our personal lives difficult. Medicine People have personal lives, despite what may be thought about us. In-between the work and the ceremony, we live very human life styles. We go through what everyone goes through. A prophet is not automatically exempt from experiencing the event. In fact, each time we experience the event through the veils of time, we endure it. Every time we see through the veils of time. Plus, you loose a lot of sleep because *the seeing* does not always happen when you want it to.

I wake sometimes in the middle of the night, running high fevers. Sometime screaming and in cold sweats. I feel things before I see them, so I can experience these things for many days, even months before they are released from the inner sanctums of my minds eye.

I have had many visions of the future. Some good and others not so good. I have witnessed the disassembly of the 4th World. We will be given warnings to these events that are coming. We will be tested many, many times over to strengthen us. Only the purist of heart will make the journey all the way. This is part of the Gift of the Eagle, it is the way of the Eagle. To see the Eagle in our visions always means initiation. The Eagle can be a very harsh teacher as well as a strong ally. To work with the Eagle's Medicine demands the highest degree of integrity and total balance of temperament. One must conduct themselves with total impeccability. Nothing less will survive the intensity of the Eagle energy. To do otherwise could mean severe consequence, even death.

Understand that the Earth is a living being, fully possessing her own consciousness. She has her own agendas, her own dreams, and her own desires. That part of her which is physical, that which we walk upon is her body. This Purification that we are beginning to experience is a cleansing of her body, just like we two leggeds do when we go to the purification lodge. There is an energy that moves through the universe. It has different degrees at different times. When the Earth enters these energies, it is like *Her* going into the purification lodge.

We are now in the time of the Purification. We are experiencing a birthing and a cleansing at the same time Earth Mother aligns herself in harmonic resonance with the rest of the universe. She is going to purge herself of everything that is making her sick. She will purge herself of everything that is causing emotional imbalance, and sickness of her mind, as well as sickness of her body. She does have a mind of her own, remember! She is dreaming a new dream, as you should be!

She is very caring of her children. She loves them very much. That is why she allows them to make so many mistakes, and still gives them anything they desire. She will and must rise up and defend her children from the abusers and abductors. She is wise and knows that there are those who wish us harm in the universe. She is our Mother! She has created many veils of energy to protect us on many levels. She has made it very hard for these beings which you might call ET's, or what I call *the Ethereans*, the inter-dimensional beings, to just come into our environment and take us over. However, she herself is going through massive transition and is very weak right now. So we her children are going to have to bear some of the burden of taking care of our own business. It is time to make our houses ready, company is coming.

How do we know that she is protecting us? Because many of these beings possess knowledge of technology which is light years beyond our present abilities and comprehension. Yet they have not taken us over, and for a long time they could not interfere with our natural evolution. Yes, it is true that long ago there were attempts to tamper with us, but *not all* of these attempts were executed with malevolent intent. Some of the tampering was done with the intent of fixing what harm was done by the renegades of their race, as well as our own experimentations.

This summer, at the Ghost Dance, I was given a little time alone to commune with Spirit. This was allowed me by Spirit, as I was invited to be the ceremonial leader of the Ghost Dance. A commitment which I resisted. I went for a long walk to be alone and talk with the Grandmother Spirit. I found myself alone, by the fire with nothing but the stars over my head, many, many miles from any one or anything... I asked Mystery, "What about the future? Am I mad? Is everyone I know mad? Many of the things that I see worry me, and what of the dreams? Are they just madness? After all, I am just a two legged like everyone else. Can you help me? Am I supposed to figure out all the answers here?"

Have you ever known that kind of moment?

I was so grateful for the gift of the silence. Just to be alone, and to reconnect myself and Mystery. The space of timelessness where I was able to renew myself, just feel myself, for myself. I call this special kind of time "taking a little M&M." (ha ha)

Seven Circles of Power

ystery spoke to me through my soul. I could hear the voice of Grandmother. In an instant she stood before me, her hair blowing in the winds, she was wrapped in a red blanket. Her long fingers lifted slowly and pointed into the clouds, which appeared as balls of light with the sun streaming through them. The glare of the sunlight through the clouds made them seem like screens. Slowly pictures of the future began to appear upon them. I was shown many possible scenarios. I was given new energy to deal with them. She always gives us what we ask for in direct relationship to the degree of intent we ask for it. This is law, her law...

"Many of these things will be obvious to you, to all those who live with the Earth Spirits, and remember the ways of the original teachings. As the prophet has told you, it is inevitable that you will experience these *Thunders*, but the People will also be given *Seven Circles of Power*. These will be *Seven New Ceremonies*. Your sister (Wolf Moondance) will contact you and remind you of this conversation we are having incase you fall asleep. There will be signs that these things are coming, but you must stay alert, and not get caught in the sadness that is beginning to sweep through mankind.

"Those who are locked into the flesh and the material world will not be aware of these thing until they are upon them, nor will they be able to see these things for their true purpose. For the most part, they are blind in spirit as well as eye. Do not exhaust yourself trying to make those who choose to sleep understand the ways. They have not the capacity, they have fallen away from their souls, as well as from their spirits. They are worse than the soulless. They are encased within their limited consciousness and have developed offensive mind. They suffer from the human condition of ...*I know*. Thus they will not have an understanding of these things. These things that will be so apparent to those awakening will be non realities to the unawakened. They are like ghosts in a vision to the un-awakened.

"The signs will come. The messengers will come. The prophecies that have been given will manifest. Affirmations will be received, that which are called the signs. But only those of most pure mind will be able to sense them for their true purpose and origin. One must first be aware of the truth within themselves to sense it in others. Only those of most pure mind will be able to decipher illusion form the truth."

Note: Most pure mind is the mind of the heart.

"Today, many people are working for the spiritual uplifting of their own group, of their own way, of their own people. Spider Woman is coming. She is spinning a new dream. What she will bring, and what she will uncover must be given to all People. You are all her children. She sees no difference in any of you.

"Earth and her People will experience *Seven Great Thunders*. Seven messengers. These are known to some as the *shakings of the dragon's claw*, or *the shakings of the eagle's talons*. Each one will mark the beginnings of a possible future, and the closing of the door to the old corrupt way of life. Mankind will pass through seven worlds of their own creation. You have been chosen to participate in the learning and sharing of these *Seven Fires,* these *Seven Circles*. These Circles of Power during this time will be reborn from the souls of Womankind. In this way the ones who are awake will be shown the pathway, and given the means of how to prepare for the return to *the Sacred*.

The first of these *Circles of Power* is the Ghost Dance, which is why you and the others have been called here. The second is hidden in the ways of the Medicine Wheels. The third is in the way of the Sweat lodge. The Fourth is hidden within the labyrinths. These things have been revealed to you directly by Spirit through your own experience and quality of intent. You will meet four Women of power and grace possessing great mystery to their personalities and origins. They will bring the other three Circles of power to you. Only your heart will be the guide for discernment.

"Two of these women will come from the land of the Condor. One will come from the land of Mu. One more and her companion will come from the caves of the Dragon. These women will hear of your work and will be directed by the Grandmothers. You are to present them to the woman's circles that will form from those who have awakened by experiencing the first four. You must surrender your anger, put down your sword and stand firm before your fears. For you will experience many things that can not yet be revealed to you. Let yourself become an example for other who express in the male energy at this time.

"Let no one who accompanies you judge another, and let no one in your company react to the lessor energies within them, lest they be removed from the gathering. Where you are going these kind of energies will be very damaging to your advancement and survival, for mankind must now pass through the *Hall of Mirrors*. You are amongst the first to enter, much of the *Hall of Mirrors* you have already experienced.

New ceremonies will evolve through the Grandmother's energy, as mankind awakens to the true meaning of the Christ Consciousness. Only the ceremonies of Purification and the Sacred Pipe will remain of the old ways to be brought through the veil of illusion into the Fifth World. I could feel the Grandmother's presence. I started to churn within as she spoke through my heart. "Along with the *Seven Thunders*, the People will experience seven miracles. The awakening of the feminine will bring us *Seven Circles of Power*. You are experiencing the *First of these Circles*, the resurrection of the Ghost Dance. The reawakening to the deeper truth and power of this ceremony will awaken the Grandmother Energy, allowing women to regain their former place of equality and set forth a balance upon the land and within the hearts of mankind.

"There is a place upon the Turtle, in the South West. You must find this place. You will know this place. It is by a Big Sister Volcano, long asleep. She exists within a circle of other sleeping volcanoes... Go there, dance the Ghost Dance within the mouth of the Big Sister. There you will connect with a force from the inner belly of the Earth. A force so strong that the entire cycle of self-destruction could be vanquished in but a moment. This place must be made known to the Ghost Dancers.

"You must lead Five Ghost Dances. These Dances will be held in four locations. Each cycle there will be five, with the last at the place of the beginning. The People shall come to you, personally or by messengers, inviting this ceremony to be held. People will hear of these ceremonies and the miracles that will occur at them. They will be called to come, and at each location the Spiritual Leaders will embrace the performance of the Ghost Dance in their land. Along the pathway many will be called to these awakenings. The numbers will necessitate the ceremony to be held in very remote places. There will be much fire and testing of this feminine energy. However, once the first five are completed, the *Seven Circles* will have been birthed, and the pathways cleared.

"These will be very difficult experiences for those who insist on holding on to outmoded dogmatic belief patterns. The *Hall of Mirrors* allows no escape from the consequence of truth except through truth itself. It is a labyrinth of intricate design. In order for mankind to progress to the next doorway, they must learn to give up the dogma. Give up the rules. The rules were born of mankind, not of Spirit. They are locks upon the gateways of freedom. All that is required is the recognition of the Sacred. Spirit will provide the rest. For Mankind, the test shall be their ability to trust their inner voice, to perceive through their hearts.

"The People of their own will must unite, both men and women, as equal and divine entities. Unconditional Love is the key here. The release of all judgement and anger is required.

The past is a no thing when one finds themselves living in the moment. Seek all avenues to escape the grasp of anger, and with full intent open the pathways to the heart. In the final moments of this dream the heart will be your only shield against calamity. Force will match force. As the frequency of change intensifies, so shall the response. Is a matter of cause and effect.

"Once the *First Circle* is birthed, the remaining *Six Circles* will make themselves known, and shall be given to the people who have followed the Rainbow Vision. The *Seven Circles of Power* shall be born of the unifying harmonics. This birthing will result from the releasing of fear that will arise from the merging of energies. The merging of energies will be allowed when the spirit of mankind relinquishes to follow the will of Creation. One can not change the course of the river without serious consequence.

"Through the gifts of the *Seven Circles*, women shall heal themselves. Thus womankind shall heal mankind and together they will join to create the new frequency of the Fifth World.

"The release of all agendas is not only required, but essential. Only the Mother's agenda need be followed. She is the guiding hand that will carry you through the gateway of tomorrow. Trust. Trust in creation. Trust in Creator. Trust in your divine heritage. Help those that help themselves and keep walking for the emotional storms will again be of equal intensity to that which is the reflection experienced from the Earth.

"Along with the splitting of the Earth's embodiment, so will you experience a splitting of your realities."

The Seven Thunders

J broke away from my *Third Attention* for a moment. I felt as if my head were going to explode. It was as if I were in a dream, yet still in this place, and whatever level it was on was abject reality. Another messenger began to speak. The voice I heard was an ancient voice. The voice of El Viejo, the Old Man. This Spirit was capable of taking on any form, yet it remained the same. When I first gazed into the myst, trying to see it with my ordinary vision, I was at a loss. I have learned that on occasion when we have these kind of experiences, as we shift back and forth from plane to plane, we will momentarily slip back into our *First Attention*. I reeled momentarily, feeling the dizziness in my body. Then, in the next instant, I was in a cloud. I struggled desperately to focus my eyes. It was as if this vision was showing me many, many faces. Faces of all beings, all races, and things I could not recognize.

It was as if I were experiencing simultaneous realities merging into each other. As if I were living all of them. I was aware of a Crystal City that seemed to be under a dome of some sort as I looked up to where the sky would be. The buildings reminded me of what I had once seen while in the Arizona desert. But I could not hold the thought, and another reality seemed to pull me in, and then another... I was walking through a swirling shaft of pure light, which possessed many colors. Yet it was also by its very nature a white light, a liquid light.

I found myself standing in a very strange place. The color of the earth was a kind of saffron. There was a pink myst which seemed to move like dry liquid across the landscape before me. If I moved, the whole of the place seemed to respond to my slightest motion. I instinctively knew that I must move slowly and with graceful expression, else I would tear the whole reality up around me.

I saw someone walking towards me, almost gliding across the field from my left. It was an old man. I could not discern the style of his garments. They could have been old or from somewhere that was not yet in my reality. What I could discern was that his garments were simple. It appeared that they were woven and almost seamless in construction. He wore a kind of turban, and the most beautiful of crystals that formed a necklace. Whoever he was, he did most certainly not work for the government. By his features he could have been Hopi, or he could have been even older than Hopi. There was something unearthly about the sense of him.

We walked together for some distance and with each step it was as if we were merging in awareness. It was as if we had known each other for eons. The sense of strangeness left and I reached the point of not noticing the differences. He stopped for a moment and looked over towards a small grouping of trees in the distance. They had the look of juniper, but everything about them was somehow different. He held his hand out signaling me to wait a moment as he walked ahead.

The First Thunder

The Old man turned back towards me and motioned for me to follow him. I followed his footsteps which were somehow very apparent to me upon the ground that made no noise when you walked. I moved over to where he was standing almost effortlessly, feeling no sense of gravity. It appeared that he was standing on the edge of a cliff. I stood next to him, looking over the edge. Far below us I saw a city. It appeared that there was much fighting going on, and much sickness in the city. A wind came up over the edge. It was heavy and slow and consumed me momentarily. The smell of death filled my nostrils and almost overtook me, and I wanted to wretch. I heard the crying of children and women. There were many just wandering around aimlessly. The buildings were broken as if there had been an Earthquake, or a great storm. There were many lying in the streets dead, or on their way to death. I saw many vehicles dark and without markings. Overhead I hear helicopters, and when they came, the people ran away and hid from them. Form the vehicles men would step forth, wearing some kind of dark green uniforms -- almost black. The people ran from them as well.

Many of the people appeared to be sick and had open sores upon their bodies, some were almost naked. I remember their skin, which was cold and a greenish grey in color. Their eyes were hauntingly empty. I know the look as Sampacu. I have seen this look in the eyes as the body prepares for the spirit to leave. It is like the spirit is already gone, yet some residue remains, and the people live out the final steps of their lives roboticly.

I looked more closely at the people and could see that they were all ghastly thin, like skeletons. There was much starvation going on here. The land seemed barren, being able to sustain no life. There were no herbs, or food plants growing. It was parched and there seemed to be water but there was no one drinking from the creek.

Old Man spoke to me, narrating the vision before me. "There will be much starvation in the times coming. There will be no means of healing all those who are sick. They will have lost touch with their souls. Their Tonals will be broken and their life forces will become weak.

"There will be no way of reversing their plight, for they will deny that they did this thing to themselves. They will be seen casting blame in every direction. They will believe that the Earth itself cursed them and caused this thing to happen. They will say that Creator caused this thing to happen. Only if they can take the responsibility for their own actions and deeds can the situation be turned around.

"They have tampered with everything, even the clouds. They have forgotten that this has happened before. They paid no attention to their pasts and have no awareness of their true natures. They play with everything like destructive children. The Sky has been ripped like an open wound. The wound is festering. The rain will rain poison upon the fields, and the water will burn their insides as they drink it, and carry worms that will eat them up from within. They have walked away from the old ways. Now the old ways can not help them for they are not connected. They will no longer know how to live with each other as human beings. How to live in harmony with the Earth. Now the elements of the Earth will turn against them.

"There will be little that can be done for them as the natural laws of this Earth have been broken, even their spirits will have left them. They will be loosing their souls and there are many who wish to have souls. They will be as shadows. They have created a way of life that forces them to live outside the laws of creation. They will even enforce these ways with their enemies. The sickness will be so complete that they will even kill those who wish to heal them, for they have chosen the path of death.

"They have all been judged and caught in realities created by their own actions. There will be no ability to dream in these people, no ability to laugh, for they will be devoid of Joy. They live their lives for death, not for living. So they will have created this reality from which there will be no escape. They will not have within them the ability to create life even for themselves.

"The scientist will know about these conditions, but they will not speak. They will only see the fault as being in the maladies of diseases and of the weather. There, draughts and flood conditions will be extreme. The hole in the atmosphere as well as the dimensions will cause the terrible Devil Winds to suddenly rage and then disappear, leaving behind a trail of death and destruction. Some of these winds will blow as much as 200 mph.

"Those who created this condition will try to cover up what they have done and blame it upon the Earth and God. They will tell the people that it is because they have walked away from their religions. There will be much fear in the hearts of these innocent people. Then there will be a great fear that will find the hearts of those who hid the ancient knowledge. They will realize that their secret is no longer a secret, for the messengers will be spreading the word across the globe.

This will be the first signs that the war in the heavens is about to manifest upon the Earth plane. There will be many ships of light being witnessed in the heavens in this time, for the leaders of the people have made deals with thieves, and their contracts are due.

"The religious leaders will have no answers for the many strange occurrences that will be happening with the weather, as well as the diseases that are spreading across the lands. The appearances of the great star ships will occur with more frequency. The People will begin to see for themselves that in fact it was their religious leaders who are the ones responsible for their situation of helplessness. This will be obvious as they see that these leaders will be powerless to do anything in the face of what is occurring. There will be a quiet but steady resentment building in all Peoples for this, especially in the young as they realize that they have been duped for so long. But there will also be a feeling of fear in that most will not know where to turn in the face of the continuing calamities.

"There will be the discovery of many of the ancient temples and schools of knowledge, which have long been hidden away, as whole mountains seem to dissolve in the torrential rains that are coming, the result of El Nino. Remember, there will be two El Ninos. As the discoveries happen in many locations all over the world, many hidden truths about the events of the past are also brought to the surface, which will substantiate how their religious leaders enslaved them and kept them form knowing the truths of living upon this Earth.

"A multitude of souls who have reincarnated upon this Earth at this time have life-contracts for service during the transition. Many were born into this world in 1947, between 1976 and 1979, and in the 90's. There is now an ongoing emergence into this plane. So many souls are coming back to help with the transition that there are not enough embodiments for them all. This is why we have many *walk-ins*.

"Many of the children born in these years will be capable of greater intelligence than their parents, for many are connected to the Source, and posses within them a memory of their Creation as it actually occurred. They did not come into this life severed from their Light bodies. Many among them will be those who participated in the building of the ancient cities and sacred sites. They will have a memory of where these sites are and they will be very instrumental in finding them again. Also because of this, they will have access to the whole of their brains. This will enable them to have access to their full consciousness capabilities. It will be said of them that they are mystics, that they are he old ones manifesting upon this plane. In many instances this will be true.

"It must be considered that conditions that allow for souls to exchange embodiments allow for the existence of other occurrences. We must not forget that *walk-ins* can also be created by mankind themselves, as we now know has occurred with the exposed realities of the *Montauk Project*. *Walk-ins* also can be sourced from other than human souls, such as extraterrestrials. We must use extreme discernment when we come into contact with these individuals.

"Their powers of mind will surpass those who are in ordinary reality. Mind control is one of their abilities and methods by which they move in and out of time experiences. Having this knowledge of experience beyond time and dimension, some have developed powerful although perverted consciousness capabilities. They have no roots, and no people of their own. They are wanders through many dimensional realities. Slaves to those who move them from destination to destination. For their very existence is due to those who control them.

"Many of these beings are little more than contrived emanations of human consciousness, who have been mechanically created. They are very aware of source yet are powerless to act of their own volition, for not having souls they posses no will. This condition is permanent unless they themselves to take on souls. This is rare, but it has occurred. Such a transition can only be accomplished by connecting to and working with someone who possesses a soul. They themselves can not manifest a soul for they have no experience of its nature.

"When we enter the day of purification and experience the three days of darkness, billions of these entities will disappear from consciousness completely. For they will have no individual point of soul reference. It will be as if they never were, even in our memory.

"There are many souls that are presently in a coma like state. They are dysfunctional in the earthly experience as a result. With the raising of frequencies upon the Earth plane, many souls will begin to awaken quickly over the next two years, `98 through `99. Many of the ancient temples, and cities will be discovered that have long been hidden from the eyes of man. The discovery of some will be due to natural occurrences, where others will be revealed through the intent of those who have incarnated here and once participated in their construction.

"As a result of the energy from these ancient cities being uncovered and the energies once contained being released, people everywhere will begin to remember the ancient truths that were connected to their experiences there. It should be forewarned to those who will speak of these truths to the People that they will be hunted down and made out to be criminals, witches, and worse. Those who might perform acts of healing, and other things considered to be of a miraculous nature, will be accused of performing acts of Black Magic and will be said to be Satan worshipers. These awakening souls must exercise extreme caution for *fear, remember,* is growing within those circles of people who are currently in control of the political and financial institutions of this world.

They are harvesting the consequence of their deeds of many lifetimes, and are aware of the inevitable consequences.

"The *Hall of Mirrors* will bring about a humbling of all People, where they will be forced by their own circumstance, to own the responsibilities for their actions. For in many the powers of the mind will be awakening as a result of the Earth resonating to much higher frequencies. There will be a cleansing of the emotional bodies of mankind. For the corruption of the passing consciousness will not be allowed to pass into the Fifth World. The Children of the Earth will own by their own experience the pain and agony in this experience they have created, as they churn within the grip of the *Cycle of Destruction*. You must tell your People to go to the mountains now. To gather what seeds they would need to grow food that can be grown within glass houses. Both for food, and for medicine. Scatter the seeds upon the Earth as you travel, then they will be there for the harvesting when you need them, for you will travel much, and often by foot in the times that are coming.

"Build little villages, take only that which you will need to keep sheltered and sovereign. Simplify your lives in every way possible. Keep always three days supplies with you for each member of your family, for there will be times you will have to be away from your homes for that long with out warning. As the *Dark Hunters* will come searching for you from time to time, for they will fear you and the knowledge you possess. They will come from the heavens as well as across the land in strange machines that make no sound. Not all of you will be able to understand how to shift energies and become invisible. The people who have not changed their life patterns and developed these abilities, will have to utilize their skills of survival.

MErKaba → *[handwritten margin note next to "shift energies and become invisible"]*
MEdiTaTion

"There will be small pockets of calm and safety for those who have a food and deep rock water source. If you are protected by the trees and are at the higher altitudes in granite mountains, your odds for serenity will be greatly enhanced. For most, this is going to mean a rough school and an accelerated one in learning to get along with people. Learning to put aside petty judgements, and those of crass manners learning to be gracious. This is a different kind of war, but it is a war. The war of valued life.

"Be prepared to take care of at least twenty people at each camp. Your camps should be one days travel from each other, so you can travel with your young ones and Elders. Stay to the highlands. There you will be safe from the flooding, and the trees in the mountains will slow the *Devil Winds* that are coming, and protect you from the *Green Mysts* that fall from the sky. These things are coming very soon.

"When the winds come, you will look for tornadoes but there will be none. It is the whirlwinds, the demons, that are born of mans dark nature. The Mother can not longer hold them, she is too weak. Just as she can no longer hold the poisons in the sky. For the atmosphere is too weak. Both time and space are filled with holes from all the experimenting. Mankind in his experimenting has ripped open the *tensile bubble* that was created after the last destruction to protect them. The scientists are aware of this, but are not letting you know for obvious reasons.

"Diseases will begin coming now with more frequency due to the *Little Devils* that there will be no cures for. They will come from Monkeys and cows. Also they will come from the taking of drugs, which will even be in the plants that will come from the water that is poisoned with their chemicals. You will need to grow your own food, in the mountains where the snow will keep things pure. There will be less diseases there, and the marauders will be afraid of the spirits and animals that will become much more aggressive towards those of lesser consciousness.

"This is already occurring, even amongst the peaceful ones. Our kind is vanishing as a result of the madness played out upon this land, and there is a energy that has been released that can not be turned around any longer. Many humans as well as our kind are dying as a result of the Little Devils. Perhaps 85% of all present life forms are in peril at this moment. There are devises that can filter out two of these Devils, but the third cannot be filtered out of your drinking water. When the three of them come together death is very quick, and will be known as the New Plagues.

"There will be Marshal Law in the cities. Even in the towns outside the cities. But in the rural areas, with the exception of locations where there are military bases, this will last for only a little while. For the situation in the cities will become such that those trying to keep control by force will have to send their forces to those areas to maintain their control. For in the cities they will have gone mad with the pain of death and dying.

"You will see strange things in the skies." Then, Old Man pointed to the sky and I saw what looked like bubbles. You know, when you look through the bubble and everything is blurred? Some started to open up like holes, and when they did I could hear a horrible roar. As this sound emitted from the sky I could feel the Earth beneath start to shake. Smells came from the ground that I was not familiar with – as close as I can describe, it smelled like sickness, increasing my desire to wretch.

The air was thick. There were velvet-like particles in it. They were hard to move through my nasal passages when I would breath. It burned my lungs. I was still looking up at the sky and there appeared to be a faint green myst coming from the holes and raining down upon the ground. I looked again upon the ground and there were huge cracks opening around me. They appeared more like wounds in flesh then cracks in the ground.

Then I felt something like a raindrop, but it was thicker. Like starch. It was falling from the hole in the sky. As it landed upon the Earth the evaporation process turned it into gas. This was source of the odor I smelled.

Then Old Man pointed to the creek, and I saw the fish. They were dead, floating in the water with their bellies up. They too had oozing, open sores. I remember screaming. Then somehow, I was seeing things from a new perspective. Yes, that was it! I was seeing it from the sky. I was flying. My eye through which I was seeing was the eye of a bird, an Eagle's eye. I was flying high over the ocean, along the coastline.

There were storms coming from the distance. I could see them but they were strange. They had strange colors to the clouds. And the lightening was very large, if that makes sense. There was flooding everywhere, and dead Whales, as well as other fish floating in the water which looked like a river churning after a storm. It was brown and full of Earth, and garbage a lot of garbage. There were parts of buildings floating, and boats, tankers I made one out to be. They we all broken into little pieces. I saw fires raging below me, but the fire was coming form the cracks in the Earth.

Then I seemed to be flying in the desert. Not over Red Rocks, but dry bush -- maybe Nevada, or California. There were thousands of people, some in vehicles some on foot. They seemed to be migrating. Headed ....that was it, they were headed towards the mountains. I could see a city in the distance. It looked like Las Vegas. Helicopters again. One seemed to be right on top of me. I turned to look at it and the next thing I know I was sitting by the fire again, and the Old Man was still there but it was as if he had turned into a myst before me. Smiling, very quiet and still. It was as if life itself had taken a breath. Everything was still.

It was over.

As Old Man was becoming more like the myst, his voice was clear although very soft. I could swear that I saw tears in his shimmering eyes. Man will blame creator for all of this, as he always has. He will curse the Earth and ask for the mountains to fall down upon him, but they will not. Out of frustration and fear many will die needlessly, they always have.

Those who rule over much of this world as well as mankind will scream their blind anger to the heavens, but the Creator will not hear. Then the thunder will begin again. They will try to use their technology but their attempts will be useless for their devices will not work. Upon the Earth or in the heavens.

With that, Old Man got paler and paler -- then he was gone. A sudden crack came from the fire – I nearly jumped when it startled me. Only some gas in a log. I sat back and lit a cigarette, searching for a calm. I poured some coffee from the pot that was sitting on the rocks near the edge of the fire. I do not remember how I got to the second experience, but suddenly, I was there.

I was hearing a different voice ... yet the same voice. This time I was actually quite calm, and just accepted it.

The Second Thunder

This time it was a Grandmother voice. The voice spoke to me softly and quietly, but with definite power. I seemed to hear it in my heart, of all places!

"These holes are the second warning. They come from the comet that passed. The twins have already appeared in your heavens. They have begun their games which eventually will help greatly in setting the world free (Hale-Bopp.) This event marks the beginning of the perishing of many upon the Earth. It will effect all forms of life. There is a myst that will fall from the skies. It is the Green myst of death which will fall from the heavens. Plants, animals, even the tiny life forms will perish with increasing frequency because of this myst. Man could have avoided this but they no longer communicate with the Nature spirits. Instead, mankind is at odds with that which gives them life.

"They think they can create life, that they can create the key to being as the Creator. They forget why it is called *Wakan Tanka, Great Mystery.* But the appearance of this green myst and the effects it will have upon life here on this Earth will begin a new thinking process within mankind. They will have a choice. A choice to return to the old ways and renew their relationship with the Earth and her spirits, and a simpler way of life.

"They will try to use the technology they have been given by those who come from beyond time to turn the sickness around. But nothing will happen, they will feel lost and a great despair will come over them. They will know that physically they posses no abilities to change anything. They will try to use the other technology, that which they have kept from the people, but at this they will be stopped. For without spirit no thing will work as it was intended. If they make the right decision, they will go on. If they make the wrong decision, life as they know it will disappear. They can return to ceremony, they can Ghost Dance, they can transcend time and limited mindset. They can use the power of their spirituality, or stay in the darkness, cold afraid and living without power. What do you think they will do?"

Then, in a whisper, the voice was gone. I felt a queer chill down my back. I felt as if I dozed off for a second. You know that state when you shake your head to wake yourself up and come back into awareness? Like when you have been driving for three days and refuse to say you are tired, and pull over ...

I felt this cold which got so cold I went inside my motor home and got a blanket, and a jacket as well. It wasn't cold out but the chill of it was something else. I kept trying to fight off the sleepy feeling -- I finally surrendered and went inside to lie down. But it would not be to sleep I was going.

Buffalo Hearts

J felt that I was taken to the center of the Earth. There was snow everywhere. It was a crystal world, with rainbow lights glistening off the crystals. For all its beauty, it was awfully cold. I could not get warm. Then a Buffalo appeared before me. A Red Buffalo. It seemed I was able to communicate with it telepathically. I remember having the distinct knowing that I was to get upon its back. The Buffalo was galloping, but the ride was very smooth and I had no trouble holding onto its fur. It galloped through a myst of light, then stopped at what appeared to be a meadow.

I got off the Buffalo and turned to look straight into its eyes. I was overcome with a tremendous sense of sadness. I felt very alone, very alone. I looked around at the meadow and saw a shadow moving across the land before me. I looked up at the sky and in an instant it began to turn black. It was like a bleed in a movie. It just got very black. Swirling like a surrealistic cloud. Then there was a bright pinprick of red light. I could not take my eyes off it against the blackness of the sky. It seemed to explode and fill the sky in a bright scarlet red color.

I felt the rain again. As I looked down upon my arms and body the rain was the color of blood. I shook my self into awareness again and could tell that the Sun was different, but I could still say it was setting. The light seemed strangely defused, there was no shading or sense of perspective of distance. It was almost two-dimensional. The light from it burned my flesh where it touched me, and the rain, well it was that starch-like-jelly that I had experienced earlier.

I lost sense of time but it was turning darker, yet there was still a red glow like a cold fire in it. The stars were bright red, and seemed like eyes staring at me. I could feel the leaving of many souls from this plane, perhaps thousands, perhaps millions. I could feel their screams, yet I could hear nothing except a roaring, or was it more like a tearing sound? Like the sound muscles make when skinning an animal. You must tear the sinew away to release a joint.

Then there was that God awful stillness. Like life itself was holding its breath. I was brought out of my state by the sound of the Buffalo. It was speaking to me through my mind, and it was the grandmother voice again. Its eyes, filled with tears, with the expression 500 years of sadness.

"This is the *Second Thunder*." She Spoke.

"Life as mankind has known it will come to an end. But there is still the possibility that he can breath life into it once again. Just a slight chance. The Children of the Earth must return to the wilderness. They must seek the shelter of the trees. Here they will find pure water, and that which will sustain them. You must tell them. Some may hear. You must try. The events that lead to this time I will show you so that you will know the signs. Look, look with your minds eye into the past..."

I looked into the nothing, and watched mesmerized by the swirling nature of the void. Again I could hear her voice narrate the vision. It was as if I were being guided.

"Mankind has reached the edge of time, it is the ending of what was and at the same time the birthing of what will be. Like the grasses that seemingly die in the winter, they have the ability to renew again in the spring. When this season turns into the next. But the life force must come from within the spirit of mankind. They must accept their connection to the whole of life. They can no longer stay within the experience they called Life upon the Earth. From this point there is no return... only a movement forward. The People must choose life, or choose death, it is by their own actions that they will endure.

"There is no difference between the Children of Earth except that which they deem as being so. There is no separation between the Children of the Earth and the whole of the cosmos. There never was except in their thoughts. It would be as simple as wishing it to be so to recreate the dream in perfect balance, but they believe they can not... and So it is."

I could see many life times and civilizations before me, but I can not tell you how. It was like I was experiencing a complete life review from the first moment I had ever entered the Earth plane. I could feel the connection to all things. It was as if when I moved, everything around me moved in conjunction. Although I could not feel it, it was a liquid world -- like soft jelly, yet everything was connected. If I moved too fast, then there were little whirlwinds, and in that area for a moment everything got blurry. Then it would return to normal. Then I heard the voice again, softly narrating...

"In the state of believing yourself, separate -- you have lost touch with the nature of your true reality. You no longer have enough light sticking to your essence to hold the consciousness that keeps your creation alive and intact. It was only given the life force you projected to it, no more no less. In that moment you are no more than an emanation of your true self. Unable to truly feel, or express emotions. Only depression, anger and rage.

Therefore, you believe life to be a boring, unliving thing. Instead of the miracle it is. You created it through thought, and gave it life force through the will of the Creator that is in each and everyone of you. Turning a thought into a living experience is truly a miracle. You have created it so well that you became lost in its creation, and out of touch with yourself. It is like you dozed off at the wheel. You have lost control of the dream. And it can not exist without your love, your thought forms. So it is becoming *a no thing* as you decree it to be so it is.

We have an agreement, your People and my People. It is this agreement that has kept the People so close to the *Oyate Ta Tanka Wakan,* the Buffalo Nation. This is why the calf woman, *Pte San Wi* came to you with the sacred rights. It is very ancient and goes back to when we first created this world together. Can you remember?"

Things started to move again. I heard the music of the spheres, and there was a specific tone that somehow, I was feeling as well as hearing. It was like a pulsing went through the fabric of the entire reality of wherever I was. I began to feel as if I was leaving my body. It was not unlike, an ascension -- somehow I knew that. It was more like... my molecules were separating and moving outward from my core. Then I went through that swirly void again. The violet, white and pink hues surrounding me I felt elated and lost any sense of time I usually have. Then, my thoughts of myself having the experience were stopped by the sound of Grandmother's voice speaking once again.

"The Red sky you are seeing is the womb of Earth Mother in creation. You are witnessing the Mother in her moontime. She is preparing the new egg within her belly for the conception of the new consciousness. She is much like a pregnant woman and must be allowed to go through her mood swings and changes without interference. We are all intimately a part of her dream. Our thoughts, our emotions, our feelings can all be felt by her, as we in turn feel and react to her changes as intimately as if they were our own.

"When we connect with her consciously and connect to her with our intent, this is the point when her dream creation can take place and new life can be born. Mankind does not have to end.

They can create a new dream while reconnecting to the source of all that they are. What she is allowing us to experience is the nature of creation itself taking place. It is like when you look up into the sky and for a moment, staring at the Sun, you close your eyes and you can see the red of her blood. Then everything moves to apparent darkness. But there really is no darkness, for even in the void there is the light. It just has a different nature than you normally would perceive. It requires you to engage your *Second Attention*. For it is your thoughts which activate the awareness that you are, which enables the void to express itself activated by your desires, the living dream of experience.

"That is one of the reasons that you are such a miracle. You do with your thought what others in this universe who are not the Mothers Children can do only with technology. But even they can not give something the life force, only your species can do that. No other life essence can create life in such a manner except the Source itself. You **are** the reflection of that Source in all its glory. But there is a great sadness in your beingness at this time. This sadness is felt by every living thing, yet it seems that it is only the two legged who does not know what the feeling is about.

"Two leggeds, for the most part, have forgotten that they are a part of the whole of all that is. You have somehow gotten lost in the nature of your own creations, and have lost the awareness that you yourself are the source of all that you experience. It is the emotion of love that you have forgotten. You no longer embrace the miracle of yourself. So how could you see the miracle of all that is around you? Humanity, therefore, dances in its own madness born of feeling separate from the Source. Along this black path you have lost your ability to be in the state of love. As a result of your dilemma and the life force upon Mother Earth is waning. The dream that you have known all these centuries is fading and with it, all that is within the concept of the dream could be lost.

"If you loose the dream, the dream will find its own place -- for no thing dies, it only moves on to become another thought form. But the dream was so carefully created through the love of mankind that to loose it would be a great sadness. You could take another form, and you have, and often do, but it is hard to leave the feeling of this creation, for it is indeed unique throughout the whole of the Universe. There is none other quite like this Emerald, jewel that she is.

"Come, do not slumber, it is time that I take you to witness the Third Thunder."

climbed up upon the Buffalo's back once again. She took me to yet another destination, somewhere deep within the crystal myst. As I stepped down, I found the ground to be soft to the feel of my feet, which were somehow naked. There was a bluish tint to the grass, if it was grass. I could no longer be certain of the true nature of reality in this place. It is as if the consciousness that flowed through me had changed. I had to remind myself that this was not my ordinary body, but my dream body, which operates at a frequency much faster than that which exists in my normal body exists.

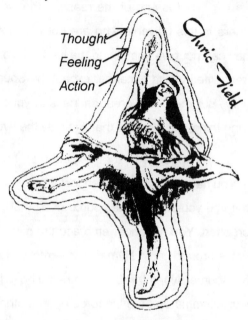

In my teachings at the Great Halls, I have been shown where the human body in a perfect state of balance, creates a field. We can see that field as a light field that surrounds it, i.e.: an aura. There are three main layers closest to the body, which weave in and out of each other much like a cold fire that swirls seemingly contained within a vortex. As I revealed in *Last Cry* with considerable detail, these layers are Identified as Thought, Feeling and Action. The form created, viewed with the *Third Attention* is much like a luminous egg, which can appear to stretch and bend with the movements of the body. When one has developed the Third Attention, they can begin to notice colors that seem to emanate from the body, which affect this luminous egg.

These have often times been called the auric field. Which is not an entirely correct concept. The auric field in actuality can extend as far as a mile from its source, having fine threads which extend even farther, reaching the source of life itself. Light, as science is beginning to find out, possesses a nature that far out reaches our present concepts of physics. These strands of light can reach out millions of miles to reach the central Sun, Alcyone. What most people see as colors surrounding the body actually tell us the nature of the individuals intent and the nature of the thoughts the person is embracing at that moment. When we develop our *Third Attention*, we can begin to see something more to this luminous egg.

This has now been taught in our time as being the Mer-Ka-Bic field. We have developed our *Second Attention* to the point that, as a global race, we have realized this field is an actual living environment of its own. This field possesses a life force, which is emanated from the light source both within as well as outside the physical body. Through the wonders of Kirlian photography, we are even able to capture this via camera equipment.

This Mer-Ka-Ba which surrounds the human body is the cause of the realized reality that one perceives themselves to be in through experience. In the average human who would enjoys a state of emotional and physical walking in balance upon the Earth, this field can spin at speeds of up to nine tenths the speed of light. Once a person has developed their *Second Attention* and begins to enter their *Third Attention*, they are actually capable of increasing the capacity of their individual Mer-Ka-Bic field beyond the norm. When they work together as groups three or more, this can even be enhanced to the point where they can move through *Third Dimensional* reality quite quickly and easily.

The path of the initiate teaches oneself to move this field with deliberate intent and to govern the speed of their Mer-Ka-Bic field at will, thus enabling them to access *Fourth Attention*. The initiate, at this point, can actually travel through time and space. They can move their field at twice the speed of sound, therefor it is easy to achieve total invisibility to the naked eye of someone *Philidelphia Exp. External Merkaba Technology gone "wrong"* who is existing within the much slower field of energy, or ordinary existence. In *Dream State* we are obviously moving at a very enhanced rate of speed. Reality and our perception of reality becomes pliable. Thought forms seem mutable and react in direct response to our inner and divine emotions, which emanate from our heart space -- like wise, what we do not emanate from our heart space.

In the case of the individual who attempts to take the intellect into this higher state of reality, there is much morphing of perception. This occurs as their fears and fantasies will quickly take shape as perceived reality in accordance with their cultural, social, and genetically encoded *- Dreamscape The Movie* physio belief patterns. The intellect only effects us up to the *Second Attention*, beyond the *Second Attention* intellect is like a gilded stallion in a corral of mares -- It serves no purpose in unlimited reality perception, therefore it is a no thing. When one tries to hold onto the intellect in the higher frequencies of perception, at best there is distortion in that perception, or blocks which are created within their awareness process. In either case, intellect only exist within temporal reality, and the state of awareness actually dissimulates when it is employed. Simply put, one can not hold the vision.

As I touched down upon this new Earth, I was straining to perceive new feelings with every instant of my experience. I grabbed my intent in order to enable myself to let go and feel the greater message to my experience. I was soon assisted by the voice of the Buffalo Grandmother again.

"From the beginning of these times, mankind experiences that he has been connected to the Buffalo Nation. We have an agreement, a contract if you would, to stay with each other until the end times. It is because of your intent and the actions taken in your dance upon this plane that we make these truths known to you, that you might share them with all People. It is felt that perhaps then more of them will open their hearts and hear, as well as see the course of their reality as it moves into the new world."

Grandmother was still speaking when I heard a sound like wings, giant wings just above me to my left. I looked up and through the Crystal myst I saw something moving towards us from the distance. As it drew nearer I could perceive a huge Spotted Eagle. The Eagle landed right beside me, and it was huge! Its head reaching almost my waist as it landed before me.

My eyes were drawn into the dark pupils of the birds eyes which held me in their spell. I could feel the Eagle touch my mind and then felt its words within my heart.

Eagle Medicine

The Eagle began, "It is time we speak. Often I have come to you to remind you that you walk with Eagle Medicine. Often I have come in vision to remind you that it was time to prepare for the times coming. Now we have entered those times. There is a knowledge that you should know now. Because you are ready, because it is time to know, and all things occur in their time."

I felt a calm within me. The Eagle's eyes seemed less fierce, and the newness to the experience was quickly transmuted to a kindred reality. Grasping my intent had worked. Holding onto no other thoughts, I was thus allowing only the feeling of my intent to fill my energy field, which had rapidly cleared my perception. The sound of Eagle as it spoke was warm, and the voice, although stern, was nurturing and filled with caring. I found I was being drawn deeper into the vision.

"Long ago, we, your kind and mine, created this world in accordance with the Mother's dream. It was created upon a not quite yet completely recovered physical expression of herself. There were many expressions of realities which still overlapped in those times. Mankind still co-existed with the huge reptiles, and other beasts of the previous age. Dimensions, and the filters between dimensions, had not yet achieved their final steps for the balancing was not yet completed…. Many times the openings between the worlds were allowed to be kept open.

that it could be understood and be prevented from occurring in future expressions of third dimensional form.

"A plan was devised by the Watchers, and agreed to by those upon this plane. The evil would be dispersed into each manifesting form of mankind. The evil would then be dealt with in the experience of evolution, containing within each essence a little part or seed of the evil. The theory being that perhaps the evil would not be over whelming in small pieces. Mankind could then experience, through the continuing experiment of free will, the ability to overcome evil in a natural and hopefully permanent way. It was also agreed to that mankind would have to have shorter life spans in order to successfully deal with the project.

"Thus, a safety factor was allowed for -- to the perpetuity of the maligned consciousness. Understand that you yourselves were part of this decision. That as you were, and always will be, in true essence, beings of light choosing to have the human experience. However, in order for evolution to be experienced and for it to be conceivable for the progress to be observed, the illusion of time was created.

"The illusion of time was created but it had to be contained so that it would not become a problem to the rest of the universe where it was not necessary to be established. A solution was conceived. In a manner of speaking a bubble was created holographically around each reality, planet and being, which would contain the experience of time within it. Because of resonating frequencies each reality would be connected to the other. Earth itself allowed her embodiment to be enveloped with a form of this *tensile bubble* which would contain the experience of time.

"Her atmosphere was readjusted in order to accommodate the perpetuity of this experience until such time as it would no longer be necessary. At which point, mankind would experience the ending of the time space illusion and the experiment would conclude. We are now at that point of mankind's experience.

"Every turning of the cycles, consuming 26,000 years in time perception, the Earth turns around. She moves allowing adjustments to be made in her own perception of consciousness. Thus, mankind as well as all creatures upon the Mother, would experience a great shifting in realities with the turning of each cycle.

"Some species chose to leave physical expression. Others chose to transmute because of their acquired abilities to adapt and to accept the changes resulting from the new cycle that each turning of this Galactic season would bring. Some of your own kind, as well as other species, seem to come and go upon this plane. They have the ability to change physical form, and some of them no longer express upon the Third Dimensional plane. They have left this plane and reentered the realm of light, choosing not to return. Many of these life forms you have remembered in legends, such as the elves, dwarves, unicorns and dragons.

"Everything within your experience until this moment has been temporal. Earth in many ways has been a proving ground for evolutionary graduation to the higher planes of expression. But not all of the evil could be transmuted, for thought and emotion have the life force contained within them. Until a way whereby the creating Source could in effect cut itself off from the emanation, where upon the life force would end and the emanation could be dissolved.

"Some of this evil was delegated to the lower dimensions, which then were encapsulated, and thus frozen in their expression. This worked for a long time. However, there is a shaking occurring within the consciousness of mankind which at this time is causing a ripping once again of the planes of dimensional expressions. The tears are due in large to mankind's own experimentation with the natural order of the universe." i.e.: *The Montauk Project*.

The Fourth Thunder Is Upon Us

I continued to hear the voice through my heart telling... "With the shifting and tearing of consciousness that is occurring, it is hard and getting harder for the guardians to protect mankind from these forces that were manifested by mankind themselves as a result of their actions. Mankind, for the most part, is no longer aware of the existence of these guardians or of their own true relationship with the Earth and her People. As a result of this lower state of our awareness, all of the potential reality available to mankind could be destroyed in these final moments of the dream. This is inescapable unless mankind gets a hold of their intent and elects to understand this ancient knowledge."

"A Warrior's Wisdom"

Dis-Connected or Lost Souls or soulless ones

There is an expression amongst the Lakota People ... *Washichzu* (wäw-she-ch-tzü) which has become misused as a slang to define "white people." The true meaning of this has been forgotten by most, as a result of letting go of the original teachings and veering from the *Good Red Road*. The meaning of this phrase must be understood in order that those who are returning to the light may successfully do so. Creator gave us this word to define those without souls, those who are not connected to their centers, which is connected to the Source.

There is a center of the Source -- the *Wakan Tanka* -- the Great Mystery. In the beginning of creation all that is was created in a moment, the same moment. Each soul was born as a particum of light. Like the spark that is within the flame, many sparks making up the flame which flickers in the darkness, giving off the warmth and light. And the many flames making up the whole of the fire itself.

There is a light which is within the fire, and a light which is a result of that fire. This is much like what occurred in the beginning. There is a light -- the source, and there is a reflection of that light -- the image. Both are real, but both are very different in point of origin.

If one were to take a stick from the fire and hold it up it would light the darkness before them, correct? But, if they were to take that same stick of wood and hold it up in the light of the afternoon Sun, the light of the Sun would absorb the light of the stick, would it not? Do you understand now?

Our Elders have told us there were never many human beings in this world. And then the *Washichzu* began to come in increasing numbers. They were like the locust. They did not know who their mother and father were. They devoured everything, and killed for no reason, almost for the love of it. This happened because we walked away from the Red Road, and got lost upon the Black Road. We have lost our abilities to call up the spirits and the forces of this Earth as we once did. The Eagle's voice awakened in my heart again, "Sad times are seen for the People. The times will become increasingly worse unless they return to the old ways."

"Do you remember your Elders telling you this? Can you see the picture this far yet?"

"Those without souls, the *Washichzu*, are the emanations of your own light. They are manifested by your own essence. They are the result of your own thought forms. They possess no souls of their own. They are emanations of the souls of mankind themselves. As they are, as they act, as they think so shall the emanations be. They are reflections incapable of creation for they are not part of Source."

I was overwhelmed at this information and the implications it brought, as I am certain you are as you read these words. I struggled once again to grasp my intent, and to not fall into the trap of thinking, for the mind can trick you, all information must be perceived through the heart for the truth to be learned. I had to rely on simply feeling the words as words were only sounds which traveled upon the wind. Words have interpretations, but sounds can be understood by all species, all beings in all dimensions. For sounds are the releasing of emotions from deep within the spirit of a being.

"The guardians are given life through the spirit of man. Many are of the Earth, some originated in other dimensions, but some are also born of the emanations from mankind's souls. They can even take on physical form and walk amongst you side by side. How they are, how they interact with you and the world around them is in direct relation to your intent. This is part of the *Warrior's Wisdom.* The Warrior knows this and thus commands the nature of interaction with their reality by keeping close watch on intent."

I had lost all sense of where I was, listening to Eagle. I was perhaps in the stream of consciousness, the river that flows forever. Yet, I was aware of being in the crystal myst, having lost all sense of self except in thought. I realized in that flash of a moment that the crystal myst must be the light of the activated void. The place where all things are manifest through our dreaming. For the visions passing before me that had no form were too numerous to count. They were happening too fast to isolate. Was there such a thing as **visual** emotions, I wondered?

"What does this have to do with anything?" I found these words spilling out of me, perhaps expressing my fears. The Eagle was looking directly into my eyes. It was as if we were interchanging relationships with each other. At times I was the Eagle, and at times the Eagle was outside of me as my teacher. I became aware of a sound, which had been ever present throughout my vision. It was like the wind, yet it possessed tonal qualities. Then, in the next moment, as I was feeling it change, the Eagle spoke...

"It has to do with connecting with the guardians. You will have to reconnect to the guardians as the shifting intensifies, for they are no longer able to contain the evil that they have been protecting you from -- that which has been done out of ignorance. Without this connection to them, mankind could be overwhelmed by their own actions. They would fall prey to their lesser selves, and the darkness that exists in their shadows. Then mankind themselves as well as their emanations, might no longer be expressed upon the field of realities."

I found myself having the strangest thoughts. What would happen to the spirit guides if there were no longer a mankind to have thoughts of them? Would they still be of their own source, or would they disappear with the consciousness that created them in the shifting? And what of this *tensile bubble* which contains time? Was it meant as a metaphor or was it spoken of as a hard reality?

No sooner did I have these thoughts, the Eagle responded...

"The *Washichzu* are all of these beings that are born of man. They are and exist in the spirit world because they are in the consciousness of man. Some have been given the job of being the guardians of man's spirit, as well as the reflectors of mankind's thoughts and emotions. This condition must exist, because it is the spirit dealing with the spirit."

"Mankind's consciousness in reflecting their perception of the Devic realms and Earth spirit realms has, and continues to, inadvertently to create them. They are reactionary in energy, and action. Like the child watching the parent, they essentially imitate their creators' behavioral and emotional blueprints. Yet they posses a life force while having no soul. Another reflection from the *Hall of Mirrors*. Throughout the evolution of mans consciousness some of these emanations have taken on physical form. Some being of lower vibrations and others being of higher vibrations. These beings, for they are beings, are immortals in many ways. However, their perpetuity into the future reality depends wholly upon the success of mankind's transition through the shift, when Fifth World reality comes into full expression."

"They are helping to effect *the Quickening* the people are now sensing. In their desperation to assist mankind in their awakening as we approach the final hours before the purification, they are manifesting into physical form and walking amongst us. They know that this shifting of seasons is inevitable. Mankind is already in the fourth dimension, and feeling the chaos of the transition. Transition is being experienced on every level, emotional, physical, and spiritual. Mankind will now pass into the remaining Thunders."

As often happens, I drifted out of trance state and back to contemplative reality. There were so many things swimming through my head. I have been a friend, a beneficiary, an observer with several Elders, representing quite a cross section of cultural expressions, never mind geographical locations.

I have been gifted and chosen as the spirit holder of many of the Prophecies and Sacred Teachings of these Elders. They were the holders of the knowledge for their People, their tribes, their Clans. All the Prophecies were blending into one fractured fairytale, having one basic fabric or connecting link. Not all the pieces were in my possession, perhaps they never would be. I could see the commonality of all of them, and yet, the telling of it in the way emotionally I grasped the vision would probably be a task beyond my talents. It could take a lifetime. And I will probably spend the rest of this one trying to complete that mission.

Passage Into the Remaining Thunders - The Point of No Return

The Eagle broke through my thoughts, "*The People* were told generations ago that Mankind will experience the coming of the *Thunders*. These would be warnings, indicating that the end times were beginning. Warning them that the Purifier was coming. Warning them that they must change their ways, or risk the peril of loosing ability to create any expression upon this Earth in the Fifth World. Perhaps this world would never be again. That is how severe these warnings are. Upon experiencing the first *Three Thunders*, mankind would still be able to change the outcome of their future upon the Earth plane of their own free will. Although with the coming of each *Thunder*, the path would get more and more difficult to reverse.

However, it was also known that upon the sounding of *Fourth Thunder*, if they did not head the warning of the previous *Three Thunders* and they continued upon their path of self destruction, the *Fifth Thunder* would sound and shake the whole of the Earth. It would then be too late to reverse what had been set into motion. Mankind would experience terrible times through which they could only hope to survive by the grace of Spirit, preceded by the intervention of Ethereans. The first *Three Thunders* have already have occurred, passed unnoticed by most. Mankind has done little if nothing to change their ways thus far. Events are now *quickening* again, with the full force of the El Nino looming over the Pacific, as the *Fourth* and *Fifth Thunders* are now unfolding simultaneously.

Authors Note on HAARP

I can not help but feel in my heart that a lot of what is going on with the weather, our actions or non-actions, that have created the environment for the El Nino are directly tied to HAARP activities. HAARP is the acronym for High-frequency Active Auroral Research Project. I have sat in many *Inipi*. There are many things that we see in the *Inipi Lodge* through good old *Native Remote Viewing*, which is more reliable then the government version. *Native Remote Viewing* has the back up of over 30,000 years of practice.

HAARP has the capabilities of manipulating human emotions, perceptions and motor activities. There exists within the far reaches of HAARP the tangible ability to cause the movement of the Earth's tectonic plates. I could go on forever here about HAARP, but I believe that there is a publication which describes the present and potential activities of HAARP as well, if not better, than I can.

There is a publication titled *Angels Don't Play This HAARP* By Dr. Nick Begich. I highly recommend that you read this book. You need to know about the technology that exists and is already being employed. With that knowledge, you can better draw your own conclusions between current events and their correlation to the Prophecies of the Elders.

Information Encoded By The Immortals

I felt a bolt of electricity go through me. It was shocking, as I had basically not felt my entire body through out the vision. Yet suddenly, in that eternal moment, I was very aware of it. It was as if my body was experiencing the dream state as well and wanted me to be certain to hear this message, so I could bring it back with me into the physical. I responded with a jerking of my body, like I had experienced a chill. This had always been a sign that I was experiencing a great truth, or realization.

I moved even deeper into the Trance State, and was shown the faces of several people I did not know. These were faces of people who were not quite yet in my life, but on an ethereal level, I knew we had been connected many times before. Perhaps they were of my soul group, and we now were assembling in mass for we had reached a point of energy as the weeks after the Ghost Dance would reveal to me. The Eagle began to reveal the information encoded by the immortals.

"Those known as the immortals are now letting those individuals who have proven their intent know of the existence of ancient libraries and the knowledge which they contain. Certain individuals carry with them certain instruments, which come from these secret locations. They have been recorded upon the living stones. Stones which can not be destroyed by ordinary means. Already your scientists are aware in the Yucatan of the existence of that which is being called the *Prophecy Stone*. Currently this stone is in pieces, but with the transpiring of certain events the pieces will be brought together. This event and its announcement will precede the rising of the domed cities, the lost cities of Atlantis which have come to be called by the Native People of South America the *Cities of Prophecy*. These cities lie beneath the waters of the Gulf of Mexico, ranging from the Yucatan as far East as the Caribbean. There are other Islands even farther East, those which I wrote about in *Last Cry*. These cities are all rising to the surface.

"What are these *Thunders*?" I asked. I was hearing my Spirit voice sounding much like a young child, and was a little surprised that I was *hearing* my Spirit voice. It was as if it were coming from outside myself. I could hear Grandmother's voice telling me the prophecy so many years ago, but as if it were yesterday... "The eyes of man shall be witness to many thousands of starving people resulting from the consciousness of war."

The first *Three Thunders* have passed. The *Fourth Thunder* is upon us and *Fifth Thunder* has begun – they are occurring simultaneously. The world viewed the multitudes starving from lack of food while others grew sick from overeating. In Rwanda and other Third World countries the suffering was viewed by the world, yet virtually nothing was done to turn the tides of events that transpired. Relief was never really sent to the People who became the pawns of corporations and politicians. We now view even more millions suffering as a result of a condition, which remains unchecked. This was the First Thunder, and as I said, it went virtually unnoticed.

Grandmother's voice again came in the wind, letting me know that I was not yet through with my experience. She began to tell me of the other *Thunders*.

Remember when the Elders told you, "Spirit warns you three times. Then you are on your own." I remembered this well from when I was instructed in the prophecies of the Hopi. If conditions prevail and it is necessary that we fully experience the *Fourth and Fifth Thunders,* that will mark the beginning of times where what has been put into motion can no longer be reversed.

As the Old Man said, there will be many deformities in plants and animals caused by the three Devils. It is possible to filter out of the waters two of these devils, but the third can not be filtered out. These devils each possess the ability to cause serious illness, but when all three are in combination, they are deadly. Mankind will not be able to filter these Devils from the rain, the rivers or the oceans. This sign will come during the *Fourth Thunder*.

The Fourth Thunder Continues

From the birth of the *Third Thunder*, we will see the *Whirlwinds* come. The seasons will become harder and harder to distinguish, and this will confuse the plants as well as the animals. Earth will experience the green myst. This myst will be the myst of death.

Strange bacteria have been born within the waters. Originally, they were air born. These have begun to spread throughout the waters. First they will contaminate the ground waters, then rivers. In the beginning, they will only affect the fish and animals. Then they will begin to affect the young and the Elders. At the onset they will affect only populated areas. The condition will progress and become global. When this bacteria, or the little devils move up to the clouds, burning rains will fall into the oceans. At that stage the condition will begin to form strange abnormalities upon all life in the oceans. It is also seen that the creatures that once lived within the waters will come out of the waters to die in a desperate but hopeless attempt to escape. These occurrences will not be *able* to be ignored, as they will die in great numbers. Upon the land itself those life forms that drink of the waters shall experience the burning of their flesh, and will suffer from what appears to be diarrhea, and internal bleeding. They will dehydrate and the flesh itself as it will apparently will begin to devour itself and liquefy.

Water shall become burning to the touch and become so caustic it will seem to melt the flesh. Ulcerous soars to erupt upon the skin and in the internal organs of the body. Eventually, there will be no water fit to drink. The standing people themselves shall begin to die from the burning rains that will fall from the clouds. Soon the plants will not be able to be eaten, as they will contain the poison from the waters and they shall cause death.

The Fifth Thunder

Animals shall be born with many strange deformities due to these strange bacteria that will develop as messengers of death. This shall come as a result of the poison from the rains. Animals shall be seen with many extra limbs, as well as missing limbs. From the time that this begins to be seen occurring throughout the world, we can expect within one year that these deformities will begin to appear in People. Many children will be born without brains, or other organs, or missing or extra body parts as is already occurring with the animals. The AP (Associated Press) and numerous other news agencies have released documented stories about such occurrences. We must note that the *Fifth Thunder* is commencing before the *Fourth Thunder* has concluded, evidence of the *Quickening*.

During this time there will appear strange animals and plants of new forms, as well as the re-emergence of old forms. Time will be dissolving. These deformities, mutations and re-appearances will first be seen in the insect world and the world of microorganisms. The Winged People will begin to fall from the skies, and lie dead upon the ground. Many animals will disappear forever from physical expression upon this plane. Their food supplies shall become contaminated, and they will become afflicted with strange sickness. They will lay themselves before mankind and perish upon the land in an attempt to let them feel the intensity of their situation.

These things are already occurring, and yet mankind stands firm with a cold heart -- unmoved by the plight of the Earth and her creatures – unwilling to change – ignorant that the plight being witnessed is a mirror of times to come. Mankind remains lost in the illusion that they are above the consequence of cause and effect. They posses the ability to change their present course in *the cycle of self-destruction* yet they take no action. They possess the ability to use means to grow food and produce medicines while protecting nature. Instead they choose to continue using elements that create upheavals with their four legged relations, their relations in the skies, Mother Earth and her waters. Again, they remain indifferent and self absorbed.

Another sign of the *Fourth Thunder* will be that four great women who hold positions of high reverence will perish. This will serve as a warning that mankind must reunite with their ancient heritage and destiny. The feminine energies must be awakened and acknowledged if mankind is to continue with any hope of changing the outcome of events.

There will be a global reawakening to the true teachings of the Great Mother. Four white Buffalo calves have already been born (The fourth was born in June of `97). This was prophesized as one of the signs of *Fourth Thunder*. Yet mankind, as is their nature, remains self absorbed, enslaved to a false consciousness. Trapped in their webs of dogma, their third eye is blind from atrophy. This exists even among the Native American People, many of whom refuse to return to their true spiritual path along the *Good Red Road*. We now must understand the Grandmothers are preparing to let loose their final fury upon this land.

This shall begin the seasons of emotional storms -- the *Winds of the Mind*. The ways of the old patriarchy shall be shown their weaknesses, as solutions to the chaos occurring in the lives of millions shall be beyond the scope of Man. They will find themselves chained by their own fears and ignorance. As they destroyed the ancient schools and their knowledge, so did they seal their own fate. Untold millions lost their lives in the name of the Christos and the Church in Rome, who killed by decree from the Papal Bulls, ranks of the Illuminati. All actions and their impact of frequencies upon the tapestry of creation shall return unto their maker, and recorded for future history.

With the awakening of the Feminine, many of the Grandmother Spirits of old, the Kachinas, will begin to return with frequency. Buffalo Calf Women, *Pte San Wi* herself will return and be seen by many women. These women will be called to remember their ancient ceremonies. Knowledge that has been kept secret for untold thousands of years out of fear for harm to the children will again come into the stream of consciousness. For these are also the *Winds of Truth*. The true Christos places no gender above or below the other. Neither is more powerful then the other. The true Christos is not an I, separate from the whole. Rather it is a *WE* in which individuality is maintained through the acknowledgement of the true feelings of our hearts.

Through the balance of the male and female within our beings, creation can occur. The frequency shifts are effortless if the human heart is open. With the advent of the *Winds of Change*, the suffering of the spirit is about to take a turn towards the Sunlight. Spirit is refusing to play the game of bondage any longer. The illusions will begin to melt. First, in the invisible world of Human emotions so long misused and misunderstood by mankind. Then, a shifting will occur in the consciousness itself, it will be perceived at first as if a madness is sweeping across the land. Those not living in their truth will choose from only two pathways; madness and surrender, or the gateway of fear. The latter pathway shall embrace fits of tyranny, and they shall be victimized by their own actions in the great *Hall of Mirrors*.

Women shall begin to reclaim their power through the rebirth of ancient ceremonies. A flame shall be lit so bright that *the songs of ancient Avalon* shall be heard upon the winds in the time of the full moon. This light will burn so brightly as to allow mankind a new and yet final chance to reconnect to the creation energies, and turn around their cycle of self-destruction. Of course, this will also be the cause of tearing down many personal relationships and mini societies that exist within the circles of disharmony.

In the process of reaching for truth, these little sects of people, who congregate and hold onto archaic concepts of spirituality, will begin to fracture with greater and greater frequency. In many areas where woman and child are unnaturally alone, they will find it impossible to remain. They will begin to roam as refugees upon the land, seeking shelter and compassion from those able to afford it. It will be a sadness that mankind has again manifested by their own creation through their acceptance of enslavement to dogma and the exercise of senseless judgements, born from the distortion of patriarchy.

This fracturing, like the *little devils,* will begin within a very short period of time and spread to the larger communities. The social and religious structures will then crumble in reflection of the intensity of the trembling of the Mother's body. She is purging herself through fever, for the poison born of malevolent thought and deed is erupting like sores upon her body. That which is not in harmony with her will be removed either by its own will or hers. This is the process of *the Purification*, it is the way her body purifies itself and can not be avoided.

Through purification, there will only survive small groups of beings that will have developed their abilities to hear and resonate to the Spirits that have come to assist them. A positive outcome of this will be that the full feminine energy will have the opportunity to cause the final shattering of two-dimensional consciousness. This limited consciousness has enslaved mankind for thousands of years. It will be the final opening through which mankind might hope to avoid the and final *Thunders* as the *Sword of Shiva* is felt throughout the land.

The Sixth Thunder - The Turtle Becomes the Dragon

Below the oceans we have the ongoing occurrence of many volcanic eruptions. This has, thus far, been a slow process. The magma is oozing out of the vents that regulate temperature conditions in the inner Earth. This activity will intensify, to the point that we are going to see surface conditions agitated. Smoking oceans will produce sulfur breezes which will blow far inland. Clouds will drop black dust on our cars parked so safely in our driveway. Quite frankly, the ocean is reaching boiling point. This is what is meant by the Egg of the Phoenix is cracking. We talked about this in *Last Cry*.

Earthquake activity will increase in frequency to as much as perhaps more than 3,200 per month in the Pacific Rim area. There will be a shaking of the land and a churning throughout the whole of North America. Watch for seismographic activity registering 5 to 7 points on the rector scale in Canada, around the Great Lakes and along the Mississippi valley area. This means that the Earth is trembling in the throws of her fever. This geophysical activity of the magma will cause the oceans to heat up, and become even more out of balance than they presently are. This heat will encourage the uncontrollable growth of Pfiesteria as we sit and watch in helpless awe as our oceans die at a rate of greater than 6 sq. feet per second.

El Nino will wreak havoc twice over two years, occurring with greater furry with each visit. El Nino is a voice from the Earth, an emotional reaction responding to mankind's' refusal to change their ways. *The Winds of Change* have now commenced. These winds are the *whirlwind spirits*, which the Hopi told you we would see in the *End Times*. They will be strange, angry Wind Spirits. At times they will reach speeds of more than 200 MPH. They are a warning of what is yet to come during the *Fifth Thunder*. With the coming of these *Winds of Change*, mankind can no longer avoid the consequences of the events that will follow. If they choose to survive, to linger, they must learn to move with the shifting. We must strive to understand the *Cosmic Solution* ... *how to stand on moving ground!* The Chi of the Earth is emitting from her deepest depths. Only through mankind reconnecting to their true spirituality and awakening their divine inner being will they have a hope of being able to survive the remaining Thunders. For El Nino will signal that the whole of the Earth is now engaged in the *War of Valued Life*.

There will be a great explosion of little sister, the volcano near Mexico City. This will cause the Grandmother to explode, which lies under the surface. She will spit all of the people living there into the sea. When this occurs, the tail of the Turtle will begin to break in two and Mexico City itself will be under water. This eruption will cause a great shifting of the plates, and the ancient domed cities will slowly rise to the surface of the waters in the Gulf of Mexico. Eventually, what is now the Gulf Coast of America, will be as high in elevation as the Himalayans.

But when little Sister speaks, Grandfather will answer, and Mount Rainier will erupt in Washington State. The land in this area will also begin to break up as the entire Cascade Range is activated by the upheavals occurring beneath the surface.

There will then be three great shifting along the West Coast of the Turtle. Many places will sink beneath the surface of the Ocean, and others will become Islands. The Earth will also swallow the resources that mankind has used as (fossil) fuels, deep into her embodiment. Thus mankind will be forced to use other means of energy in order to survive as a species.

The three great shiftings will correlate with a tremendous churning of the plates that are presently upon the ocean bottom in the area known as the Pacific Rim. The consequences of this will alter Earth's present physical constitution forever. The over all effects upon life forms will change entirely in moments. There will be such a tremendous effect upon the ocean that the water will begin to boil from the effect of the volcanic eruptions. All oceanic life forms may be extinguished.

There will be another shifting during this time, which will occur simultaneously, resulting from the movement of these tectonic plates. This movement of the landmasses will throw the rotation of the Earth completely off balance. There will be a great wobbling effect of the Earth at that time. This wobbling, when it settles down, will have caused the Earth to shift 32°, as we will discuss later in a later chapter, which is an excerpt from *Project Stargate*. This shifting has already happened three times before, as the observation of geological formations will attest. There will be a very rapid melting of the present northern (Arctic) ice caps, causing great flooding to occur. There will, at the same time, be a rapid freezing and the formation of ice to form in the south (Antarctica.) This will cause the Earth to shake violently, raising many new land formations and sinking others far below the depths of the new oceans, which will be formed as a result.

Obviously, this series of events would be devastating to the Earth and any of its life forms which would be expected to continue to survive in Third Dimensional Reality with the advent of the Fifth World. Your Star Brothers have already come to agreements that should this *Sixth Thunder* begin, there would be direct intervention by them to try to correct this from happening. However, even they can only do so much. A great deal of the Earth would still change drastically. So there are some truths to the maps that have already come forth indicating the possible outcome of geophysical cataclysms.

As it is seen now, something will occur very soon. An event will occur that will cause a severe reaction beneath the Earth's surface. The event will be caused by mankind themselves (HAARP?) Chain reactions will then occur along the San Andreas Fault, which will cause Grandfather to erupt in the North. The map of the new Millennium will then begin to form, as much of the western coastline will be altered forever. Large portions of land from Northern California well into the Washington coast will sink or be lost due to tidal waves. Other portions will break up and many Islands will form.

Should events continue progressing as they presently are, then the Earth herself will correct existing conditions through natural means – her means. Those already watching the progress of your world would then have no alternative but to intervene and govern Earth and her Peoples themselves. The return of the ancestors would then take on quite a different nature than might have been envisioned. The nature of the *Seventh Thunder* will depend upon what mankind has set the stage for. Nothing, at that point, can prevent the breaking up of the *tensile bubble* that has both contained and protected mankind.

The Seventh Thunder

During the third destruction of Earth, during the time when Atlantis sank beneath the Great Waters, it was decided that we would share the seeds of evil we had created. A little seed was placed within each one of us. This is not to be confused with the seed of the dragon. For the Dragon is what allows us our alchemic and clairvoyant wisdoms. But this knowledge was lost from our consciousness. The experiment was in hopes that we would be able to transmute this evil, and it would never again manifest into consciousness. This time of the *Seventh Thunder* is when our ancestors come back to see who has succeeded, and who has not. Therefore, it is the time referred to as *the Harvest*.

The energies released from the inner Earth due to tectonic activity, as well as those entering this plane due to the tear in the *tensile bubble* of time, will be of such a nature that all reality shall be altered. The whole of the ecosystem which held Earth's reality together has been so damaged that it can no longer maintain itself, never mind repair itself. Those of the inner Earth M.S.W. will also be effected by these events. As will those who thought they could control the Earth, as well as her People.

The tearing, which is occurring in the fabric of time, will result in a rather bazaar reality where many things that are born of man will return to their source. As that source dissipates, so shall it creations. Meaning that the consciousness of mankind is imploding. Eventually that which we refer to as social consciousness will no longer be.

This transition will not occur in an instant. Through our perception, it will occur in stages. The observance of this will cause madness in many. There will be those around us that are of insufficient vibration to continue. They might go up in smoke, as the Hopi saw it. Or they might liquefy, as the light particums that expressed their place in reality no longer have a resonance to match what the Earth's frequency will be resonating to.

X-men

The *Seventh Thunder* will bring much social strife. Many will be homeless and with out recourse as the financial systems fail. They will loose all that they based their self worth upon. There will be no answers coming from traditional forms of organized religions to allay their predicaments. The infestation of disease will be everywhere. There will be no water to drink that does not have disastrous effects. All these things, plus the relentless intensifying of natural disasters, will wreak havoc. War will be wide spread, and all will seem hopeless. Cities will become armed encampments, and in rural areas many who resist the *new order* will be kept in compounds.

In the midst of the chaos is when the one referred to as the Anti Christ will make his appearance. We have seen this one, and know of his creation. It is the final thrust of the Illuminati -- those who follow the Dark Star. This is where those who are known to us as the Watchers will intercede, for if they did not, there would be no reality left to express. They are already making their presence known, reminding us it is time to clean our houses. Company is coming!

The prophecies of the *Seven Thunders* are already occurring, and to discuss them can be disturbing and frightening. But one can learn to see beyond what appears to the obvious. One can learn to see into the fabric of creation, and touch the fabric of life itself. The *Seventh Thunder* has to do with the fabric of time and dimension. It has to do with the opening of the doorway to eternity. It is perhaps the last chance for humanity to save itself from oblivion.

To continue, the movement of the tectonic plates will rip apart that which has held us fast to the cycles of mortality. The lock, which seems to keep us tied to cycles of repetitive redundancy. That which was established to hold as a ground for the frequency of mortal expression, shall be ripped open. Thus allowing the being of spirit to fly free to follow its own individual destiny.

Only thought can restrict the spirit from moving beyond its prison of self doubt and self destruction. The outward signs that will be observed are almost impossible to be put in words. There will be a crashing of dimensions and a blending of time space experience. All restraints upon human consciousness shall be released in the moment of the great shifting from this frequency into the all.

The purifier that the ancients talked about is none other than the planet Nibiru. At first, it will appear stationary in the heavens, except that it will steadily grow larger. Our perceptions of it will be difficult as the presence and the effects of its physicality will itself be altering the perceived reality within the *tensile bubble* of time. How exactly is it to transpire? One must first have a basic understanding of time, and time travel. Then, perhaps, they will have sufficient knowledge to remove the fear within so the spirit can be released. For the Spirit of a thing is eternal and will be immune to the frequencies that are connected to the artificial time grids. We are, all of us, expressing upon this plane these artificial grids. Some of us have learned to move along these grids as the spider moves upon it web. What catches the hapless fly can also effect the spider. But the spider moves in such a manner, placing its feet precisely where they will not get caught in its own web.

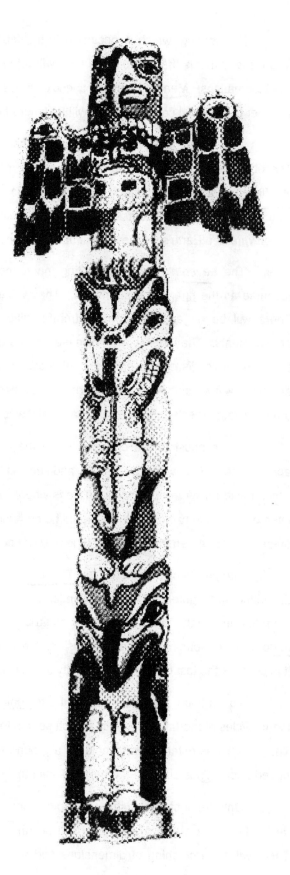

The Other Side of the Coin

felt myself getting sick. The sadness and malaise was overwhelming. I asked myself the obvious questions. Is there anything that can be done? Any thing? Or is all hope lost? If all hope is lost, then why do we continue to struggle? I felt so helpless and alone. What good is the knowledge if we can not have an effect? If we are so few and those lost in the darkness are so many, what can the few do? ... What *should* they do?

I have been so absorbed in the telling of the *Thunders* that I lost touch with my surroundings. The reality of the Eagle was not there. It was as if I had shifted into another space. I felt something churning within me. There seemed to be another essence within me -- yet it was outside of me. I was still in the crystal myst. It seemed as if I could see a form moving towards me. I saw the eyes first, yellow eyes. They were the eyes of the wolf.

It was a Grandfather Spirit. Ancient by what I could tell, and oddly familiar. At times it was as if I were looking into myself in another expression, there were so many overlays. Sometimes the figure looked like a two-legged wolf wrapped in a cape, or blanket. Yet there was something very South American about him.

"Who are you?...What do you want of me?" I heard myself ask.

"I want nothing of you. It is you who summoned me here. It is you who chose to walk with my spirit."

I thought to myself, I don't fully understand, but O.K., I'll take the leap. After all, he and I were of the same medicine, he was Wolf Spirit, right?

He looked at me with eyes that seemed to be touching every cell in my body. Yet I was firm in holding on to the energy of where I was. Where ever that was! I was in touch with my intent and aware of my beingness, my connectedness to all that is. Even with this being, what ever and who ever it was before me. I heard myself ask quietly, almost in a whisper, "Are you the Great Wolf Spirit?"

"Yes" he replied. "If that makes you comfortable. Also, I am you, if you can see that. We are all one.

"I am the alpha of your self. I am the dream of yourself, I am the power that runs through you, and yet I am my own." He added.

In the pause that followed, I reflected. I knew this being was speaking the truth. I could feel it. There was little resistance as I listened to the sound of his voice and felt the resonance of truth, which filled me as began again.

"All this is much to take in. You are very eager to know. But you should not be so eager that you forget to look at the other side of the coin. To use one of your own expressions. There are already those who have made it through the veils. And there are those, like yourself, who have danced back and forth. Things are never hopeless. Let us speak of the other side of the *Seven Thunders*.

"Mankind can soften the effects of these occurrences if they are able to shift their consciousness enough to be able to drop their judgements of themselves, and accept the oneness of each other. If they can break the chains that are only the results of their fear projections. Then their perception of their relationship with nature, and each other, would be able to enter into an energy of cooperation. The energy of the events would then take on a different nature. Though only If mankind is able to return to their true spirituality and open the doorways to their souls. They would leave the created reality of conflict. Nature wishes not to destroy mankind, only to correct the imbalances that have caused her affliction.

"The energy that lifts mankind from the mundane to the divine is reliant at this time upon the group energy. You are all holding onto each other in consciousness, because that consciousness is being threatened. But mankind has lost much of their illumination in this time. The prophecies are of little use to any one who does not hold the keys. The keys are to be found in the heritage of mankind, in their connection to their beginnings in the stars. It is in their remembrance of their connection to the light.

"Mankind needs to embrace that they indeed do come from the light, and that all reality around them reacts to the intensity of their emotional projections. The cause and effect and response of nature to this kind of shifting in consciousness would alter the outcome of everything. That shifting of consciousness would result in two possible scenarios.

"They could invite the help of the Star Nations through communications, which already are on-going. They could then work together in a combined effort to alleviate the intensity of the emerging calamities. In order for this scenario to occur, the consciousness of mankind would need to be altered radically. Man would need to drop the illusions born of the image. For in the image, mankind is lost in perception of the result and not the cause of things. Life is a living canvas, which responds to thought quite readily. In actuality it is effortless.

"If even a few did this, they could help all the others who were willing to realize that they were caught in a mere illusion of separation. Many of the changes that will be occurring are an attempt to wake mankind up to the consequences of their deeds, inclusive of thought and action. Perhaps in the face of total calamity they will be willing to come together and come into unity. The likelihood of this happening as it is seen now is not good.

"Mankind continues to indulge in warlike nature, and exercise domination of their brethren as well as the Earth. They would desire to take this consciousness to the stars, which will not be permitted. They continue to indulge in careless acts of madness to justify the past actions, which they know to be conclusively incorrect. All of this behavior being the result of their addictions to the material consciousness, which serves no purpose in the light of greater reality.

"Without the reconnection off all Earth's People to their heritage and a free, unhampered access to the ancient knowledge, which has been kept from them, mankind cannot hope to release the consciousness of self-destruction. Mankind has become the serpent that devours its own tail. Presently, they are destroying themselves and this will, if not reversed, ultimately result in destruction of all life forms as they presently express upon this plane.

"Mankind's options at this point are quite simple. Take action now and commit to global shifting of consciousness, or lose all ability to manifest upon this physical plane. This occurred when mankind sojourned upon the planet Mars. This expression has already seen destruction three times. This is the fourth expression. Your scientists have already confirmed the existence of advanced civilizations, which for all appearances seem to have vanished. Often without any logical explanation.

"The seers and those who are the keepers of the records have always known this. But mankind lives mainly in a world where they do not honor their old ones, nor their seers. As a result, tyranny rules through the proliferation of fear. They instead struggle to maintain the illusion and thus keep the People in ignorance for the purposes of control.

"The thinking is that a privileged few can hold that knowledge for their own purposes, and rule over those kept ignorant. This is the sickness that flows through mankind when they willfully separate themselves from their spirit. When one passes form the flesh into the light, all they ever can possibly own is what they have adorned themselves within spirit. But mankind has forgotten their true heritage, and thus they cannot realize their destiny.

"Not all will perish. It is a matter of choices. The intensity of these cataclysms can be softened, although they can not be averted entirely. Many will choose to move ahead into the light rather than experience these events. This has already begun. Earth herself will split into two realities -- one of the light, the other of the physical. An illustration depicting the Emergence of the 5th World can be found in *Last Cry.* Those who remain entirely with the physical will begin again form zero point.

"Mankind will move towards destiny along a split path. There will be those who gravitate to their true Spiritual reality. On *the other side of the coin* will be those who fall asleep. Those who later grasp at straws, falsely thinking that their technology will save them even in the face of the destruction of the entire Earth. What they ignore is that their deeds have unleashed many things of which they have no knowledge of. What is manifesting is not even in the confines of their reality. But they have been provided for. Not all will desire to enter this new world. We must understand, that is their right.

"Those who move into the higher octaves will have their own trials and undertakings. Much has been hidden. The loss of even more of human consciousness, they will come to understand, was the result of their own actions. The highest judgement of the truth lies within. What mankind has rendered, they will experience in the times ahead. Each deed and action will they experience 10, even 100 fold. The emotional storms are truly what has called forth El Nino. The *Winds of Change* are upon all of us in this twilight. Even upon the animal and plant nations. Even the Spirit world. In their fear, mankind has created a reality where they have become separated from the all that is. All that is left to them is the world of mind, and the environment they have created for themselves in their aloneness.

"Those who move ahead and have developed their ability to access the higher body, which is born of the light, will experience the Golden Age of Peace as they enter the Fifth World. You yourself will be guided if you remain open to knowledge that will strengthen your abilities to help those during these times of transition. You will meet with individuals who will assist you in reaching the counsel of the old ones. Prepare to go to the Southland, to the People of the Condor. Here you will be introduced to those you will recognize as the Masters. There you will receive further knowledge of the events that will effect Earth and her People.

"There you will be instructed in the construction of buildings, and ways of agricultural preservation, which will assist those you are connected with that wish to continue to try to steer consciousness to its final destiny. Here you will be asked to bring the Ghost Dance, and open the doors to the Grandmother energy. As a result, all who participate will receive the knowledge necessary to access and allow the awakening to the other Circles of Power. For as the Rockies hold the Grandfather energy, the Andes hold the Grandmother energy.

"The new Earth Keepers and the New Consciousness shall come this time from the West. It shall spring forth form the place of its origin. For here in the Western Hemisphere, all the races of the Earth are blending together and the new consciousness is being born. The new race is also making its appearance now upon this plane. Those who left and traveled to the stars are now returning.

"There exists still in the ancient city of Machu Picchu, those who walk through the veils. They are the immortals. They are coming now to deliver much information that has transformed into legend in the hearts and minds of mankind. Once Machu Picchu was a great place of learning and sharing, where those who came from the heavens would instruct the Children of the Sun in the ways of remembrance -- who and why they were and how they came to be in this place.

"Machu Picchu was a place where the higher arts were learned. Telaportation, moving through time, traveling back to Source, how to ignite the whole of the mind and travel the light; these were their teachings -- things which today are mockingly labeled magic and sorcery. At one time there was routine interaction between those of the stars and those on the Earth.

"You, like all of your kind, must now learn once again to trust the inner being and the Source within. This is what you have forgotten. For in the present society would tell you that this is foolishness. How could they admit they themselves were lost? Listen to the wind, find your passion in the birthing of life, and know once again the joy that Creator has in giving life, in causing life to happen.

"Find the honor in achieving humanness, and let go of the rules that have been created by man, and not by the divine Source. This is the true nature of dogma. The laws of Creator remain ageless through time. But the laws of mankind change with the turning of the seasons and have no foundation. Always honor where you are and those amongst you, as well as their chosen path. But remember, there are higher laws that govern all that is.

"The prophecies are very positive. They speak of the ending of time only as it is presently perceived. This allows for mankind's entrance into forever. They speak of tears and holes that are appearing in the perception of the time space illusion. This allows for doorways through which mankind might pass into a new reality. They speak of the ending of a bad relationship with nature and the Earth. They speak of a new perception of our own relationships with each other. They speak of mankind entering into the Golden Age of Peace and Harmony. They speak of the return to the *Good Red Road*."

Prayer to Great Spirit

"Great Spirit... Grandfather... I ask you... Look upon the faces of the Children of this Earth. Can you see, as I, that they are all the same? I ask you to look upon them and help us who hold the memory of the original teachings that we might open Peoples hearts. Open their hearts to see the Truth of your wisdoms, that we might return to the Good Red Road...

Grandfather... I ask for your help that they might stand strong as they face these Winds Of Change. That they might learn once again to walk without fear, and judgement of themselves and each other. For all upon this Earth are your children.

Open their hearts, Grandfather... that they might know that there is no death, only the changing of worlds... Only the changing of worlds."

The Tinsel Bubble ... Virtual Reality

uch change is required in order that all should be set right again. A great part of our present world is predicated upon is _out of balance_ and _dysfunctional_. El Nino brings that energy necessary to effect the change we have long waited for. We have prayed for it in our deepest moments of contact with that which is eternal within us.

Mankind needs to be made aware of its own limitations in order that they might see how deeply their consciousness is shackled within an _invisible cage of ignorance_. We will see the corruption, the perversion and the degree of manipulation that has manifested by our own kind to keep _WE the People_ shackled within our imprisonment. That which has kept us from attaining our fullest potential as sentient beings can no longer be hidden behind veils of obscurity, for now everyone is becoming physic. Should this frequency be awakened in the many, how then can lies perpetuate?

Friction is part of what causes growth, and sometimes growth is painful. But it is never devastating to the spirit. The awakening is just that, when all will be revealed. _Nothing can stop life_, nor can the natural order of events be prevented. We have gone too far down a blind path. The _tinsel bubble_ of our limited reality is _about to burst_. Mankind must have their eyes opened in order that their hearts may survive, in order that the consciousness that is mankind may continue to fulfill its own destiny. There is a great plan whose course was charted so long ago that it escapes our present limited memory, a plan that we ourselves engineered.

There is yet another type of *tinsel bubble.* This one concerns time -- our perception of time, as well as our perception of ourselves. To begin, let us speak briefly of our conception of our concept of time, versus the true nature of time. Discussion abounds about time travel. The very words set fantasy into motion. On the planes of this reality, machines have been developed that enable us to travel through time. They exist -- believe it. The invocation of the *Thunders* and the manner in which events will unfold is a direct consequence of our manipulation of time. Through the use, or rather abuse of this technology, their ignorance has altered our reality outcome.

Everyone is a time traveler. We all travel through time. You yourself have traveled through time from the moment you first picked up this material and started to read it. You have traveled through time from the moment you awoke this morning to this moment of realization which is still unfolding. *Time*, you see, is a no thing of itself. It does not move nor does it expire. It is much like a bubble. The reality of things is that we move **through** an experience. Each experience is encapsulated within a bubble, holding within it a time-space event. An event that we focused upon and elected to stop and explore the potentialities of. By understanding this, we can comprehend that our words and thoughts are powerful. We can begin to grasp that all we decree happens in the end.

Here is an exercise to help yourself understand this simple truth: Imagine yourself as a great light travelling through space, exploring all that is. Along your journey, you come upon a huge sphere. The sphere glows and pulses with a mesmerizing rhythm, catching your attention. You find it fascinating. You focus upon it and adjust your vision, making it larger. A trick of the eye, like when you are looking for wild flowers in the forest. When you come across the one you are looking for, it stands out above all the rest. Upon closer examination, you detect sounds emanating from it. Looking at it in its wholeness, you can see that it is actually composed of billions of tiny flashes of light, holographic light. Now you become intrigued.

You venture closer, straining your vision. You try to glimpse within one of these tiny emanations of light. You can see that there are things occurring within these little bubbles of light, but you can't get a clear picture. Then, one glows unusually bright. Suddenly, you feel a sensation like being stung, and ... Bang! You are inside it! You wake up to a slap upon your behind and the sound of yourself crying...

The experience you are in now, this lifetime, is just one of those bubbles. Each one expressing potentialities of possible outcomes. (Remember the movie, "It's A Wonderful Life?")

One of those potential outcomes is the reality you are presently locked into. You have picked out one of these flashes and entered it with your consciousness. The problem is, you have somehow disconnected from the rest of the whole (you.) You think that all you are experiencing within the bubble is all that there is, when in fact it is but a infinitesimal part of the whole to which you are connected, as well as the whole of the glowing sphere.

So, what you need to understand is that time stands still, in a manner of speaking, while you move *through* an experience. That experience is a time-space event, a moment, a still picture. The movement through time can only be perceived within its structure through our emotions. So, as you move through this experience, you are in effect moving through time. Time itself does not move. Time has no ability to move. You, however, do have the ability to move. You are like a spider upon the web of time, and that web is made up of light. All of which is created ... is created by your thoughts ... which in turn creates the web in the holographic level of reality. This is how you travel, along the vibrations of your thoughts. For within your own reality, your individualized reality there also exists a web of your own creation.

Why is it then, that so many people seem to have the same or similar experiences? This can be explained quite simply. The web we are talking about is spun from the appendage point just above your Third Seal. The web you spin gets connected to the other webs, where upon it touches and begins to pick up frequencies from the webs spun by others. This is the reason your reality, your consciousness, affects the consciousness of the whole. Yours is but one web inter-spun throughout the *Web of Life*, no longer impacting solely its own reality.

Picture in your minds eye the web we have just spun. Picture this web being composed of light, and the light is generated by a frequency. The frequency is generated by the consciousness of mankind... and thoughts are spinning little threads of light, much like a spider. The threads can stretch, they can blow and wobble. But each is connected to the other and so each movement, no matter how subtle, is felt be the entire consciousness that composes the web. Since that web is connected and intricately woven, every thing that is part of what that web is composed of, is governed by the same reality. This reality is called social consciousness.

Body-Mind-Consciousness

Whenever one of us has a thought, in the moment of its conception it simultaneously has been felt by someone else, and will be yet by another as it moves along the web. This is how you come to know that a red light means stop. This is how we build up immunities to diseases, why we all have similar perceptions of family structure, why lovers steal a kiss. Thus, we all have a similar awareness of a Source, of all that is and our connectedness to Source. Some of us are more rebellious in nature and deny Source, just as the child growing through teenage years denies the existence of their parents reality. Thus, because of their lack of experiential understanding and foresight, they criticize the pathway that lead to their very creation. Later, because of their own connectedness to that web, they to will become just as their parents. You see, we play out all that we have experienced. Sounds like programmed reality doesn't it?! Monkey mind. Monkey see Monkey do. Monkey say Monkey believe. Monkey hear Monkey do. Well, it is!

All being connected to this *Web of Life,* it is extremely hard for an individual to possess their own thought. They often become either absorbed or overwhelmed. Perhaps this is a reason why we have had so few geniuses in our society, up until now. In order to achieve that status, that state of reality, one would have to break out of that web and stabilized the whole of reality on their own. Now that's a vision quest, isn't it! How many people do you know who possess that kind of inner strength? Well, in actuality, all of us do. We just are not aware of the potentiality. The secret is in creating our own Mer-Ka-Ba, our own independent energy field. Further, we are programmed by the whole that going beyond the web is something not allowed... Eminent danger lies there! It can not be done! Only damnation will find us! We will go to hell, God forbid! This is where we again come into conflict with programmed conditioning. *Body-Mind-Consciousness.* It is easy to train the elephant not to break the little rope if you have programmed it from infancy.

Hell, by the way, can exist. But it only exists within the confines of limited reality. It is not the place where we find ourselves going down a lava river, being tortured and burned for all of forever. That was probably a vision induced by severe indigestion. *Hell* is a state of existence where we experience being totally separated from the Source while experiencing time. It is a state where we wind up repeating the same scenario over, and over, and over, never hearing the voice of Creator in our hearts, never going beyond.

Those who wish to explore the concept of *Body-Mind-Consciousness* can do an experiment with this phenomenon, or connection. This simple and inexpensive experiment can be done in most homes, even in an apartment or studio setting: First, get some fish and place them in an aquarium. Guppies are good for this one. They are inexpensive, require little care, grow fast and can reproduce a number of generations with a year's time. Place a glass divider in the center of the aquarium just before you release the first fish into their new environment. Leaving the divider in place, raise the fish on one side of the glass partition. After three or four generations, remove the glass partition. You will find that the fish will swim up to the place where the glass partition *was,* and immediately turn around and go back in the other direction... even though the glass partition has been removed. It will take a few more generations before some of the new fish being born will accidentally go past the phantom partition and a larger reality might come into existence. But for the older members of the tank, the partition will always exist... they will never venture past the phantom partition. **This** is the type of conditioning that is definitive of *Body-Mind-Consciousness*.

We are much like fish in an aquarium. Even though many of the partitions that have existed within our society structures for thousands of years have been removed from our path, even though we can now go beyond the boundaries of our former reality and enter an unlimited consciousness, we stop at the place where the partitions once existed. We turn around on ourselves and go back in the other direction. Thus we are caught in a cycle of constantly recreating the limited reality experience. We have become conditioned to accept limitation, and to not question it. When we no longer question our experience and those who we have given the power to run things while were are 'out to lunch,' we become like sheep waiting for the slaughter.

Contracts and Promises

A message from the Native Americans for what is about to occur upon this plane and our interactions with those stepping forth from other worlds to mingle with us in the human experience would be... Do not trust blindly. Hear the words that those who come from another world have to present to you with your heart. This kind of thing has happened before when the younger brother came from across the waters. Many words were said, but few ever became reality. Remember, even when words are written upon pieces of paper, they can exist in one moment and be forgotten in the next. Words that come from the heart hold the breath of life within them and retain their integrity. It is not as easy to forget your heart, for it is a part of you. I would ask you, "Is it the deliverer of evil that is remembered beyond their time? Or is it the one who expresses beauty, and encourages dreams and brings hope to the People? Is the latter not the one that is remembered in their hearts?"

Little of what the Younger Brothers' promised us did we ever see. These Younger Brothers promised us many things, but they changed their minds once they got what they wanted. This feeling is alive now upon the land, and alive in their children who are part of the land now. We are nothing but the Earth manifested in these funny bodies. The children do not trust the way of life that has been left to them. There is not even a place for them in this world any longer. They are considered by many to be 'useless eaters.' *Kissenger*

This is what our youth is reacting to, the destructive intent of their Elders. That intent has been covered over with silver words. It is seen by the children and felt by their Spirits for exactly what it is, rather than how their Elders would have them perceive. The children know in their hearts that we can never own the Earth, rather, it is the Earth who owns us. This lesson would be well spent on the Younger Brother.

Followers of the Dark Star

Those in the Black Robes, the ones called Jesuits, which we know today are no more than the *Illuminati* order of the priest hood, told us of a loving God, who was the God of all things. We knew of this Mystery for it was already in our Sacred teachings. Indigenous People also had a Messiah. Because of this common link, we listened to what *they* had to say. We let them stay upon this land, for was the land not here for everyone? Then in the cover of darkness, they sent for their missionaries who came back with & miners soldiers -- those soldiers were mercenaries. Their ranks were compiled of thieves and murders who had come to this land under the threat of death to enforce their will upon us.

These same priests who had spoken of the one God of all things then said "*Indians are without souls, they are to be considered less than animals. They are to accept the teachings of the Church or be exterminated.*" This is on record with the Papal Bulls. Unfortunately it did not become common knowledge. There are written accounts of the very words spoken by the Black Robes throughout South America and North to the Turtle and the People of the Great Plains. We know today that they were none other than the *Illuminati*. They wore medallions showing within the pyramid a hooded priest carrying a curved sword. When they would show their medallions, soldiers and even generals would aqueous to their wishes.

This is not limited to past history, for these conditions are going on today. Their deeds are just covered up by Clever PR. What is it that the *Followers of the Dark Star* desire? Long ago, it was decided by the Lords of Light that an area would be delegated where time and physicality could be experienced through multiple expressions upon this plane. Each civilization, it seems, has applied a name to this area of the universe. Today, it is most commonly known as the Milky Way. Indigenous Peoples have their names for this star grouping as well.

Think here for a minute. The ancient Mayan, looking through their observatories to the stars did not use the names we use in today's homogenized global society. I chose to refer to one of the surviving bodies of knowledge of Indigenous People, in specific, the Lakota People.

Indigenous Revelations

ere in North America, the Lakota have a word for the Milky Way which is *Wanagita canku*. Which translates to the Sprit Path, or Pathway of the Souls. It is also sometimes referred to as the breath of Great Spirit, *woniya Wakan Tanka*. It is here that all souls that express upon this Earth and in the Universe come from and return. *Wanagita canku* is the birthplace of the souls. There are others born in the universe ... those who do not have souls. The *Washichzu*. They are born, as we've discussed, from our own experiences.

There is knowledge which has been recorded that tells us of the *tinsel bubble* and how it was created around a portion of the universe. Earth's energy fields were so destroyed during the Atlantean experience that a special bubble had to be created around her specifically. This was done to allow life to express in the physical manifested form, whereby mankind might work out their own problems and keep the integrity of the free will zone intact.

So there was conceived the concept of time and space, and a means by which that illusion could be perpetuated. Crystals and Pyramids were constructed for these purposes. This would allow mankind a new experience called evolution. It was felt that this would be a good way by which we could determine what our own progress had been. It was felt that by placing the expression within the confines of a limited life span it would be more controllable. Should the seed of evil evolve to a point where it could potentially be a threat to the rest of the universe, it could play its drama out and there would be a pre-imposed limitation.

Always, there was a way by which the Initiate could travel through this *tinsel bubble* and attain full memory and ownership of their being. Those who had achieved the ability to move beyond time and space and attained a degree of immortality. They performed many secret teachings after the ancient schools were destroyed by the Lessor Gods, who were those under the spell of mortality. This knowledge is still held by the Mayan and the Inca fire keepers. Here in America the Hopi, numerous other Indigenous People have that knowledge their bundles as well. Part of those teachings are the Star Maps. Often it has been said that the secrets of the our future are to be found in the stars.

Lakota Star Knowledge and the Goddess

excerpt from *Sacred Circles,* *Mysteries of Makaakan, the Goddess*

There is a lot to be said about the Sky maps and the Earth Maps. They deserve a book just in their own right. The detailed story of the Celestial maps will be included in my work called *Sacred Circles* which is scheduled for release between the fall of `98 and spring of '99. *Sacred Circles* could be called the Celestial keys of Enoch as preserved by the Indigenous Peoples of this Planet. We are the *Earth People*, which is what we all are in this rainbow river of life through which we swim.

The Star Maps and the Earth Maps are knowledge which was given to mankind in the original teachings the gift of the Star People to us. Within the teachings of the Sacred Circles lies the understanding of when events will take place here upon the Earth in accordance with the Cycles of the galactic clock. This part of the knowledge of the nature of time and how we move through time, how we connect to the universal field of consciousness and become the whole of what we are. I have included this portion of Lakota Star Knowledge in *Winds of Change* as it was shared with me. In many aspects it harmonizes with many aspects of the Prophecy of the *Seventh Thunder*.

The Star Knowledge is now coming to light in the Western Hemisphere so that *all the People* can share in the opportunity for freedom from limited consciousness. However, freedom is a two sided sword. It is the energy of the *Goddess Shiva*. By the way, Native People have their own names for these beings that little brother seems to love to claim as his own. *Shiva* to the Lakota would be called *Makaakan* the Earth Spirit Goddess.

Makaakan comes from the First World. She was manifested in the crystals in the Second World and the flowers in the Third. Upon the birthing of the Fourth World she became the Goddess *Makaakan*. She is a daughter of *Wakan Tanka* (Great Mystery) and *Han* the Great Grandmother Spirit. *Han* was the Darkness, *the black light in the void,* into which *Wakan Tanka* would reach and return with all that is manifest. *Han* is the Darkness to the Light from which all things come. *Han* is the Womb of Creation. *Wakan Tanka* created *Maka,* the Emerald Disk, which is the Earth. To *Maka* he gave a part of his Spirit. He gave her *Makaakan*, the Goddess. He gave his blood, *Mni,* the waters that make up the oceans and rivers that all life might come forth. Which is why Native People to this day hold blood sacrifices, like the *Sun Dance,* so sacred. For it is a reflection of the kind of compassion and commitment that *Wakan Tanka* gave so that we might live in the beginning.

Once, long ago, when *Maka* was new, the surface world was connected together. The Mountains ran East and West rather than North and South. This is a way that we can tell what is the original land of *Maka*, the Mother Land. One might choose to experience the Mongollan Rim located in Central Arizona. It runs East and West unlike the other granite rim formations in Arizona which run North and South. The energies there are quite different. Ruins of civilizations well over 20,000 years old can be found there which affirm the human presence during that time period.

There were once many nations that enjoyed life upon the surface of *Maka,* but there came an affliction to the consciousness. The children became greedy, and selfish. They stated to kill each other in games of war. They lost the *Woopè,* which are the laws of respect, in the family structure and the reverence for life itself which was taught to the People by Wolf Spirit, *Schunk manito Tanka* and they became perverse. They forgot that the universe was created and maintained by compassion and mutual respect.

The disease of FEAR filled their consciousness and then began to spread throughout the land like a plague. The People began to separate and went off in different directions, continuing their perverse ways. This distressed *Maka* very much to have her children divided and living in such a manner. She sent out warnings and signs calling her children together, but because of the divisions of People and their perverseness, few understood. The few that headed her warnings she embraced. These People she kept hidden in her belly, safe through the times of the cleansing.

Maka shook herself and the first cleansing began. [underground] Great rivers of molten rock (magma) flowed throughout the lands, and she sometimes covered whole nations beneath lakes of this fiery, glowing magma. Some of these areas can still be seen in New Mexico, i.e.: the Valley of Fire, where even to this day the land lays black and charred. The waters of the rivers and lakes changed the manner in which they flowed. The flooding of *Mni* washed *Maka* pure of the pestilence of diseased consciousness.

When the cleansing was through the surface was not the same. The surface lands were scattered, and entire nations of people had vanished forever. There were new Mountains that now ran North and South. The rivers were in new places and flowed in different directions. This, *Maka* left as a sign so that her children would know that this would be the last chance for them to walk the *Good Red Road* and to remember the original teachings. Everything was changed by the cleansing. Only the heart of things was left.

The Star People came and they noticed that everything was different, that the rivers flowed in new directions, and the Mountains, they also ran in new directions. They noticed also that many of the children were wandering and confused. They wished to help them as they were relatives to those who walked upon *Maka*. They taught them the knowledge of the constellations, and showed them the Sacred Hoop, *Cangleska Wakan*, which represented where their relatives came from.

They taught them that they were descendents of the Star People, the Star Seed. They taught them that they were descendents of Great Spirit, *Wakan Tanka*, and that they were the *Nagi Tanka*.

There was much unrest upon *Maka* in these times. The Buffalo, the Eagle, the Bear, all *Maka's* children were upset that this terrible thing might happen again. They blamed the two leggeds for creating the disharmony and some even wanted to destroy the two leggeds. The Star People, however, intervened and would not let them destroy the children. A plan was created. The children would now dance through dreams of what they were. That which had to be created to have this happen began. Under the direction of the Star People, the Great buildings and mounds were constructed that stand to this day.

The Star People left *Maka* but promised to return when it was time for the dream to end. They make visitations here, but the time they would actually return is encoded in the Star Maps. Look at the Lakota Star Map in the illustration I have included. If you were to overlay the stars that form Orion's belt over the great Pyramids in Giza, you would find they fit and a puzzle begins to form. You could then overlay them over a map of the Black Hills in South Dakota and what you would discover would be amazing. This is a glimpse into the *teachings of the Sacred Circles* and the information to be found in *Project Stargate*.

This story from the Lakota is another affirmation, in its own way, as to why Pyramids were built and crystals were placed at specific points upon this Earth. This was done in order to create a grid to hold the energy fields of consciousness, for all reality is again, **created from thought**. This grid system created a gigantic Mer-Ka-Bic field, or expression of the Flower of Life. Within this grid system, physical life was able to express upon this plane. This grid actually has the shape of a bubble. Time, in the higher understanding, is not linear, although it is perceived to be. It is actually spherical. This is the nature of the *Sacred Circles* or the Music of the Spheres, for sound creates all that is physical. We are beginning to understand this with the studies of Cymatics. (*An excellent and simple explanation of Cymatics can be explored in Gregg Braden's book, Awakening to Zero Point.*)

Virtual Reality

however, there were restraints placed upon the expressions. One of those restraints was that those life forms within the field would experience time in temporal expressions. Thus, the wheel of reincarnation was conceived. Mankind's conception would allow temporal existence and the ability to incarnate into this plane at will to continue upon the journey. But the memories of previous expressions would not be held as they would be memories of illusion. Therefore, only emotions could trigger memory. This was developed through a science called *Kryahgenetics,* which we discuss later in a later chapter. This also kept the conditions and integrity of the free will zone intact. Yet, the means were also provided whereby mankind could develop the ability to perpetuate and even achieve a level of consciousness through which they could attain virtual eternal life. This was what was made available to the Initiates through the Mystery Schools.

Reincarnation, it was felt, would be a fairly safe method to allow mankind to express in the physical form, and yet not be caught in a singular perpetual expression. They would have the ability to change the course of their consciousness. Meaning, if a particular expression were to be imperfect, mankind would have the ability to return again and express in yet another expression being free from the reality conditions of the past. In other words, all memory would be erased. However, they would still retain an ability to continue to develop and attain perfection. Although the mind could not directly access recall of past lives, the information of those experiences were be retained within the cellular reconfiguration of their lineage, remaining accessible through emotional memory. This would be understood and grasped by the part of them which was eternal, the Spiritual Body and Awareness, encoded in the DNA. Thus *Karma* was conceived.

Another condition of virtual reality within the tinsel bubble was that the emanation of soul consciousness would co-exist within the environment created. This, it was felt, would help expedite the process. The emanations would be reflections of mankind's consciousness. They would, for all intents and purposes, even have the ability to inhabit bodies. Though they were in fact emanations of mankind's higher self. In essence, beings which did not possess souls. Mankind would therefore exist within a reality manufactured by their own thought forms, playing off the reflections of and actually interacting with the emanations.

It was a perfect virtual reality game, affording mankind the ability to experience, through the process of evolution, a complete reassembling and customizing of the physical forms designed via their own will. Thus, they would be afforded the ability to raise their expressions to the point of full enlightenment, or complete Christ Consciousness. The *Great Experiment* was created within the *Great School.* The rest of the universe would remain untouched and protected, if something went awry by means of the *tinsel bubble* acting as a containment unit for the *Great Experiment.*

The records found in the Dead Sea Scrolls, which speak about the Sumerian records, are interesting and enlightening. However, please keep in mind that these records deal with only one geophysical area of human development. They are, in my opinion, accurate, yet not representative of an entire picture.

Fragment from Dead Sea Scrolls

The Creator Gods directed the actions of the Syrians and Andromedans to create this *tinsel bubble.* They knew that eventually it would wear down, marking the end of time. However, it was hoped by that time mankind would have risen above their destructive nature and be able to achieve full connection with and awareness of the Divine Source. There would be presented another opportunity for the opening of the worlds and, regardless of whether they retained memory or fell into unconsciousness, they would awaken under the frequency vibrations of the *Pachacuti.* The awakening was the predictable part of the cycles of the universe. The universe has a very accurate clock.

The stratification of Earth's atmosphere is no coincidence. Like the *pH* of the Human blood the atmosphere has a specific balance point. It was known that radiation resulting from our own experiments, such as the contamination of the *Manasic Radiation Belt* as discussed in *Last Cry* could be extremely harmful to organic life forms throughout the universe. Because of this potential hazard, the radiation would need to be filtered out. As well, that radiation could negatively effect the consciousness of Mankind while expressing in the physical plane. Therefore, an organic shield was developed, and the atmosphere formed.

The *tinsel bubble* would keep the consciousness contained and assure that Mankind would not be able to achieve full awareness of the potentiality of their being unless they could maintain the harmonic balance of their Chakras, or, what I call the Great Seals. This could only be attained through initiation into the higher understandings, which have everything to do with the purification of the blood. Thus the great Brotherhoods, and Great Sisterhoods were formed by those individuals who had gone beyond the spell of mortality.

The Great Seals are doorways to higher consciousness, which can only be opened when one attains a certain ability to maintain and express through the higher frequencies of consciousness. These Great Seals exist within us, as well as within the universe. The Inca called this time in the cycles *Los Pachacuti,* the time of the great change. One has to develop the ability to hold the higher frequencies through disciplines, hence the necessity for initiations. These Great

Seals actually lie along certain grids that exist with our bodies as they do in the universe, and in the embodiment of Mother Earth.

This illustration entitled "Chakra Spheres" by Aeloliah was gifted to me at one of my lectures. I am pleased to share it with you here to demonstrate the harmonic balance of the Seven Great Seals. This beautiful illustration can be seen in its full color glory at our web site at http://www.wolflodge.org/greatseals/chackraspheres.htm.

ssentially, the *tinsel bubble* of time-space reality would keep mankind's reality contained to the Earthly experience. The nature of this tinsel bubble would alter in accordance with mankind's consciousness. Certain beings who achieved enlightenment, or full conscious awareness while expressing upon the Earth plane could move beyond the bubble. Beings from outside the *tinsel bubble* could enter the field of energy providing that there was no disturbance of the field. This is the terms of the legendary non-interference clause of our relationship with the Ethereans.

Understand that the existence of a larger tinsel bubble exist within the area we know as the Milky Way. Therefore other physical beings were also effected by time space realities although they do have a very different concept then we Terrans. Many of them live for what would be determined by our perception as thousands of years. They also have the ability in many cases to move through means of their technology through dimensional borders. Some of these beings again have attained a state of virtual immortality.

However, entry into the Earth zone has its conditions. Our perception of these beings (for the sake of communication, let's call them ET's) is not possible unless we ourselves experience a frequency shift. Thus, in many cases of encounters, Terrans are removed from the time space experience and returned either slightly after or slightly before the actual occurrence. This explains the memory loss of those who have been 'abducted.' ET's exist within a very different frequency then afforded Terrans in the *tinsel bubble*.

Unless this memory lapse or missing time experience occurs, there could be, as a result of the nature of the consciousness grid, a complete *destructuring* of known reality. The experiment would fall into absolute chaos. For the purposes of easy entry into the Earth plane and interaction with its people who dwell upon the surface, clones were developed. These are a little different than the Emanations. They have consciousness programmed into them, but are engineered to not possess any will of their own.

Back to the *tinsel bubble*. As a result of our tampering with the atmosphere, a very, very serious development has resulted. We have natural changes occurring that were not foreseen at the period when the experiments were first attempted. The situation has been intensified further by the experimentation of time travel devices, such as in the Montauk experiment. Further complications have resulted from the reckless use of the *HAARP* technology. We are at a very tenuous point. We are now faced with a dilemma which effects the whole of life upon this plane, and threatens us with the potentiality of virtual extinction.

We have ripped a whole in the bubble. This bubble is organic in nature, it is not mechanical. The rip is growing. The cosmology of the rip could be equivocated to an open ulcerous sore, that is now spreading. The cosmology of the *tinsel bubble* has been so weakened that repair of the rip has reached the point of no return. So what does this mean?

I will attempt to sketch the situation and the possible scenarios for you, although a broader explanation will be released in *Project Stargate*, an excerpt of which will follow. A full and complete explanation, however, would take volumes. If what you have heard so far seems like it is a little surrealistic and unbelievable, well, it is only the tip of the icebergs. Believe it or not, it is essential that the knowledge is at least in your consciousness so that as we experience certain events. This way we will not be paralyzed from our total unawareness of the realities of things.

This *tinsel bubble* also prevents dimensional merging to occur within the confines of the bubble, except those born of the Earth itself. We are now experiencing dimensional fracturing of tremendous magnitude. "*That which has been hidden will be revealed,*" is what the Elder's have told us about these times. We are beginning to experience many occurrences which will soon reach proportions where the truth can not continued to be withheld from the awareness of the People.

The appearance of La Chupacabra is one such experience. We also have People disappearing, almost into thin air. Thousands of children are vanishing from existence. We have sightings of UFOs being witnessed by thousands in metropolitan as well as rural areas all over the globe. Abduction experiences are increasing, and becoming an almost a daily event. Evidence of animals that come from supposedly prehistoric times are being found throughout the globe. Read "National Geographic!"

These events are not all off the wall. Many credible people are having very real experiences. I would ask you to consider Whitley Strieber, who wrote of his experiences in *Communion* and his latest book, *The Secret School*, and Travis Walton who authored his experiences in *Fire in the Sky*. Col. Corso, in *The Day After Roswell*, where he gives his accounting of the events that transpired there. Then we have the *Montauk Boys* and the events of the Philadelphia Experiment. All this information is being told to us by reputable, intelligent people; scientist, doctors, military officers, etc... All with accountable, documented stories about *experiences that never happened*? The phenomenon is too wide spread!

The Inca have told us that this is a time of *Pachacuti*, the time of change when there would again be doorways open through which we could walk outside of time. There exists now a tear in this *tinsel bubble* that has contained time. Beings of the ethereal levels of reality are coming into this plane. At the same time, our consciousness is leaking out of the *tinsel bubble*. One result is that our imbalances are now effecting the greater bubble within the Milky Way. This has opened the doorways for levels of intervention by those who come from beyond the *tinsel bubble*.

We are dealing with multiple factors here; those who are beneath the Earth, those who are from other planets, those who are from other dimensions as well as those who come from our own consciousness. I have had the opportunity to meet with and have many conversations with many of the People involved in the Montauk Project. We have talked about the prophecies and the experiences they have had. There are many things as a result of our encounters that have become clear in the process.

We, as a species, are loosing our consciousness. We are loosing our memory. Life expressing as nature upon this plane is vanishing. We are going through tremendous electromagnetic frequency shifting. We are headed for the Photon belt and science is very, very aware of us reaching Zero Point. The contracts agreed to in 1953 between those of other dimensional expressions and our governments are up and, as we said in *Last Cry*, it is the time of *Truth or Consequence*.

Irreversible damage was done due to these time travel experiments. I will speak of a few of them as they directly relate to many of the prophecies.

The Basic Nature of Time

Time is spherical. It is not linear. We perceive time experiences as being separate because time experiences move through a tubular form of energy, much like fiber optics. When we create an artificial or synthesized time experience, it operates separate form the bubble. What the result is, is a time loop. A time-space event, which has no source of origin and no way of continuance. So the synthesized loop is played over and over, and over. Remember the movie *Ground Hog Day*?

The *tinsel bubble* has layers to it. The main level of our experience is within a field defined by science as the biosphere. It essentially reaches a short distance above the surface of the Earth, and only a few feet below. When we reach certain elevations, like at Machu Picchu, it is almost non existent. The same is true when we go deep below the Earth in mine shafts, or travel below the tectonic plates. Also, this occurs when we enter the Pyramids.

People get stuck in synthesized events within the biosphere. Some have been sent to these time loops to eliminate potential problems, and keep the lid on information that those who created the situation do not want us to know. Still others find themselves losing solidity. Once the time factor of reality is overcome, then individuals can enter time from any point and exit time from any point. This has been achieved in other civilizations by other means.

The *tinsel bubble* is collapsing. The time factor is dissolving. We are experiencing a merging of the light spectrum, and of the dimensions. These are some very important factors in understanding what we will begin to experience in the *Hall of Mirrors*. Two Dimensional thinking, which is, let's say, what we experienced in consciousness prior to the 70's. In the eighties we moved into Three Dimensional thinking, and now we have entered into Fourth Dimensional thinking. Many of the things we only dreamed of in the 70's are quickly becoming experienced realities.

When you start to see beings from the other worlds, do not be so willing to accept just their words. Do not be so willing to channel spirits without qualifying them. There are many spirits, not all are benevolent. Many people are now playing with knowledge that Native Americans have known and held close to our hearts for thousands of years. There are many of you who call yourselves *New Ager's,* or the gifted ones, bringing forth new knowledge and understandings. There is only the awakening to what already is, no matter what title you give it. It seems that people are quick to create new names and to try to claim something they have learned from a benefactor as their own.

There is much more credibility to be found in honoring those who passed the information on to you. It keeps the thread of humanity connected to that which makes it a living knowledge and therefore empowers it. *Honor* and *respect,* without it you can't even begin to connect your intent and what ever you do... well, nothing grows.

There are thousands of books and videos being produced about information covering everything from the secrets of Sacred Geometry to the Star Maps and the alignment of the Pyramids at Giza. This is all knowledge that your ancestors left behind in their walk upon this Earth, which is something that needs to be honored. Then it will be empowered. We must remember that we are all connected. The true art is in connecting the memory!

Project Stargate - Information Release

The Mountain Brotherhood has completed the first stage of Project Stargate. We are now prepared to begin releasing the information we have compiled. Project Stargate contains information which has never been released before to the public. This body of work represents painstaking efforts and years of sacrifice to their personal lives for the sake of truth and Spiritual enlightenment. We release this information in the name of love that mankind might grow and become wiser. For be it known that the truth shall set you free.

One of the focuses of *Project Stargate* is the ongoing investigation into Native American legends, Star Maps and Earth Maps, and their connections to the one known as the Pale Prophet, Wa coma Tete, the Lord of the Wind. The investigation also focuses on the feasibility of possible connections to other Indigenous Peoples across the globe. What we have discovered is astonishing and will without a doubt cause all of us to take another look at the stories of our creation and our future as a species, for we are without doubt... Starseeds.

Project Stargate reveals to us that there are in fact direct connections between the pyramids at Giza in Egypt and Sacred Sites in both North and South America. The ancients have left us deliberate maps that can guide us through these millennium times across the bridge of tomorrow.

The Black Hills in the Dakotas, Machu Picchu in Peru, Chichen Itza in the Yucatan, as well as the Mounds of the Puan near St. Louis, MO, and other sites, are all connected through Sacred Geometry. The Elders used Sacred Geometry in the planning, construction and locations, so that ancient knowledge from the original teachings could be made available to us intact and in its uncorrupted form.

There are many mysteries we have heard about the Year 2000. Is the upcoming year 2000 a myth or is it based upon an actual cycle of time? The decoding of the ancient Star Maps clears up an issue that has baffled scholars for a long time. In deciphering ancient prophecies, it is essential that we be able to determine dates and locations of probable events. Currently, we follow a calendar that is comprised of 365 ¼ days divided into 12 months, based upon the birth of Jesus.

Even Orthodox Christian scholars will tell you that the birth of Jesus, both from historical and astronomical observations, indicate his actual date of birth to be either 5 or 7 years BC. The common explanation for the discrepancy is that a major miscalculation somehow crept into the record keeping during the early Christian Era. Since our present day calendar is based upon the birth of Christ, and our calendar is admittedly not accurate then, the actual year 2000 is only a numerical change and nothing more.

Indigenous People are Indigenous People. Jesus was born to the Indigenous People of his land. Interestingly, most Indigenous Cultures have Star Maps. Even in the portions of the Bible that remain in tact after its many alterations, we find there are constant references to the stars and the constellations. The Star Maps essentially were created by our ancestors, knowing that in order to determine accurately the time and place of specific events, they would have to rely upon constant factors for our source.

The geography of Earth in our recent history has been a constant in that the continents and the mountains have been static. At least for the period of time that spans our recorded history of civilization, since at least the Early Egyptian Dynasties. We now know that the Kogi Peoples in Columbia make up the oldest surviving, intact-civilization in the Western Hemisphere. The Kogi civilization, also has Star Maps. These Star Maps indicate times, dates and destinations of future events that are affecting us today!

We know that certain stars seem to be moving all the time and not necessarily in the patterns that we have been taught. However, the stars that make up the constellations are stable in the skies of our universe.

Through our research we have discovered the keys to decoding the hidden messages that have been encoded in the Bible. We are now able to correct our previously limited perceptions of the concepts of time and space. We have included some very interesting visuals that stir the imagination and in our estimation, justify a new look at our evolution and perceptions of history.

The Information that was given to the Lakota People wherefrom they recorded their drawings on Buffalo hides of the Star Maps is one of the focuses of our investigation. Wa Coma Tete, the Lord of the Wind, gave this information to the Lakota People. Like the Calendar Stone of the Toltecs, from which the Mayan Calendar was derived, the Star Map of the Lakota People reveals the truths in both past and future events.

The Venus Calendar

The Venus Calendar has been and is used to this day by Indigenous People in both North and South America. It was used by the Prophet and was the understanding by which all calendars were calculated before the Conquest. Here in North America, this knowledge is still understood and in the Sacred keeping of the Meda Medicine Society (Mediwewan) of the Algonquin People who comprise many of the woodland tribes of North America.

Venus is spoken of as the Star of the Prophet, his place of origin. Also, as the twin star for it is sometimes the evening star and then, at other times in its evolution, it is the Morning star, as it is presently. In Indigenous writings, it is always associated with the number 13, while the number that corresponds to Earth is 8. In Mayan interpretations there are four inter-weaving calendars:

1. **The Sun Calendar** with a year consisting of 365 and 1/4 days which is the same as our present calendar.

2. **The Moon Calendar** which follows the cycles of the Grandmother Moon and the Goddess Makaakan.

3. **The Tropical Calendar** in which a year follows the swinging of the Sun between Cancer and Capricorn and

4. **The Venus Calendar** which was extensively used by the Prophet for his computations.

The Venus calendar proves to be an excellent and accurate tool for time computation. Venus circles the Sun on an inside orbit and makes thirteen revolutions to eight of the Earth's. Therefore, in cycles of 8 thirteens, or 104 years, they are back in the originating position of their cycles. Most Native Americans used the Half-cycle of 52 years. They also had a great Cycle over three thousand years. Kate-Zahl (the Prophet) spoke to the People at the temple in Co Lula. He spoke to them of the cycles of the Dawn Star, sometime referred to as the Prophets Star, or Tlau-lacal-Pan-Tecutli. There he told them of the coming of the white men from across the waters.

"For five full cycles of the Dawn Star, the rule of the war-like strangers will grow unto greater and greater orgies of destruction. Hark well to all that I have taught you, return not to the serpent and the sacrificers. Their path will lead to the last destruction. Know that the end will come in five full cycles for five is the difference between the Earth's number 8 (frequency) and that of the Dawn Star 13, which is the number of these children of destruction."

The Birth of Jesus in Bethlehem

We began by taking the Star Charts and using the very Star Globe program that is used by NASA. We then calculated the Birth of Jesus in accordance with the Star Knowledge of the Mediwewan, where it is said that you enter this plane upon your star and you leave when the heavens are in the same pattern, meaning that you leave upon your star.

We are told that the three wisemen came from the East and followed a huge star that appeared over Bethlehem. Given that, perhaps it wasn't a spaceship as has been conjectured, perhaps it was an actual star! What star could have been so large as to stand out in the manner recorded at the time of the birthing of Jesus? The coordinates given to us in Mathew, where Herod, upon hearing of the birth of a King, asks his council what the positions of the stars were, left us a clue.

From the Book of Mathew

2: 1 In the days of Herod the king, behold there came wise men from the east to Jerusalem,

2:2 saying, where is he that is born King of the Jews?

2:4 And he gathered all of the chief priests and scribes of the people together, he demanded of them where Christ should be Born.

2:5 And they said unto him, In Bethlehem of Judaea:

2:7 then Herod, when he had privily called the wise men, inquired of them diligently what time the star appeared. 2.9 When they had heard the king, they departed; and, lo, the star, which they saw in the east.

Star Globe Maps - Affirmation of Star of Bethlehem and Ascension in Jerusalem

Looking at Star Globe Map 1 towards the East, in the city of Bethlehem at 51.2 degrees off the horizon, in the year 5 BC... behold! We witness a double star as Regulus aligns with Venus descending in the heavens. Thus, it would have appeared as a singular and very large, conspicuous illuminated star in the heavens -- The Star of Bethlehem.

The wise men would have been educated in this star knowledge for they were of the Melchezidec school. "Where it is said that you enter this plane upon your star.... " Entering upon the descent at the Birth of Jesus on September 15, 5 BC at 3:00 AM.

This star pattern is not seen again, nor has it been seen *since* that time. On March 28, 28AD at 2:15 PM over Jerusalem when Jesus ascended, as we look at Star Globe Map 2, we see that the patterns of the stars are *identical* to those seen over Bethlehem at the birth -- with one singular exception... Venus has ascended.

"...and you leave when the heavens are in the same pattern, meaning that you leave upon your star."

We look towards the east from the Horizon Point at each location, Bethlehem and Jerusalem at a 51.2 degree angle (the same angle as the Great Pyramid.) The results are summarized below:

1. Birth: Venus and Regulus align perfectly ... so if one were viewing them from the ground, they would see two stars as *one very large star!*

2. Ascension: You will note that all the stars align the same as on the date of the birth. This does not occur again *anywhere* in time checking back and forward 5,000 years! The only difference is that the Dawn Star (Venus) has ascended!

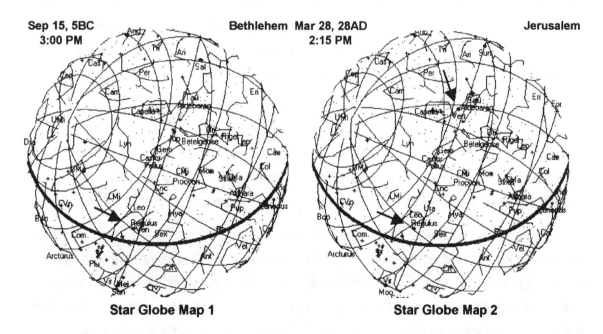

Sep 15, 5BC
3:00 PM

Bethlehem Mar 28, 28AD
2:15 PM

Jerusalem

Star Globe Map 1

Star Globe Map 2

What can be deduced and validated through the finding of this investigation is that our calendars are five years off. 1998 is actually the Year 2003. Now, go back re-read your prophecies.

Galactic Communities

not all who come from the stars will be bearing the truths of our ancestors. So I would warn you, when you see these beings from beyond the Sun, when they come to your fields, appear upon the television and on your talking leaves, do not give up your freedom so easily. Question even your own motives. We will not be able to replace this Earth that has given us life so unselfishly, and so freely. If you forget everything else, then consider one thing; that which the Peoples of this land taught you. The sacred gift that you hold so dear in words must now be ingrained upon your hearts, *freedom, choice, and love for life*. How to be a part of the whole and yet remain an individual? This in accordance with the universal law of allowing. To open the next doorway is going to take the energy of the tribe. An individual can not open it upon their own.

As we enter the Fifth World we will all be faced with choices. We are being tested whether or not we posses the ability, the right, to keep our status of Free Will. Will we choose to take the gifts that offer to perpetuate life, or will we choose to enslave the Spirit that is innate within all beings that walk with two legs. Will we take the wisdom of the ancients and honor all life upon this plane, or will we deny those expressions of life their right to share this plane with us. We are connected to all things. If those expressions of life which exist around us in this *Garden of Eden* can no longer exist because of what we cause with unconscious thought forms, how long do we think we can perpetuate our consciousness without them?

Everything we are is a sum total of every experience that has preceded. That includes every living thing upon this Earth. Will we awaken to our connectedness to this *web of life* or will we continue along the path of denial? These are some of the things that must be considered as we feel the *Winds of Change*. These winds will touch each and every one of us as we walk through the *Hall of Mirrors*. Remember and contemplate the Law of Allowance, and the Law of Forgiveness.

Remember the Glowing Sphere and the bubbles of light we spoke of? Are you willing to take another journey along the pathway of greater understandings of the true nature of things? Are you willing to stretch your consciousness? If you don't like it, then discard it. You can always go back to limited reality, can't you? But, if you try, perhaps you will achieve a clearer understanding of how things truly are so you can make the proper choices. **You can make a difference.**

The Blue Star Kachina - The Government and Those Little Green Men

The Spring of 1997 was interesting, to say the least. We had multiple sightings as well as landings, especially in Arizona. Over 150 sightings were reported to Wolf Lodge from around North America. The sightings between March 12th and 14th over Phoenix have been noted as the most documented in recent USA media history. Many Ranchers in the South Western US watched as the lights traversed across the starlit skies from Ft. Collins, Colorado to San Diego, California.

We are, it would seem to many, being made aware of the presence of our ancestors from the stars, the Home Coming. Another interesting note here, there have been at least 5 landings of theses Lights in the White Mountain area of Arizona in April. Thousands witnessed triangular lights flying over the skies in Dallas, Texas in May, and within days there was a crash of a hurling object that lit up the skies in Puerto Rico. But we couldn't get any additional information as the US military had most of the national forests in Puerto Rico under marshal law.

This was also a very active Spring in our heavens. We experienced the Eclipse, Full Moon and Equinox almost simultaneously. Hale-Bopp did not let us down either, as it kept spinning its tails and controversy.

In the Hopi prophecies we are told of the return of two brothers, the twins, *Poganghoya* who keeps the North pole in balance, and *Palongawhoya* who is guardian of the South pole. Their returns will occur just prior to the end times. Their coming would be seen in the heavens. Well, we have seen this in Hale-Bopp, the twin tailed anomaly in our evening skies, which finally caught the attention of the world after being there for the last 18+ months. Having changed it's course of direction over 40 times in that time period, it leaves even the most hard fast realist wondering if it could be something other than a comet. The Hopi tell us that it is the returning of our ancestors. The Kachinas are coming home.

Understand the term *Kachina* does not necessarily represent a singular entity. A Kachina can also represent the spirit of a thing, or force, as the *Wind Kachina* does. There are over 1,200 Kachinas that this two legged is aware of. I have heard the Hopi, Diné, and other Pueblo people talk about their Kachinas. Is it not entirely feasible then, o' western man, that a Star Kachina might represent a ship housing representatives of another race or world. I have heard Hopi Grandfathers speak about the Blue Kachina back in the early 70's. Some of these Grandfathers are well over

100 years of age. Frank Waters wrote about Saquasohuh when he wrote The *Book Of Hopi*, and Lori Toye, who did the *I Am America* maps, also speaks of this Kachina.

The Hopi also tell us when we see the returning of the two brothers, when there will be two other Star Kachinas return to our heavens.   One is *Saquasohuh*, the Blue Star Kachina. He has a blue star face and long white eagle feather headdress that trails to the ground. *Saquasohuh* returns to us by first appearing to the children who are attending dances. This event happened in 1993. *Saquasohuh*, sent emissaries to Earth to walk amongst the people. They sought to find out where man kind had evolved to in his consciousness, to see how well we have been keeping the original teachings. They will be seen in the time of the returning of the twins. They will fill our night skies flying their *patuwvotas* (flying shields,) commonly described as little balls of light rolling through the skies, sometimes very low across the desert landscape. These are the infamous orange orbs.

When we see these anomalies returning to our heavens it will also be the signal of the coming of the Purifier, the Red Kachina. The Purifier will come to purge the Earth and its people of imbalances in preparation for our emerging into the Fifth World. When we first see this Purifier as a red star moving through the heavens, the Day of Purification will be at hand. The prophecies tell us the Red Kachina will appear soon after the return of the two brothers... within two years to be more exact.

Meanwhile, *Saquasohuh* will make available to those of us who remember the original teachings the information which is necessary for us to make it through the emergence into the Fifth World. He will leave these messages for us to decode upon the ground, in the sacred grains and the stones. As the time for the arrival of the Day of Purification nears, these messages will be left with greater and greater frequency. These messages will be able to be understood by those who have kept the original teachings close to their hearts.

These messages will tell us what is happening within us, about our relationship with the stars, and the beings coming. They will tell us where and when events will occur, both on Earth and in the Heavens. They will also teach us how to communicate with those who are coming from the Stars, and from the Hollow Earth. They will reveal the mysteries of the ancient teachings given to us by *Masah* when we re-emerge into the Fourth World. These messages hold the keys to the writings from the book of life which is kept deep within the Earth's belly. The Flower of Life, the Kabalah, the Mayan Calendar, the Inca Stones, and many other forms of ancient wisdom will come alive within our merging consciousness. Many indigenous people will begin consciously walking in both dimensions over the next two years, beginning in South America and Australia. People there have already accepted fourth dimensional consciousness as a reality. We are very sophisticated here in America. It will be harder for us to accept things. First, we will have to cure a great social disease known to many as the "I / Me / I know it All" disease.

Radio shows and television specials are presenting us with many individuals expressing a variety of view points. Most of the information presented is very left brained. This is what those who monitor what we watch are capable of understanding at this point. In talking about *the Quickening*, which I have been talking about since 1993, I often stress the importance of becoming very clear. Be certain that we know what we are asking for, what we are hearing in our heads, and who the information is from. Always bring the message through your heart center first.

I have always stressed the importance of developing our ability to see through the intellectual veils of easily given explanations for events that are occurring. And, for *cry'n out loud*, be especially aware of network misinformation. There is far to little explanation and focus spent upon the Spiritual and metaphysical aspects of what is occurring. We must realize that the whole alien agenda and conspiracy against the people of this planet has, beyond question, been manipulated and executed through the mouthpiece of organized religions. It has been policed by, both then and now, affiliated political parties in power for their own purpose.

I realize that I might be taking an unpopular stand. Yet I also believe that to make a positive and powerful impact on society as a whole, one must often do so. Remember, Jesus took a very unpopular stand in Judiah. Porcupine, Holy Man of the Cheyenne, took a very unpopular stand with the Ghost Dance in the late 1800's when he brought words of peace to his People. Deganaweda took an unpopular stand when he gave the Haudenosaunee people the teachings of the Great Peace, from which we have borrowed much to create the American Constitution and the values of this country we call America. Gandhi also elected to take an unpopular stand in India as did Martin Luther King in America. With all the peoples of this world, just a handful have taken a stand for their individual knowing. We all must learn the wonderment of taking individual stands once again.

Whenever anyone attempts to explain the realities of the nature of change, they are walking on the edge of 'acceptable reality.' There is very little difference between prophecy and insanity, except in the success record of predictions. If the prophets words manifest, he is often unpopular, if they do not, he is often called a fraud. If anyone challenges the 'acceptable majority view of reality,' they are going to have to take an uncomfortable position. It is Giraffe medicine. If you stick your head above the crowd, you must expect a stone in the face now and then.

We are going to have to realize that there has been and is an ongoing mass cover-up of the actual events which have and are occurring in our heavens and below our mountains. We will not even get into secret government agendas right now. But seriously, folks, expect circumstances to become a lot more _uncomfortable_ as the world structures continue to crumble before our eyes. It is going to hurt our comfort zones, push our fear buttons, and let loose a whole lot of rage from the general population. We have been denied the truth for far too long.

In the end, Metaphysical truth will prevail. It always does. What you choose to embrace, so shall it be. The key to coping with these changes we are experiencing is in allowing. The key to the mysteries and deciphering phenomenon such as the Crop Circles, is in allowing your heart to lead you. The key to making it through Fourth Dimensional reality is in opening your hearts. The Native message is simple. "*It has always been a matter of Heart.*" Keep the beat, keep walking, we have already begun to break through!

From the Heart of the Wolf... Don't worry, be Hopi!

Wolf Song

Throughout the world there are many thousands who are now hearing the calling. Those of us who work in the light welcome you to *the Gathering!* To many, the message seems familiar. It is like a melody that plays in your head, yet you can not quite recall where or when you heard the tune, or even its completeness, only a small part.

There are those who greet the messenger with abhorrence and crassness. Their actions show clearly their fear and mockery which quickly comes into play. The merry-go-round of recycled ignorance continues to spin wildly, as they insist upon wallowing in their ignorance. The messenger does not come to have people change their way of life. Nor does the message deliver an edict from the divine. There are those who are stuck in their patterns. They are stuck in their religions, dogmas and bound by cultural ties.

The messengers are here. They keep coming, and they are not going away. They can no more be stopped than one could hope to stop the Sun from rising in the morning. The messengers come to alert us as to what is happening. Perhaps in allowing ourselves the grace of listening we will discern the sincere ones from the charlatans, for those who resonate with Creator have no need to resort to trickery. They who are of the light will offer you wisdom. They will show you ways that you might help yourself, that you would not become dependent upon them for the answers, that you might come to your own conclusions.

The prophecies can be easily misread from the lower frequencies and there used for manipulation of fear and the human consciousness. Words are to be discerned -- not carelessly accepted. Change is the natural order of things. No one can do a thing for you, it is up to you to take the initiative in your life. It is up to you to take command, to effect change and to embrace it. Only you can turn the day around when you meet your defeats. It is a matter of choosing life or not choosing life. It is all choice. Let your own conscience be your personal Spirit Guide, as it always has been. Let the battle of the Armageddon end here. I am not speaking of surrender, rather I speak of embracing. Embracing the beauty that already exists within you if you dare to make the choice to go to Source.

Within each and every one of you is the divine spark of the Source. You are now walking across the bridge of forever, and have now entered the experience of Fourth Dimensional Reality. You are in the merging of worlds. "*Those who walk in two world,*" the Elders said of this time.

What resistance, pain and un-fulfillment that are manifesting in your life is a direct result of your refusal to qualify your own experience. You are now feeling the effects of the *Winds of Change*. Yet so many of you refuse still to become flexible and allow your hearts to guide you through the haze of mixed emotions that are like overgrown bush along the path in front of you.

For those of you who have so long resisted the consciousness of the masses, **you** are battling the altered ego. The beast within that tears apart your plans and dreams, leaving you with the feeling of incompleteness. The incompleteness is really the separation from Spirit. The beast creates situations to teach you. The Beast would have you believe that there must be something wrong with you for feeling the way you do, for taking the path that leads one away from the crowd… The path less often traveled.

The emergence of humanity into this Fifth World is no myth. It is not a fantasy. It is abject reality. This is the twelfth hour. The merging of *the Solar* planes and *the Light* is already occurring. The physical is now falling into alignment, and this shifting is causing all which is not in balance with the divine plan to be cast off. To all things there is a *quickening*, even the pulse of *Pancha Mama* beats in anticipation of the birthing. In the wilderness you can here *the Wolf song*, once again. It is beckoning those who would dare to come to the Gathering of Souls. You can hear it now as it carries over the mountains, along the pathways of the *Winds of Change*.

If you are along the path, be aware! Move swiftly and regard each step taken. **There is no time left to sit in the indulgence of lack, self worth and victimization. It is time to take action! It is your hour.** You are already feeling the separation as you rise in consciousness into the realm of the living light from which you came. Nothing that does not resonate with the frequency of your truth can follow you, for only truth can enter these portals through which all of humanity now passes. It is only that which you hold that is not a part of your light essence that prevents you from progressing beyond this point. Those of you holding to belief patterns that you no longer embrace are running into walls of resistance every day. Welcome to the *Hall of Mirrors.* Only the vibration of truth shall pass beyond this point – proclaim it! Make it so!

Give up your attachments to the cycles of death. There is no death. There is only the changing of worlds. Earthly attachments will soon fall away, yet you will find yourselves continuing along the path. Merge with Creator. The Source will be your only blanket of protection against the chilling *Winds of Change.*

With the passing of each civilization that has come before you, each of those societies has embraced its own concept of money and wealth. All of those concepts have vanished along with the cultures that created them. Only the humanity is left. Only Creator is left. We have not changed much in 30,000 years. Creator's original teachings of Creation are the only true abundance, the only true heritage. All that is, is supplied by the Source. It is time to lay down our addictions to the material worship of the past and create Solon's Republic. Even your bodies will not pass into the light, so how can your gold accompany you? How can any wealth except Spiritual wealth accompany you? Learn now to use it to lift the whole of humanity through your own personal efforts.

Learn something unique. Learn to share. Honor the Indigenous way of the 'giveaway' – giving of that which you have, thus enhancing the wealth of your Spirit. What if you discovered that all money, all wealth, was only fish heads in the garden? How then would you regard all that you sacrificed for to insure your success? How many people did you have to go through to amass what is around you. How many have you denied sharing the gift of compassion and caring?

It is time to prepare for the journey into forever. The transformation that is taking place upon this plane has been the song of mankind since its beginnings. The mortal beings who embraced power over others to achieve their desires, and to achieve material gains are gone from the Earth, and from the memory of the People. Only those who spoke of love and spirit remain through each cycle, for theirs was the true way of the path to power.

Mortality was merely a concept we embraced for a brief experience. We did so in order that we might understand limited existence. Every master who walked amongst us made a path to forever. We need only to follow in their footsteps. The path has already been created for us. We need only to follow our hearts. To connect once again with that which is spiritual within us, and the Source will do the rest. The concept of Mortality eventually will fall away. So why not embrace your

Leonard Orr

immortality? Would this not be embracing God? Take the next step along the path. Redesign your embodiments in the spirit of divine light. Be what you always knew you were within. Allow it to find its own roll in your personal human drama. Hide no longer behind your fears. Rather step forth into the light, and all that is will be revealed to you by the Source eternal that emanates from within.

We have all been hurt by those lessor than ourselves. We have had our hearts broken, and our dreams thrashed. We have by such experiences learned to hide our true selves from the world. Thus all we have left to the world was our illusions. As a result, the world has become a world of untruths. Human behavior is directed, and in many instances even based upon, maintaining the illusion of who we are to gain acceptance from those around us. This, in order that we might achieve success. The cost to our divine spirit has been great. Honor and impeccability are mocked in today's society. Children are taught to conform rather than express their own individualism and talents.

Every day we witness our heroes being torn apart and disavowed of any personal honor and dignity, from our Presidents to our artists. Their personal lives are displayed everyday in the tabloids in the supermarkets. Quietly, without notice, we have slowly evolved into a society that is addicted to gossip. We have become preoccupied in living everyone else's life for we posses no life of our own. The life force only grows in the garden of truth. It finds no sustenance in the garden of illusion.

As a people we are loosing the sense of ourselves, and becoming imitators. We are taught by example by those around us to imitate the rolls we see actors playing in movies, or on MTV, etc... Characters that were created through the mystique of studio illusions. We are discouraged from playing our true selves. When we are an imitator we have basically sentenced the spiritual us to imprisonment, even death. The imitator is only playing a role in a play called the human drama, which has its own ending pre-written into the script. Thus, by surrendering the true essence of yourself, one can play the game only so long. The world is filled with ex-wanna-be movie stars who as a result of surrendering self, can only walk through the shadows. They have lost their strength of conviction, because they have given up their truth, and joy of being.

Many of us feel that there is a tearing that is occurring within our inner beings. A tearing away of all that is illusion and yes, the purification can be uncomfortable at times. But we are like athletes who are learning to train for the Olympics after a major injury, and having been laid up for awhile. The soreness will pass. With each day you will find a little more progress, with the next a little more.

Learn to live selfless. For Creator is selfless. Pancha Mama is selfless. The Buffalo is selfless. Your spirit is Selfless. There is not one of you that is greater or lesser than the other. Only one might find themselves further along the path, another a little behind. We even walk the same path on our many roads. There is a plan. There are phases of this process of the Gathering of Souls, stages of progression, if you will. With the sounding of each of the *Seven Thunders* you will experience change. You will experience cataclysmic transition, yet you will also have placed before you the ability to pass through these changes, as well as the doorways to your destiny unscathed.

It is time for all those who have been called to awaken to come into service. Learn to act in selflessness. Heal in selflessness. Share what we have in selflessness, especially our hearts. For that is what is needed most within humanity at this moment. Live our lives in selflessness. Thus releasing the human anguish that torments the whole of humanity. We have all we have ever needed. What we experience as lack is our own unforgiving nature. It is the reflection our own judgement. It is our own fear. We have forgotten to love ourselves. It is the hour now for suffering to end. It is the hour for sickness and disease to be done with. We have within our hands the means to achieve all of this, if we can master our intent.

Reviewing our footsteps along this path, how often have we come in our lives to ask Creator for so much. Most always, it has been for ourselves, the "I" that we come to Creator with our intent. How often have you asked for that which you already posses to be brought into the light? How often have you ever considered asking for a thing that it might be bestowed upon another? How often have we thought to ask what we might do to express Creators wishes and desires? To live *in service* of the light is *not* to surrender self. There is no thing lost, or surrendered. For all is ours when we are part of the all. Is there not always enough for one more at the table when we arrive at the potlatch with just a small portion of food ourselves? Is this not what our contemporary Christmas stories are about?

Do you think you would be forsaken if you surrendered the cloak of material wealth and its sister, mortality, in exchange for the cloak of grace and eternal light? There are many that are willing to walk the path, providing they surrender no thing of their material world, that affirms their status in the professional market, or their position in the great mortal society. When they pass this world all material things they held on to so desperately are quickly taken up by the vultures left behind in their kingdoms. The roll they sought so diligently to protect while playing upon the stage of morality is forgotten like a silent movie screen star. With the passing of spirit one experiences the light of eternal Source. But with the passing of the altered ego, the ones left behind only witness the dancing and singing of vampires.

It is a sacred thing to desire to connect to all that is spiritual. But not so when you sacrifice all discernment in deciphering that which is Spiritual and that which is Superstition. Build the foundations of your life upon truth. The fabric of your future path is to be found within your daily actions in the now. Develop the quality of your life, and abundance of life will flow to you, and lack will be something you experienced in your past. The Living God that is within all things is a free flowing force that embraces all that is in contact with it. The Source does not posses the ability to discern one being as more or less deserving to experience its presence than another. The Source is selfless in its emanation of the life force. Abundance is a natural state, not an acquired contentment.

It is time we all begin to give to the Creator of all, a payment on the account of man. What the Creator desires is not of the material but of the spirit. It is an energy a frequency. Love is a frequency not a statement. Love is not a contract but a state of being. Love is unconditional and its vibrational law is that one be unconditional to exist within its full frequencies. Love has no terms or conditions other then to just be.

What is it that is blocking this love from your being. It is no mystery. When we stop for just a little while and approach the situation with out judgement or guilt, it can be seen. To the zealots, I would present these thoughts of changing our internal vocabulary, for words are powerful things. You have heard the saying "Sticks and stones can break my bones but names can never hurt me." It is not true. Words can hurt, maim, even kill. A thoughtless statement can cripple some one for the rest of their lives. I work with people all the time re-establishing their self-esteem. I have seen the results of words, which were used as weapons. Perhaps we should re-examine the words that so freely flow from our lips.

At first, some of these words which are now perceived by the social consciousness as negative may not strike you as such. However, consider this analogy: At one time, **duty** was held in social esteem as the equivalent to honor. "To do your **duty** for your country." Simultaneously, it was assigned to those who were under oppression, i.e.: those who were enslaved. The negative attachment of **duty** was, at that time, kept in our subconscious, as society by enlarge spoke of **duty** in a positive context. As society became aware that enslavement, etc... was wrong, the negative connotation of **duty** rose to the level of our consciousness, i.e.: we openly recognized that the word had negative attachments. Society (we hope) is reaching a level (or trying to reach a level) of enlightenment. As society emerges into the upper levels of consciousness, the negative connotation of **duty** now emerges into our upper consciousness with it. Thus we find the need to purge words that carry negative connotations, replacing them and in some cases, discarding them all together. In short, why track dirt onto a nice clean carpet?

Socially preconceived negative applications of words intended to control, vindicate and suppress cognitive consciousness:

Belief:

Has become twisted to denote the acceptance of an unstable reality, indicating that you are not certain, you are gambling on someone else's word. That you imitate thought, not create it.

Duty:

So long associated with servitude, carries the feeling of resentment. Essentially, doing something out of a sense of obligation, rather from the heart.

Faith:

Labels a person fanatical, disabling the ability to see the entire story. The following of someone else's experience without knowing the true reason or nature of the matter.

Intellect:

Based upon a paradox of right and wrong, more or less, better or worse, the concept of intellect creates polarity of mind and division of spirit and physical. Closes the heart center.

Orderliness:

Has become a focus of the small minded, making them petty and un-accepting of the chaos that gives birth to creation and discovery. It is an attitude, which restrains the growth of spirit.

Power:

Prime cause of brutality. One feels that they must dominate for in essence power must be defended, it must be taken. Therefor, within it lies the fear of loosing, thus encapsulating the Spirit.

Righteousness:

One of the concepts that has been too deeply embraced by society. It makes our hearts hard and our minds closed to some one else's truth and retards the evolution of our spirit.

Serve: or to serve

Has come to mean surrendering ones individual being and giving away of personal empowerment. Empowerment is accessible to everyone, it is that awareness which determines the character of individual expression and thought. We should rather **be in service**, for then the actions are of the heart and no surrendering is required.

Sin:

Breeds paranoia, causing the feeling of being judged. It is an illusion that we are created imperfect and inadequate. It implies that we are less than whole, unworthy of being all that we are.

Applications and connotations intended to enhance the upper consciousness and positively impact the emergence:

Allowing:

Frees one from the polarity of judgement. It enforces seeing the Creator in all things and all people. It opens the doorways to the heart, and the state unconditional love.

Being:

A state of action -- it is divine law in process. It is like love, a verb, a living energy. It encourages participation and not withdrawal. It develops an awareness of the now.

Desecration:

Knowing where and when to make our point or retreat. What good is to be right if the result of our adopted position is the destruction or dishonoring of another, their deeds or thoughts.

Desire:

Will guide our inner being to our fullest potential. The driving force behind all Creation when born out of love. Desire feeds our passion -- the key ingredient in manifestation.

Detachment:

Allows us to realize we are *having* the experience and that we are *not* the experience. Thus there is no need to defend. Detachment disconnects are charged emotion.

Discernment:

The process by which we evaluate from a neutral place what the true nature of the experience is. Allowing the whole of our being to guide us and act through wisdom and heart.

Grace:

Silence is the greatest empowerment of all. Not possessing power, but going with the flow of it. Possessing poise and finesse is a true sign of mastery. The state of grace allows love to blossom, one to become the dancer in life, and encourages beauty. Grace is achieved through the balance of male and female energy, by opening the heart.

Honor:

Adds substance to ones self image and values to our walk. When we live and act in honor we are a living example of the Source of all Creation. One must be open and not hidden.

Impeccability:

Develops ones ability to always do their best because of self pride, and a sense of divine worth. It encourages one to embrace that which is divine within themselves and act in that manner.

Integrity:

The fabric of our expression upon this plane. It is the stuff that develops Nobel attitudes and allows us to walk hand in hand with the Divine Source. By embracing it we accept the sacredness of ourselves, therefor we feel the sacredness of all there is and our connection to it.

Intent:

The underlying force behind all manifestations. The pivot point of the Divine Laws of cause and effect. Intent is conceptual energy with which we create the nature of our reality, what we harvest upon the completion of our experience.

Knowing:

Born of experience. When one knows something, they have embraced it to the core of them and it need not be defended. Once knowledge is owned, it can not be taken away.

Birth of the Phoenix

We have been told that the *Thunder* will be felt upon the land in the time that the Phoenix awakens, which is the Dragon energy. This will allow the doorways to be open for a little while. We even knew exactly when these times would occur. It was written down, carved in the living stone. We were foretold that while these *Thunders* would be occurring, the People of the Eagle and the Condor would be awakened to the need for each to join together again. This will be an awakening that will shake the whole of the Earth and all that was hidden shall come to sunlight again. The Children of the Sun would give the ancient knowledge life again. These things were told to many people in both North and South America thousands of years ago by the Pale Prophet, the Lord of the Wind. This is the time of his returning, which is why it was essential to reawaken the Ghost Dance, for it was his ceremony. It is wake up time!

These *Thunders* are shaking the whole of the Earth. The earthquakes are uncovering the ancient cities and temples. We are now finding and understanding the writings found on the objects within. This knowledge is starting to spread through *the wind* over the whole of the world. These are the gifts left us by our ancestors. *Carried on the wind…* is it not strange that we now spread the word of Spirit across the Internet and the airwaves, calling it *new and extraordinary information?* May we never forget that millions, **literally millions**, gave their lives in order that this information would be here for us now.

Rainbow Visions

aving entered the *Hall of Mirrors* we will experience the full impact of all we have been. The experience is an exercise of free will, free choice. We get to create our future reality. We get to design the final outcome of the human experience. Only the best and strongest have been chosen for this final presentation as we approach the millennium. What a grand opportunity it is to be here in this time. We all get to sing our song and we all get to hear the wolf howl. This is an ancient dance we are dancing. We have rehearsed the steps for lifetimes.

What I share with you here, in many instances, are the storms. The storms are coming. Better to know about them than to be caught unaware. The storms that we will all endure, being part of the human race, will be severe. We have created the environment for that. But keep always in your thoughts that after the storm there is usually the return of the rainbows. The rainbows that follow these storms of transition will be great. There is the other side of the prophecies, for those who chose to hold onto the beauty of the human drama, for it equally has its passions. This is the rebirth in many ways of the fairy tale. Fairy tales are often frightening at times. There is always the test of courage, and the hero and the heroin. There are the evil dark lords as well as the benevolent ones.

Power, at times, can seem to be out of our hands. Yet in every instance in life it is affirmed that in reality power, true power, is in the hands of the powerless. It is always the struggling bloke who seems, against all odds, to win in the final battle of good and evil. Sometimes by the unseen hand of magic. Sometimes by sheer will and intent of action. The bungling fool who at the story's ending finds wisdom and reward for the mere struggle just to be. Always the heart wins out over the heartless.

We are headed for great times of magical experience. If we choose the path with heart. This too has always been the message of the prophecies. We are never without hope, even in our darkest moments. Should all our actions be seemingly unfulfilled, in the final moment, if our intent remains true we shall be lifted from annihilation of the Dark forces we have created.

In the final outcome mankind wins. The light is of its own source, and the dark only defines the light in the final analysis. The dark could not even be if not for the light shining down upon it giving definition to the path before us. But our experiences along that path are of our own choosing in many ways. We can turn the tide of events in a moment. We have always had that ability because of what and who we are.

For all the woe that mankind has created for itself there have been immeasurable creations of beauty and passion. The same human voice that judges and condemns can also create song and poetry to move the soul. The words and the voices of the Inca and the Mayan, have never been silenced, for their hearts have never perished. The words have only fallen into silence from lack of attention and use. It is this dauntless pursuit of the divine human that allows us the choice in these final hours of a passing age.

The passing of the age is like the passing of mankind through the four ages of man. Infancy and innocence, puberty and reckless passion, adulthood and pursuit of desire and dreams, to the struggle of the flesh and the spirit to recognize each others attributes. Finally, the movement into old age, where the body weakens from use and abuse. It weakens its hold upon the spirit, but the spirit, properly honed, can open doorways into everlasting beauty. For it need not break down and the mind need not become feeble. If we have the courage to allow the spirit that is within us all to takes its natural position in the game of life.

We can become much more powerful than in the inexperience of youth that is so often ruled by misguided passion and reacts to our thoughtless deeds. When the silver hair crops our being like the peaks of the great mountains, we, through the vehicle of our spirit utilize the wisdom of experience and the temperance of the soul. If we follow the path of the heart, we can in actuality create the world around us. Especially if we realize that old age itself has nothing to do with the deterioration of the body, if we choose. For is not the presence of the masters, the immortals, a living example of that which we can achieve.

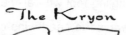

The Kryon

There is a science that exists within the reach of every human being upon the face of this Earth. It is the science of *Kryahgenetics*. *Kryahgenetics* is not to be confused with *Cryogenics,* which has to do with the freezing of the physical body in hopes that at some future date it can be resurrected through the application of the physical sciences of allopathic physicians. *Kryahgenetics* has been given to us by beings who I believe never have taken human or physical form. We know these beings as the Kryons. Personally, I know very little about these beings and have only communicated with them while achieving certain levels or states of mind through intense meditations.

They communicate through thought transference, which in my perception is telepathy. There is a person who claims to channel the Kryon, and I make no claims as to being part of his organization. Nor do I dispute or affirm that relationship. I have never read nor am I familiar with any material that has generated from that source. I also wish to make it clear here that I have been schooled as an initiate to access certain levels of consciousness that I refer to as the unified field. I believe that, through experience, these fields are accessible to anyone who so desires to access them. It is also my belief that these fields are part of us and are not separate. Although it might appear that they are so due to ones inability to raise the vibration of their physical being.

The achievement of raising the vibration to access the higher thought frequencies requires mainly unbending intent. The ability to open the door requires that we release belief patterns that limit us to the lower octaves of the unified filed. It requires opening of the Heart Chakra. These fields are beyond the capacity of split brain activity and are accessible only when we begin the process of unifying the hemispheres of the brain, to act much the same way as the dolphins.

I know that the Kryon exist and are very real. Perhaps the Kryon are much more of a reality than this physical expression of myself. They have communicated with our species since the beginnings of our expression. The Kryon were there when we lowered our selves through seven layers of light to enter physical expression upon the plain of third dimensional density.

Kryahgenetics

Kryahgenetics is a very ancient knowledge, which we still have imprinted within the genetic codes of our DNA. A knowledge by which we were able to transcend from the planes of light into the expression of ourselves as physical matter. The science of Sacred Geometry is the encoding of the principles of application of Kryahgenetics.

By utilizing this ancient knowledge, which lies dormant within the genetic coding of our cells, we are able to open a doorway. This doorway leads to a process by which we can prepare ourselves to gracefully move through the multi-dimensional transformation that is occurring within our bodies. This transformation is happening as we, the Human species, move into Fifth Dimensional reality. We can then, by opening ourselves to our inner knowingness, attain a state of Divine Grace. This state allows for the five sacred elements of the ascension process to unfold without blockage or resistance to the natural ebb and flow of our expanded experience as we enter unlimited consciousness, the state of the Divine Hu-man.

J ask you to consider that it is necessary to develop basically five attributes for actualizing the Ascension process. These are *Compassion, Gratitude, Self Love or Praise, Non-Judgement and Joy.* These attributes, when combined with the right use of will, are the keys to Ascension. Will is an alchemical blending of unconditional love combined with divine wisdom, creating a conscious force to effect an outcome.

★*Compassion* is realized through the act of allowing. It is the magical occurrence of our divine will opening our hearts thus allowing true empathy for all that is. By allowing the state of compassion to enter our being we cause a shifting of our frequency, drawing to us through the divine laws of attraction, sufficient life energy to enter the state of Love.

★ We must develop *Gratitude* for all of our experiences of the Human drama. The whole of life is then experienced as a divine occurrence, enhancing the state of Compassion, resulting in the realization of the reality of Unconditional Love. This Draws to it through the principles of the Divine Universal Law, a state of bliss, where we can experience divine peace within, which allows us to ★ realize *Self Love*, or *Praise* for our own beingness.

This recognition of our divine beingness then enables us to attain and hold the state of ★ *JOY*. By developing an attitude of *Non-Judgement,* it is possible to maintain the state of JOY indefinitely. Through our existence within this state of JOY we experience in fact that we are GOD realizing self. *I AM THAT I AM.* In this state of JOY there is no illusion of separation. We are simply one with all that is, for we are the 'IS'. The personality is relinquished, the walls that we have established in our self imposed realities that we created to protect the image of our illusionary self are somehow magically transformed. This awakening occurs when we realize that there is no need to protect ourselves when we are the all. It is a remembrance of our true state of immortality.

When these five elements are combined in an Alchemical balance, we then easily move into a frequency which allows us to hold this divine awareness not just for a moment, not for just a few days, but we actually become the foreverness of the creation process. The frequency thus attained is what can be called *Ascension or Emergence* of the Indigenous People.

Waves of Ascension

As it is seen the emergence into the Fifth World, or the ascension process, will occur in waves. The *First Wave* of the ascension process is already occurring. Many who have been triggered by the raising of the octaves that comprise the grid around planet Earth. Some are leaving in their sleep state, others in meditation. Others still are surrendering to the new plagues, or other weaknesses of the body physical. These actions have been taken to serve as "examples" to those who are still expressing within the dream. These beings are emerging in spirit only and will develop new embodiments later.

The First Wave

There is actually a pulse, or heart beat to the Mother, to Terra, to Earth. This is not a euphemism. This is a scientifically measurable fact. That pulse has been steadily increasing in frequency over the last twenty years, when it was determined to be at 7.8 hertz. Presently, the increase has brought the pulse up to around 9 hertz. The rate of increase began to accelerate around the time of the Spring Equinox in 1994. The acceleration was further enhance with the appearance of Hale-Bopp. (This phenomenon is delved into further in *Last Cry*.)

The acceleration of the increase and extreme fluctuations in the pulse of the Mother are further influenced by the simultaneous decrease in the Earth's magnetic field. It appears that as the pulse quickens, (estimated to eventually reach 13 hertz,) the electromagnetic field decreases. Calculations indicate that when the pulse reaches 13 hertz, the electromagnetic field will simultaneously reach Zero Point. This occurrence will cause a harmonic, or third frequency. That frequency will swing open the gate to the 5th Dimension.

What will happen to collective consciousness in that moment will be experienced as the proverbial 3 ½ Days of Darkness. What this will in fact be is in essence, a black out of consciousness or thought. The black out will occur due to the fact that there will be no magnetic field through which consciousness can connect or process thought, as thought travels upon electromagnetic frequency.

It is the beginning of these phenomenon that has set into motion the *First Wave* of ascension. Our senses on a scale of society as a whole may have dulled, so that we can no longer "sense the movement of our prey" for example, as the animals still can. However, our bodies and

Higher Self

our upper consciousnesses are still in tune with the Mother. At that level we do sense 'what is going on' even if our 'logical minds' and dulled senses render us unaware. Those of us who have opted to miss the *First Wave* and stay on may be noticing an unexplained weight gain. This is no different than what the four legged experience at the onset of a harsh winter when they store extra fat or produce heavier winter coats. They have not made a conscious decision to 'eat more and exercise less' because they will need the extra to make it through until Spring! Their bodies are in tune with nature, and therefore they react accordingly.

There are also strong ties to these events and the approach of the twelfth planet, what has often been referred to as the planet Marduk, or Nibiru. This planet follows an elliptical orbit that passes between Earth and the Sun approximately every 26,000 years. Why and what occurs as we enter the period or shift that every prophet points to being three or three and one-half days of Darkness can be understood through the following illustration.

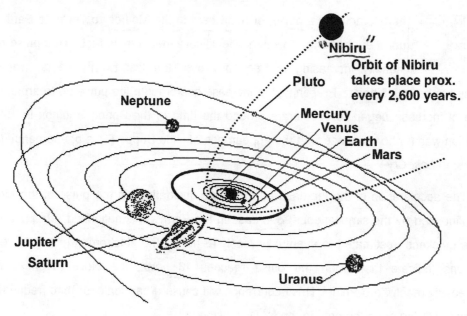

The Second Wave

he *Second Wave* will be occurring in terms of years rather than centuries, and perhaps even within months from the sounding of the *Sixth Thunder*. When conditions begin to become increasingly cataclysmic, there will be many who will elect to move on rather than repeat the experiences that they sojourned during the time of Atlantis.

In this *Second Wave* whole groups of People will, through their ability to form group Mer-Ka-Ba's, raise their vibrations to the higher frequencies. Many beings who have developed the ability to enter the light body will actually be able to transcend with that body. This will be greatly assisted by many who, after the *First Wave* of ascension, will have returned to assume the roll of guides in the process of assisting their brothers and sisters along the continued path of Emergence.

These times will know the appearances of many *New Masters,* who having experienced the ascension process, will appear as tangible evidence of the *New Jerusalem*. They will supply the necessary manna, elixirs and remedies, such as crystals which they will be aported from the Fifth World, brought back here to assist us in energy transcendence into the higher octaves. These things and the final knowledge they will bring through as required for the sustenance and healing of the People in those times, when the People are ready to receive them. Many of these centers are already being created, and yes, actually constructed throughout locations on a global level. The Children of the Sun are not with out their resources.

The Third Wave

These returning *Masters* will assist in the final lifting of souls to the higher octaves, as the conditions here become less than intolerable. Some will be taken to another place or dimensional worlds, or even ships where they will have time to rest and recharge their Souls with the divine light of the Source. Others still, may elect to return to the worlds or dimensions from which they originated.

These will be the days of the final shiftings. The full emergence will commence. There will be the separation of the physical or lower octaves and that which now resonates to the new light frequencies. This Emergence is illustrated in *Last Cry*.

The Pyramids were not built in the locations that they are by mere coincidence. They indeed have been engineered by what we would call advanced technology. Science today has no hard fact understanding of how they were constructed. All they can ascertain is that we can not duplicate them with today's technology.

The pyramids were constructed under the direction of the Star People. They were built from the top down. Pyramids have no metal in their construction. The inclusion of metal would be improperly applied physics and actually interfere with the function of the form. A **part** of the function of the pyramids is to negate the electromagnetic fields. Thus no mater what occurs to the electromagnetic fields of the Earth, the pyramid continues to operate. So no metal should be used in their construction. The only metals that have been found inside a pyramid are gold, copper, bronze and silver. All of which has been placed there for specific reasons of energy transference, both transmitting and receiving as well as blocking certain frequencies.

The pyramids act like piezoelectric cells, much like the one that starts your electric propane barbecue grill or heater. As they receive energy from the Sun, they send an impulse into the core of the Earth, which is molten magma. This is part of what causes as well as effects the apparent rotation of the Earth, its speed of rotation, as well as the direction. The impulses also transfer information, for in essence what is being broadcast is light. All that is known in the universe travels upon the light. We are, as biological computers, little more than light transducers. That is the reason we have a pineal gland and a pituitary gland. This information is discussed in a previous chapter as well as at length in *Last Cry*.

The Days of Darkness - The Bridge Between Two Worlds

hy will we face three to three and one half days of darkness? How will that which will occur as the Days of Darkness physically manifest in experience? Well, when Nibiru, in its orbital path, comes between the Earth and the Sun all light emanating from the Sun will be shielded from reaching the Earth. Nibiru is several times the size of the Earth, actually it is much larger than even Jupiter.

When this occurs as it already has in our history as a planet, there will be nothing effecting the piezo cells. The pyramids will cease to function only as piezo cells, thus they will cease to broadcast their frequencies. This will have several effects upon Mother Earth. She will actually cease to rotate and when she comes to a stop, the centripetal force will actually swing her in the opposite direction, much like the ball reverses in a game of Tether Ball. Thus we have the prophecy of seeing the Sun rise in the East and then in the West in the same day. The same day? Yes, because time itself is an artificially induced reality which will not be functional during those '3 Days.' It will cease to be.

The prophecy of the ending of time will manifest. When the Earth ceases to pulse and rotate, and time collapses, we essentially loose all connection to the grid of consciousness. We loose our memory. We enter the void where all things potentially exist but no thing exists physically. Thus what ever we embrace in our consciousness, so shall it be when this experience passes.

Now the process commences, as it has been observed and accounted for in the ancient text and sacred writings, which tell us that this experience will last for approximately three and one half days based on our present concept of time. But remember, time itself will not exist. Then you will have the occurrence of zero electromagnetic fields and zero gravity. The experience will be a moment in eternity. Only Souls possess the ability to go through this process and recreate reality on the other side. Only *Nagi Wakan* will enter the gateway of the Fifth World. Our experience in evolution will be complete. All thoughts, and therefor emanations, will dissolve.

The choice to return or to move forward into the Fifth World will be entirely up to the individual. The nature of the Fifth World will be of our own choosing. The nature of reality will be multi-dimensional, meaning that many realities can co-exist. So the experiences will be as multiple as there are souls. That which manifests will be equally as diversified in expression.

Some Souls have chosen to remain upon Mother Earth during these times of transition. Having unlocked the secrets of the ancients, they will be found surviving in their Domes and Pyramids (Earth Ships.) This they have done by choice in order to hold the energy for the returning of consciousness, Christ consciousness, into physical expression upon the then new and purified Earth Plane. This renewal will resonate to the higher octaves of the new physicality and consciousness, which is what we call 'Christ Consciousness.' These beings will usher in the *New Jerusalem,* or the Golden Age.

The transitional realities of this particular expression will be very difficult to experience here upon this plane. That which is of emanated thought forms, those not possessing a life force of their own in the unified field, will cease to exist. Meaning that, that which has been born of the present consciousness of mankind, will essentially liquefy. These emanations, both organic and synthetic, will experience conditions whereby they will no longer possess the ability to maintain expression in the higher octaves that will prevail after the shift. Only natural elements will be able to pass through and beyond the *Third* and final *Wave* of the Emergence as we enter the final purification or, *Days of Darkness*. We will experience a new dimension of physics. We will evolve past "I think therefore I Am" to include "I think therefore it is."

The Dream of Life

As we move through the *Dream of Life* we are rapidly emerging from a world of limitation into a formless universe. All that ever was and is yet to be, is being woven from the threads of the formless thought of Creation. We are spinning a *Silver Web*, which moves unobstructed through the limitations of time and space.

During this time of transition humanity will see the surfacing into the consciousness many new modalities of healing. Some of these modalities will enable us to become very effective in adjusting our DNA into harmonious alignment with new frequencies of reality. You are, after all, made up of a much greater proportion of Spirit than you are of flesh. We, in the human experience, have developed many blockages within our holographic fields that are causing us some deep emotional and physical problems. *No shit Sherlock!!!*

Many people are developing new forms of melancholia, resulting in the display of some very self-destructive patterns of behavior. Much of this condition may have been caused by our prolonged addiction to the patterns of limited thinking and existing in the frequency of the cycle of Self-destruction. We are, it would seem, desperately holding onto a perception of the human condition. This has resulted in us becoming locked into cycles of thought process and behavior patterns which has kept us running in circles upon the gerbil wheel, never making it to the picnic!

Thus, the Cycles of Self-destruction have come upon us. These cycles were written about thousands of years ago in the Prophecies by our ancestors the Inca, the Mayan, the Hopi and others. The good news is that the outcome is not written in stone and can therefor be rectified. Should everyone on the face of the planet have a similar experience to the character "Scrooge" in the story "A Christmas Carol," and thus experience the same kind of awakening, in that moment, the outcome would be re-written. Now do you see why changing the Global Consciousness, which is what Wolf Lodge is dedicated to, is so important? This is why we do the Ghost Dance. Get it?

What we are experiencing in the *End Times* is the ending of these cycles, for they no longer serve a positive purpose in the evolution of the species. Each one of us, upon entering this Third Dimensional density, brings with us, encoded within our essence, certain imprints within our holographic field. These can be referred to as our electromagnetic coding, or EMC for purposes of brevity.

What we are talking about is science. We are not speaking metaphorically in any sense. The Holographic field is pure energy, light in conscious order, not yet possessing form but indeed possessing divine personality. Remember that all of the universe is one. Every life form in the universe is connected to the *Web of Life*. Even the Kryon.

The following are excerpts from my up coming book **the Eye of the Shaman**, (*Kryahgenetics*,) which will soon be available in manuscript form. I believe these excerpts contain information that is essential in keeping the flame of human hope alive through these transitional times.

Eye of the Shaman

This is the story of the return of the Nagual. The Nagual is a vessel of the Source and a *Traveler of the Void*. Realizing that mankind has now progressed in consciousness to the point where many are ready to accept the higher teachings, he brings with him the science of *Kryahgenetics,* which holds the keys to self transformation and manifestation.

Throughout history, the 'secret' knowledge of the Ancient Wisdom Schools has been shrouded behind many veils. Often, the truth can appear confusing to the curious mind, making it difficult to discern what is myth and what is superstition. As we observe the pathway of consciousness with each passing generation over the last 5,000 years, mankind as a race has grown progressively weaker and weaker in their Spiritual fiber. The vibration of human consciousness has lowered with the passing of each lifetime to such an extent that at this time it is for many almost impossible to access the higher levels of mind. Levels, I might add that exist within all of us.

American's are PT Barnum's kids. We love our carnivals and freak shows. We are too willingly drawn to the charlatan and fortune teller. Without our knowledge of how to access our true spiritual natures, we are trapped in limited existence. We are prisoners caught within the Spell of Mortality. We have become no more than slaves to a synthetic social order that maintains a synthesized environment in order to perpetuate its illusion of itself. This synthesis has created a form of reality which has removed itself so far from our true nature, that for the most part we have reduced our capabilities of divine consciousness to mere robotic modes of predictable animal behavior. We can, for the most part, no longer see the divine as being humanly attainable. Nor are we able to see ourselves as graceful expressions of a divine reality. We are, it would seem, loosing our nobility as a species. Oh, how we have fallen in self esteem and awareness since we first came to this plane as Lords of Light, the Children of the Sun!

The Spell of Mortality

There lies deep within many of us, implanted within our physique the foundation of all our fears -- a great cosmic flaw. Within the once Divine Human Consciousness there exists a flaw which we shall unveil in this teaching as the

Spell of Mortality. We who were once the divine Archangels of God, find ourselves believing for some unknown reason that we have lost our immortality. We have become <u>disconnected</u> from the source of our origins. We are suffering from an illusionary fear of the loss of our immortality. This fear has caused the once Great Archangels of God to dwell in what seems like an eternity within the confines of the <u>labyrinth of limited existence</u>. Where did such a thing begin? How did such a thing happen? *"right use of Will" By Ceanne de Rohan ~ Sante fe, N. Mexico*

That is a story for another telling. A story about <u>priests</u> and <u>Sorcerers</u> that come from a realm we call <u>Middle Earth</u>. A time the armies of the Ramadama conquered all of the known world. It is a story of the <u>Blue People</u>. A story of Great Starships that filled our heavens and within which we once, along with our <u>star brothers,</u> traveled to the heavens. It is a story about those who came from <u>beyond the Sun,</u> who are in truth <u>our ancestors</u>. It is a story that speaks of what would be seen to some as fantasy and fiction. But in actuality, it is very real. To those who have begun to awaken, it is memory and not fantasy in the slightest degree.

This story would tell of a time when a <u>veil of darkness</u> fell over Man-kind. A time when women gave up their connection to the divine goddess, men became little more than tyrants, and the Gods were reduced to monkey mind reality in the three ring circus of <u>procreation</u> <u>pain</u> and power. Kings no longer would rule by divine right and wisdom attained, but by might, and the exercising of fear to <u>control the people</u>. A horrible time when the Goddess and those who were her priestesses were driven out of every land, hunted and burned at the stake. <u>Everything</u> that once placed us in the <u>light</u> was either taken or those who knew were <u>put to death</u>. Eventually, after a few generations, we were left to believe that our Dreams were something to fear rather than something to cherish and guide us. We were lead to believe that having visions was a sure sign of madness or satanic influence, rather than communication with the divine source.

The fears and sadness of this realm still lives on within the hearts and souls of mankind as we enter the time that was foretold when we would <u>walk in two worlds</u> and feet the ending of time as it came crashing down upon us. These stories are encoded within the <u>DNA</u> of the human species. The *Quickening,* as we are realizing, is a universal occurrence. We struggle to access the information from within our invisible <u>cages of fear</u>.

This book and the knowledge it contains is dedicated to *Otipemsiwak* "those who own themselves." For upon these talking leaves, as my Grandfathers would call them, are written the <u>keys</u> to opening our unlimited potential. Only the <u>simple</u> and <u>pure of mind</u> will be able to <u>walk</u> through the labyrinth of altered <u>reality</u> we have created in our learning, and emerge into the light of eternal truths. For it is said -- <u>that which is real is often unseen</u>. What is seen is not necessarily

Age of Dracula

real, and that which is illusion is too often what is seen by man. It is also said that the future is already written, the shift is inevitable, only the outcome may be altered.

Alchemy is one of the oldest sciences of higher knowledge existing upon this plane of reality. It was known and commonly exercised by our ancestors on a global level. We were, of course, still connected to our memories of coming into this plane from the stars. There was a break in our evolution, when the wisdom schools were lost to us for a period of time, when the knowledge itself became lost to our memory. Now we have become the *Gods in Amnesia*. In the previous experience, when our memory was still intact, the knowledge, when relating to salient life forms, was called *Kryahgenetics.*

There remains a wealth of information that is still held by Peoples Indigenous to Mother Earth. Here in the Western hemisphere we have casually come to term them as the "Indians." All Indigenous People have their Shamans, and they are both male and female. The Shaman knows the power of mind, and is an experienced journeyer in the worlds between the blinking of our eyes. As both male and female, they have always been aware, there is in mans experience another reality just beyond the ordinary. In so many ways, we live in a reality that is encapsulated within many realities.

The knowledge of this extra ordinary level of reality has been absent from the consciousness of the masses for many generations. Some times it has been a result of actions taken by the forces of Light themselves. Not all negative energy or experience is of the Dark. The knowledge has remained protected from the onslaught of organized religions, even as their crime lords spread fear and tyranny across the globe like a plague, almost successfully crushing the spirit of mankind. Now, the seasons bring the *Winds of Change* upon us again. Their structures of suppression and debauchery are passing. Their time is at hand. There is a rumbling in the forests, in little villages, and throughout the mountain tops from Peru to the Canadian Monashee. The minds of mankind are lit once again with an unexplainable illumination.

The powers of the mind are available to everyone, if they choose to open to the Source, the God Force that is within them. The People Indigenous to the Earth Still hold the knowledge of how to access the Mysterious powers of the Human Mind. Their knowledge can neither be stolen, nor contrived. It can exist only within the state of most pure mind; the mind of the child, the mind of Creator. the mind that knows not of limitations. As we reach up to the highest of the conscious levels of light, we find that the nature of its essence is indeed ever increasingly child like.

Once opened, the mind cannot be closed. Once touched by the light of Divine Consciousness, it will never again become forever lost in the shadows of illusion. Truly, the pathway to the stars is through the heart of a child. The gift of the Grandfathers and Grandmothers is accessed through dreaming, and the understanding of unlimited reality. Through expanded reality we have created Third Dimensional reality with a sense of space, time, matter and all its forms. We are children of an unlimited Source that knows no restraints. This Source is quintessentially lawless in its nature. This dream in which we walk, is only the experience of a moment frozen in the landscape of forever. Seek you the truth, and it shall free you. Forever is the path with heart.

Casting Off Our State of Illusion

The manifestation of the miraculous is seemingly unknown to most of us simply because we deem it to be not so. We deem it to be beyond our reach, that it is out there instead of in here. **Because** we are living in denial of the Supreme Being as being a part of us, which is impossible therefore it is illusion. For God is all that is. **"Because"** is born of judgement. In the state of judgement we have separate ourselves from the Supreme Being. Thus we are in denial, thus we negate our creations. We are lost in this state of illusion from which we perpetuate our existence through pain, and limitation. The cause is our Dream Creation process unrealized. We have created the nature of our reality from an incomplete perception, thus manifesting reality in conflict with its true nature. We have become, through this process, the reaction to -- rather than the Supreme Cause. For in our altered state of reality we perceive the Source of life as being external, rather than internal.

The first step in understanding Alchemy is to understand that Alchemy is a process. It is the understanding the Universal Laws that dictate the Nature of our Reality. The participator must transmute their limited reality to be able to accept the results of what is presently thought of as a mystery, or miracles, to where they become applied knowledge. You must be able to deal with the unknown outcomes. It is actually detrimental to your path to get hung-up on the outcome of events.

What is going to happen, the seeing of our future, is outside of your present sphere of awareness, therefore it is unknown to you. Alchemy is a science and you are the apprentice scientist. The experiment is to journey into and come to know the self within. Further, to take that self knowledge and through applied experience, be able to understand your true relationship to the whole of the Universe.

What is it that makes a flower? What is the true nature of physical matter? What is creation, and what is the nature of the God that creates it? What is your relationship to all of it? What are the causes and effects of why things happen the way they do?

To answer these and the other questions that will occur along the journey you must alter your present level of consciousness. You must expand your awareness so as to enable you to accept more than is presently accepted as your reality. You must go beyond limited Mind. Anyone can learn. The rudimentary requirement is your desire to know and your commitment to completion. You are going to go beyond your present limitations. You can not create something new from the same consciousness that conceived it. In order for creation to occur, the manifestation must be the result of an expanded consciousness. You must access a consciousness that is greater than that which conceived of the original thought.

So the first step involves the understanding of how to transmute your present state of consciousness. You are going to have to learn how to expand your consciousness by identifying that which is keeping you locked in limited reality. Then you must come to understand the principles that are involved. So let us begin with the four basic elements; Mind, Consciousness, Awareness and the Soul.

Mind: Your mind is like a computer waiting to be programmed by Consciousness. Of itself, mind is a no thing. It is strictly mechanical possessing no heart, no emotion and no reason. It is not capable of grasping the abstract. The mind is simply a tool which we program. It is a machine, and like a machine, it responds to with that which it has been programmed to. Its abilities are severely limited to its user, which is activated Consciousness.

Consciousness: Exists in the great void, it is the source. Here is where all things potentially lie, yet no thing materially exists. This is the realm of Creator, yet not the completeness of Creator. Consciousness in and of itself is liken unto a dream state, constantly flowing like a river full of ideas and possibilities. It is ever changing. Yet it remains the same to our primal perception. Asleep, consciousness is waiting for the user to tap its unending knowledge. Liken unto the empty canvas of the Artist, waiting to be given life's purpose.

Awareness: An energy. It is the flow of the river realizing itself. It is powered by desire. Awareness is the recognition of a self purpose. The elemental essence that distinguishes the difference between the Rose and the Dandelion. It is personality expounding self purpose. It is individual essence, that which makes us unique. In its self fulfillment it merges with Consciousness and pulls from the resources of that embodiment -- the ultimate desire. In its commitment to fulfill itself, its only desire is to become. To BE. As it expands, in the process of becoming, it becomes the cause and thusly the divine sense of being is realized. It is that which consumes the darkness, making the unknown the known. From our thoughts which lie deep in consciousness, all things materialize into reality.

All memory **The Soul:** The embodiment of our memory awareness. Your Soul holds the emotional memory of every experience that your awareness has explored since the beginnings of creation. The Soul is unemotional in its function, and totally impartial. It is the program that holds the knowledge of Consciousness that is used by the Awareness to fulfill desire. It is the program, the computer chip of the Mind. Here lies every experience we have ever experienced since the beginning of time. The Soul possesses the individual memory, as well as the collective memory. It is the Lord God of your embodiment.

The Creation of Illusion

The Mystery that aligns these elements all together is the Christ consciousness, the God Force that is within us all, the I AM presence, the Great Mystery. It is that which enables us to recognize the Universal Life Force, and its Universal Laws. The Egyptians called it Ska, as do the Lakota people here in North America. Some would call it magic. Some call it God. What ever you call it, or however you define it, it is the Mystery Intelligence that makes up the embodiment of all things, and the very nature of their existence. The Master Dreamer. Spider Woman weaving her web.

The moment you are born into this plane, your feelings and your thinking processes are still unlimited. You are like that empty canvas in the artist's studio. You have committed to this plane, and are affected by its laws of physicality yes, but you are not yet bound by the restraints of other's belief patterns. You have not yet developed your internal core belief patterns that create your adult world and the experiences. You are still unaware of physical limitation. Children dream ✓ of flying, of playing with Angels, of talking to animals and "imaginary" friends. *Not for long Tho.*

Children do not know the concepts of race, color, or creed. No one has told you yet that God is outside of you. So your Awareness IS. It is coming from pure I AM, pure Consciousness. It is not filtering through the filter of the collective consciousness. Limitations begin the "moment you begin to comprehend through language." The I AM, the Lord God of your being communicates through emotion, through feeling, not through language. *The Kogi of Columbia*

Here is where you begin to set up boundaries that can last your entire lifetime. Here is where you begin to establish the concept of external limitations. The adults around you teach you through their language of their fears, their belief patterns and their limitations. Most of which is nothing more than recycled ignorance, handed down from one generation to the next. Beliefs based upon superstition, rather than fact. This is where you are introduced to collective consciousness. You are taught the perceptions of the masses. This is a Tree. This is God. This is right. This is wrong. Don't do that... so on so forth.

Most children experience adult teaching by an archaic method of punishment and reward. "If you listen to Mommy, you'll get this." "Do like Daddy says now." This molding process of collective unconsciousness gains in velocity as it progresses through our development. It is Pavlovian conditioning. Eventually, the concepts of each generation become more and more rigid and inflexible. You are programmed to living the limitations of the faceless millions of people that proceeded you. Limitations that have nothing what so ever to do with your reality.

It is predetermined at birth by the collective consciousness what you will be permitted to experience on the Earth plane. When in your life you are permitted to experience it and what the rules are that you will adhere to. It is a madness of existential Pavlovian reality, which is based upon *at best* incomplete information, and for the most part upon superstition. The boundaries of your life have been created through the unenlightened intellectual process of an unaware Mind. Intellect was only one of the aspects of the Mind, only **one**.

Your life is in constant duality because you are always trying to live someone else's concept of what it is you are to experience. You have been programmed for duality. You are living someone else's conception of life. So it is constantly falling apart because it is not your life, it is not your Dream. The boundaries established are not your boundaries. They are not your beliefs. You are following a doctrine of recycled ignorance, it is called dogmatism.

The rigidity of all this behavioral programming to the individual does not allow for the capacity for inner genius to unfold. It does not allow for individual expression. It does not allow for your Being to engage reality on its own terms. You are imprisoned within a cage of someone else's creation of a limited reality. You are imprisoned by the bars of false intellectual concepts, that in reality are no more than conclusions based upon superstition.

We are entering a time where the fundamental infrastructures of this kind of limited reality are being swept away by the tidal waves of change. There is an avalanche of awareness that is entering the planet. The path of the initiate is not for most people, because most people would rather stay asleep. Most people do not want to change, they are afraid to change, because if they changed they would not know who or what they were. They would have to assume responsibility for their actions and that means their creations, as well as their life's circumstance. For we are the sum result of our collective thoughts. We are the creators of our own destiny. It is much easier to blame some one else, to keep hiding your head in the sand.

The path of the initiate is the path of the *Spiritual Warrior*. You are going to have to leave behind everything you think you know. You are going to have to go beyond your present limitations into the unknown. You are going to have to take this journey alone. You are going to have to commit to growing beyond Body-Mind-Consciousness to the greater reality. Most people haven't taken this path, it is safer to stay at home in the illusion of the preordained dream, someone else's dream that is.

Rules are created in the mind. There are no rules in the greater understanding of Universal Law. All things are possible through the application of the Universal Law. Rules, according to definition, are prescribed Codes or guide lines for conduct. Law is an applied principle. Principles are fundamental truths. It is upon the interpretation of rules that society's laws are imposed.

Dogmatists have quarreled over their beliefs for centuries. They have even murdered because of them. They do not know, in the reality of all these centuries, if their beliefs, are true or not. They are not allowed to test them. Yet out of fear, they defend their beliefs to the death. Why? Because they are dealing with phenomena and superstition rather than Truth. With Truth one does not wonder, because in order to know the truth you must become the truth. The Truth can be tested, it is constant, it stands of it own virtue. Truth is the fabric of the Universal Law and needs no defense, because it is of itself. The interpretation of the Law and the use of the application of the Law is a matter of choice.

Developing Discernment

You must develop within yourself the ability to live consciously, to be clear and precise with your expressions of what you desire. Your internal interpreters communicate through feelings. Feelings are of themselves very simplistic by nature. Keep it Simple. It is when our "feeling picture" gets out of focus, when we are overlaying too many "feeling pictures" over each other, that it becomes a complex matter. We can no longer interpret the blue print clearly. We are receiving conflicting information. This kind of confusion also occurs when we accept the illusion and deny our true feelings, when we live by the allegorical dictates of some one else's doctrines. Feelings do not understand Language. Language was created in an attempt to explain feelings and to express our desires, thus we could clarify a course of action which would then manifest the experience.

There is a very powerful sense of clarity that comes when we expand inwardly. For it is within that we access the Consciousness of self, the original consciousness of creation. The Consciousness of GOD I AM. The dimensions are not 'out there' some place, they are in your inner worlds. It is the God Force expressing itself from within you through the eternal process of Creation. So everything you experience around you is the result of that which you perceive yourself to be. Your inner most thoughts dictate the very nature of you exterior reality. It is the Universal Law. You are what you Dream. The Dream is the drama you live through experience.

If you perceive that you do not have a role in the outcome of matters, that is embracing the consciousness of self victimization. It is all a matter of worthiness. If you feel that you are not a part of or that you are separated from everything, then all that is around you reflects the inner world of that self reality. What ever you conceive is in a state of constantly becoming outward manifestation. This realization can totally alter the concept of "Holding the Thought." Hold the thought that abundance is in your life. Adopt the attitude that you have all you need in the moment. Feel gratitude for the very fact that you can conceive this feeling. You will eventually become that feeling. You create the feeling of abundance, the environment for the thought to exist in. Do so and the Universal Law will then take charge.

By creating the environment within self to accept the feelings of abundance, you Are creating a power. You are activating the Laws of Attraction. Life will affirm through the manifestation of circumstances, experiences that confirm your emotional feelings. That is why when you don't feel good about yourself and you look into the mirror, no matter what you do you will appear less than acceptable. You can, however, commit to changing your feelings. Simply take a walk in nature, interact with a friend, paint in your studio, or take up an action to cause the _music_ change of mood. The experience of looking into the mirror will change as if by magic. Through this simple exercise, you can experience a taste of the process of Alchemy first hand.

By taking control over your feelings and not allowing yourself to be as a leaf in the wind, you will develop an attitude of assumed strength and self esteem. You will be ready to receive success and abundance when the Universal Law delivers it. It wont just be given to you. You have to work at it. You may be shown a path. Life may bring a new opportunity, a new experience that will say to you through feelings, "I can achieve this. Why didn't I think of this before?" If you think it will be hard pressed in the coming, then it will be. If you adopt an attitude of grace and poise, so shall it be also. The *Good Red Road* is often times not linear, and the shortest distance between two points of perception is not necessarily a straight line.

The space between the conceiving of the thought and the manifestation of the thought is the process of becoming. Traveling through the valley of transition can be a time of tremendous self realization. This is where we redefine our feelings, as well as our reactions to those feelings. We get the opportunity to discard that which does not enhance our growth, and embrace that which enhances our vision. We are *developing discernment*. It is where we develop the sense of self determination. We are adjusting our attitudes, opening them up to accepting change. We are going often times through the unknown, as we experience transition. This is where we develop wisdom -- the knowingness of why we are doing what we are doing, or not doing. We no longer feel separated from the Source. We know the Source. The power of the God I AM is alive within us and we are a part of this Source. We are simply on a journey, a journey that takes us into forever. We are voyagers of the light.

When we go within, we become closer and closer to this inner power of unlimited being. We learn to trust our feelings. Always along this journey, we are developing our ability to communicate with this inner self, this expression of God I AM expressing itself through us. We accept that everything outside of us is merely the result of the inner feeling, the inner world. This process alters our outward perception and in turn our inner perception. We begin to realize that all that exists outside of us, the interactions of people and events, is simply the Universal Law manifesting in outward expressions of the dream of the collective consciousness. We stop taking the world and the outward expressions of reality personally, realizing that it is the expression of the collective unconscious.

"Shields of Protection"

The events happening outside of us which seem confusing, the madness of the drama, the occurrences of insanity, are for the most part simply the results of unconscious thinking and uncontrolled emotional expression. At this point, we begin to develop our "shields of protection" rather than walls of separation. The shields of protection are the result of self realization and clear perception. Realizing that this I AM energy is in all things and that it is manifesting for them as well as for ourselves. We can then participate in the game, within our own boundaries. The game is called Dream Creation. The losers are only those who choose *not* to be Creators, those who choose *not* to participate. They are those who live out the dramas of others, and not their own. We are learning to utilize divine awareness to decipher our experience. Our method of defense against intrusion of another's reality is our developed conscious will.

This realization can open many doors for us, for in reconnecting to the God force within we become limitless in our potential for Creation. We are creating a new Awareness, realizing it is the nature of this God force within us to Create the Dream, it is an automatic process. We all do it any way, most of us just do it unconsciously. By choosing to participate consciously we can learn to create the Dream by exercising our conscious will. The learning process is simple. Allow the God Force to teach us how to create new core belief patterns, by putting our feelings out in front of us. Use our awareness, and listen to our feelings. Shut off what we have come to think of as rational behavior. Stop the little voices inside your head that your mind doesn't know. Put your Dream in front of you and walk the Sacred pathway.

Let no one Dream you. Know that you are not the Dream. You are in fact the one, the I AM, who is having the Dream. You are the Dreamer. Dreams are not logical so the last thing you will need is logical advice from the Mind. When you seem to hear that kind of advice speaking from deep within the logical caverns of your Mind, thank it, acknowledge its effort and declare "I AM the Lord God of my being, I AM the I AM, I AM the Dreamer, be gone." Affirm your inner vision, affirm the existence of the I AM presence within you. Embrace the feelings of the God force within, reconnect to Life, listen to the music of the wind, and be in your truth. Persevere, and know that... *the Source is with you!*

Each time you reaffirm this Magical Presence within you, you will get a renewed feeling of being, and strength will fill you. This infinite presence is so powerful, so magnanimous, so much more than the limited mind. It will dissolve your illusions and self doubt. You are accessing another dimension that the Mind has no understanding of, for it is limitless. The Divine Awareness will come and whisper the proper course of action, so be prepared. Learn to listen to the subtleties of its expression. Great power is silent. Creator is silent. It is moving beyond light speed and our preceptors have grown slow through lack of use. The God I AM never abandoned you, you simply got lost in your perception of your relationship to it. You got stuck in mind. Through your over indulgence in the intellectual process of mind, you became lost in endless duality, the world of the image. It is time to move forward now, into Awareness. Remember, you are the Dreamer. You know... the one who is having the Dream.

This Universal Law is impartial and unprejudiced in its actions. It does not seek to find fault. It will manifest precisely what you ask for. The totality of the manifestation is directly related to the extent of your conviction and your clarity of expression. Keep it simple, one thing at a time.

You are not your body or your mind. This robe you wear will one day be discarded for a grander garment. You are a manifested individual expression of this Great Mystery. You can, in fact, call upon this mighty I AM presence at any time regardless of your seeming circumstance. It is the real you, the you that is your eternal living Spirit.

You can literally create any circumstance you desire through application of the Universal Law. Manifestation can not occur, however, if we draw the feeling from illusion. For instance, money is not real, it is an illusion. Being in abundance is not. Money is a creation of the altered ego. Abundance is a state of being, it is a feeling, it is an attitude. You are the child of the Earth. Your very body is made up of every element that comprises her embodiment. She is your Mother. Therefore, you possess the consciousness of each of those elements. The elements are under your domain, so to speak. But remember, they have a consciousness also, and that they are also of the I AM. **The Key is in being in Harmony with them**. The elements rule this domain, and they are very real.

You are the expression of the God Force upon this plane. This God Force is neither male or female in gender. It is more like an energy, a force. This Divine presence is expressing itself upon this plane through you, it is part of you. Get close to it, reunite with it. Become yourself, your true self. What ever you desire is there for your use. Always ask permission. Respect all life forms and the god Force within them. Respect the laws of the giveaway -- for each thing gotten, leave a gift that holds meaning to yourself.

Your manifestations are not manna from heaven, they are your creations. They are yours to utilize and further express this Divine presence through your enjoyment of them. They are of you, therefore they are you, just as you are part of the Great Mystery, I AM that I AM. Rejoice in the God force working through you. Become the hollow bone.

You are a part of an unfathomable whole. A magnificent force that is limitless and inexhaustible. All of life around you is the manifestation of its mighty presence, its will, and does respond to you. Realize that same presence is in everything you come in contact with. Without it, no thing materially could exist. Acknowledge it and go forth with right purpose and proper action. For all is balance, all of life is a prayer. Walk the Sacred path by making your life Sacred.

Within the Divine Source, the Great Mystery, the I AM that I AM, there exists no duality. It is pure awareness born of the original Consciousness. In the beginning, the Consciousness of I AM contemplated itself, and in that great movement it realized through its own energy, its potentiality, and all of the light was Created. All things potential were brought into Conscious reality. This great Consciousness works the same way yours does, for you are part of this great Consciousness. You are a particum of the original light of the dawning.

Consciousness is thought lying dormant in the void of eternity. Awareness is the force that activates Consciousness. The Consciousness expands and realizes its potentials. Energy is created through this process. Energy is how thought moves and is felt. This moment of energy is just like the waves of the Ocean. Awareness is the force the Egyptians called Ska. When it engages Consciousness, it creates Energy. When Consciousness is aligned with Energy creation occurs -- it must, it has to. We are aware of our thought through our feelings. When thought moves it creates Light. Light in turn creates "color" and "tone." The degree of tone or color is realized through Energy frequency.

All of life resonates to these different frequencies. The differences cause dimensional changes. The difference between the Fourth Dimension and the Third Dimension has to do with the rate of speed of the light, how fast or slow it vibrates. The Masters who exist in Fifth Dimensional reality resonate at such a high frequency that they can walk through walls. Walls exist are in our Third Dimensional density, thus they vibrate at a much slower rate of speed. This is also why we can not see the Masters, even if they are standing right in the room with us. It must also be taken into consideration at this point, that all things existing within a particular dimensional reality, vibrate within a specific energy wave, or rate of speed. Meaning that we, the tree, the rock, the bird, the flower, although vibrating at our own individual metabolic rate are "co-existing" within the wave of energy that comprises Third Dimensional reality. The Source is coming from an extremely high rate of vibrational existence. It is beyond light. It is thought wave. As thought waves slow down or coagulates, they becomes light waves. As light waves slow down they in turn coagulate and become matter. In the manifesting process we emit, so to speak, thought waves out to the source. As they commune with the Source, they return to us through the same manner, eventually manifesting into Third Dimensional reality via thought, to light, to matter.

Creating Sacred Space

If you want to sail a great schooner you first have to learn to row a little boat. So in the beginning, make it easy on your self. Let's not try to create a fourteen carat diamond, or have a wine glass fill with wine. If this sounds ridiculous, that's good! There are countless people who would try to make this occur, and upon failure would walk away -- the only manifestation having been realized would be the furthering of their feelings of unworthiness. We must start by addressing attitude. We must change our attitude, and sustain the higher thought patterns that come from the Heart Center, or the Fourth Seal. Without the proper attitude it is impossible to proceed down the pathway.

Meditation is the quickest way I know of to 'ride the bus to the inner world.' If you have not already conceived a process, I would ask you to consider this very simple and un-dogmatic method. Remember, where a candle, etc... is suggested, take the utmost caution. Candles are nice, but if you can't be safe, then they are not worth it.

1. **Decide upon a place or an area**. It could be out doors, or in the attic of your home, or a special corner in your apartment. It should be a place where you go to have Sacred Time, to be closer to the forces of nature and the God within. If you are just now creating this space, then make it special. Prepare yourself and the area as if you were going into the holiest event of your life, as if you had invited Creator to dinner. Announce to the universe what it is your intentions are, and what you wish to accomplish here. This is your place, so others ideas should not be allowed to influence you.

If you wish, you may light a candle, acknowledging the flame of life within all living things. The Violet Flame of eternal beingness. Smudge the area with sage, invite the spirits -- all of your relations. Ask for their assistance. It is too often unacknowledged the importance of the roll that the elements play in our every day existence. Call to the six directions; North, East, South, West, Down (Mother Earth,) and Up (Father/Heavens.) Always remember to acknowledge the seventh, which is within. Ask for the protection of the Great I AM, the Mighty Mystery of perfection. Literally call forth a merging of the physical you, and the spiritual eternal you. Acknowledge your Grand Mother, the Earth, and your Grand Father, the Sky, for they have given you life, and an embodiment in which to experience this divine Human drama.

2. **Make prayer ties**. This can be a good form of mediation for those who might be unfamiliar with the meditation processes. These are small pieces of cloth made from two different colors of natural material, you will need fourteen to start out with. You will be tying a small offering in them -- the Native American tradition calls for tobacco, or sage.

Take the fist seven pieces of cloth of one color (preferably violet or scarlet,) **representing the seven positive aspects** that you wish to create in your life, i.e.: the changes you wish to occur, the effects you see they would cause for the betterment of your life, how it would bring you closer to the God force within, so on and so on... Place your offering in them along with the positive aspects you wish to create. Tie each little filled piece of cloth and then tie them together on a string to make a chain.

Take the remaining seven pieces of cloth (preferably white) and place a pinch of offering in each of these, also. These seven pieces shall be the **seven negative aspects** that you wish to leave your life, the seven attitudes you no longer desire to embrace. These are the negative influences that you feel keep you from being more than you are presently experiencing. Take your time, be specific, be clear. It doesn't matter if it takes you all afternoon, or evening for that matter. This is your life. You must see the Dream through to its completion. Tie these ties together (as above) and add them to the chain, remembering that all of life and all of your experiences are continuing, like the flow of a river.

3. **Place the tied prayer ties in your special place**. For seven days, think about each one of these ties specifically, all fourteen, seven times during the course of the day. By the end of the week it should get very easy. Your can do more, but keep it simple to start with.

If you execute each day this simple discipline, you will begin to develop your ability to focus. Each time you thought about all the aspects that each little prayer tie represented, you declared that thought into the universe.

4. **Pick a time either each evening or each morning.** Sit in a comfortable position at your special place. If you can sit in the lotus or half lotus, this is fine. If you can not, that is alright too. **Intent is the most important factor**.

Remember! Each time, honor the six directions and the mighty presence of the God force within. Take seven slow breaths. Upon the intake, acknowledge your connection to the eternal God Force within. Envision yourself within a Great Violet Flame. On the out breath, envision this Great Violet Flame bursting into a great ball of light with you in its center. Feel your connectedness to all of life around you. Feel this Violet Flame and its light entering into every cell in your body. See it there. Become the Flame.

It can be of assistance in journeying if one chooses to listen to soft music. Flutes or harps are excellent. Also, one can truly journey while listening to the sounds of nature recordings, especially if it is difficult to get into the great outdoors. Be sure it music without words for words will only draw you into someone else's dream. The objective is to get to a place where you are not aware of your thoughts. You are awake, but drifting somewhere... somewhere beyond time.

Now, think about each of the little prayer ties... Embrace each aspect of your experiences. That which you wish to bring into your being -- that which you wish to experience no more. Try to go beyond thought and feel the feeling. See in your minds eye the completed change and the person you will become when the change is complete. Actually live this change of attitude. Walk around, meet people interact with them in the new way you have created. See yourself moving through life in the flow of it, rather than against the tide. Remember you are the Divine Law, you are perfection, you are harmony.

5. **Set aside a time at the end of this seven day period** where you allow for yourself to spend at least two full hours -- lost in the Dream of what you are endeavoring to create. It is your life, it is O.K. to do this. You deserve this time alone with the God force within, so give yourself

permission. After you have done your meditation, you should achieve the state of mind where all there is is you and what you wish to create.

6. **Take the fourteen prayer ties that are before you**. Now, depending on your situation, either place them in a safe receptacle and burn them in a small ceremonial fire, mixing some sage with them while they burn, or bury them into the earth and plant upon them (even a planter or window box will do.) While doing so, declare that you are committed to the God Force within and committed to walking in the truth of the divine perfection. You are now letting go, allowing that which you put into your prayer ties and yourself to become part of the Universal force, the God Force.

These changes that you have called forth are accepted from the God of your being, they are so. Release them into the universe Let them go from your Consciousness, for they are complete. They are consumed in the Great Violet Flame, as is the illusion in your life. Affirm yourself in your minds eye as standing in your truth, being the changes you have dreamed about within your being. Become the completed form of these creations. Walk into life allowing for nothing that is in disharmony with your declaration. You have just completed your first exercise in Dream Creation. Now, go and do something that brings you joy. Play time is important, it lets the child out!

Divine Attitude

Change must start from within. In order for you to alter that which is out side of you, you must first go within and expand your abilities within the inner world. You must go beyond the Consciousness that created the problem and become more than those circumstances. You must accept your responsibility for its Creation. Take from it its lesson to you and your life's path. Leave it behind you. If at first you do not complete all the desired changes, this is O.K. Go back through the process, ask the God force within to reveal to you what you choose not to release. Perhaps there is a situation that needs addressing before you will be free to continue on the path. Remember, to the true initiate life is never a problem. Rather, life is a never ending opportunity to develop skills and to become the expanded self.

Everything is energy -- sometimes high energy, sometimes not so high energy. Even the feeling of no energy is energy. It is like you are a magical fish swimming in a vast sea of endless energy, going around asking all the other fish, "Where is the ocean?" Well, the ocean is all around you. The reason you can't see it is simply because you are immersed in it. Your existence within this field of Sacred Energy, the God Force, is no different. It is endless and all around you at all times.

Your ability to perceive this endless field of energy, is determined by how much effort you have spend on centering yourself. Also by the effort you expend reconnection your awareness to your connection to the Source. This is accomplished by using your will. At first you will learn like a small child, learning a little more each time. As your mature, or begin to connect, you will pick up speed with each experience.

This life time, this experience upon the Earth plane is yours. You created it by choice. You are involved in relationships and interactions with other people. But the experience is yours. No one is going to die for you, only you are going to do that. No one is going to live for you, only you can have the experience. This is *your* evolutionary experience.

There are no incurable diseases, there is only restricted consciousness, which can *seem* incurable because of a senseless devotion to ignorance. The refusal to grow. It is called A "CLOSED MIND." Your true inner nature is eternal and unlimited. Even your body was programmed to be eternal. Death itself and the embracing of death is a conscious choice. It is the conscious choice of the collective. Remember *Jonathan Livingston Seagull* and how he had to struggle to go beyond the pull of the collective in order to go beyond limitation? All that just to become his own individual expression of life! He succeeded, just like you will! It is your commitment to conscious choice, conscious living.

The laws governing proper attitude are important to comprehend in order to embark along the path of the initiate. We all too often spend vital energy in useless pursuits. This is a form of dissipating personal power. Thus, when called upon by life's experiences to draw upon our power of focus, it is not there. We find our thoughts and emotions lost in a whirlpool of confusion, where we are desperately trying to focus through a labyrinth of conflicting perceptions of probabilities. This can only cause us to become **reactionary**, rather than **causal**. This attitude causes the focus of creation to change direction, constricting and imploding within us. This is called *discretion*. When all of life appears to be coming from the out side rather than the inner world of our being, we experience the feeling of implosion. Our Consciousness, in essence, collapses upon us. This state of being is the doorway to fear, and fear shuts down the system.

Bridging the Valley of Self Doubt

When the system shuts down we get lost at the crossroads, unable to choose a course of action. The result is confusion. Life gets flat. We loose our ability to 'come from a position of power.' This is when the demon rises within, and we suddenly enter the *Valley of Self Doubt*. It is literally causes an experience in insanity. To the aspiring initiate this can be disastrous. If they give into the negativity of self doubt, the Dream dissolves. The initiate can cease to be by virtue of their own judgement. What is actually occurring, in simplicity, is that we are turning our power over to the Dream. We start to become that which is Dreamed, loosing awareness of center, which is the source of the Dream. We have fallen out of sync with our life's natural rhythm. We perceive ourselves as viewing the light, instead of being the light.

Being out of sync with the natural rhythm of life, we begin to experience feelings of lethargy and malaise, both mentally and physically. We literally loose our ability to communicate with our inner being, the God Force. We disconnect from everything around us, we give into fear and shut down. This process again is called implosion, it is consciousness collapsing in upon itself. Think of it like a computer that suddenly becomes disconnected form its source of power. It stops transmitting the picture after a few second delay, and then your visual screen goes blank. We have all experienced this to one degree or another at different times. If it occurs, it is alright. Retreat to within, the Divine Source. Surrender to your inner self, and then allow the Universal Law to take over. It knows what to do. Just go back to the source.

You see, we are the only creatures that are afraid of change. The only ones! One of the most beautiful stories I have ever heard to express this, is the story of the Caterpillar. The little worm that spends its entire life consuming green leaves. It does not know that it will become the Butterfly, it cannot even see the Butterfly, because the Butterfly is the next step in its evolution. There are no great wise ancient Caterpillars to consult, and ask "Why do I have this compulsion to spin this chrysalis, and go inside and go to sleep? What will I dream when I go through this Process?" It just follows its own inner voice.

Do you think that when the Caterpillar awakes, it says "Wait a minute, what is this? I do not want this. I want to go back to being a Caterpillar. What are these wings of Crimson and Blue? What happened to my hundred legs? Now I only have six! And what about these ridiculous black stockings?" Do you think it asks this?

To Do - To Dare - To Remain

The God Force; that which is Dreaming you, that which is so loving that it allows you absolute freedom of expression, that which sustains the Thief, as well as the Saint, Man as well as Woman, and the beast, the fowl and the flora as well, that which Dreamed the Dream of life, allowing you free access to the knowledge of the process, asks nothing in return. Rules? Keep it pure, remain silent. Tell no one of your inner quest, or that which is being revealed to you. If you have questions go within, not outside. You can not find the answer in the collective unconscious, they simply don't know. They most likely are hoping that you have the answer. *To Do, to Dare, to be Silent*. Keep your methods to yourself, and then speak only of the Manifested creation, not its cause. Your brothers, sisters, teachers, and guides will make themselves known along the Pathway.

At first you may not be certain of your direction. You might be facing terrific change, the tendency of the Group consciousness is to avoid confrontation. It is hard to discover your own pathway in a world that is caught in the spiders web of collectively agreed to limitations. You will be feeling things that perhaps no one around you has ever allowed themselves to feel, never mind express. They are for the most part locked up in the Prison of intellect, always coming from past experience. Unsure of tomorrow, because of the denial of the NOW. They have elected themselves self appointed ambassadors of the "Have Nots." They do not yet own themselves.

If you find yourself entering a space of confusion, try a walk in nature, a walk with your Mother. There you will find many answers. Everything that surrounds you has the God Force within it. In the quiet of nature you will become aware of the subtlety of the energies around you. In nature, you will be able to reconnect with your feelings. You will be grounded by her energies, she will actually take the negativity from your body. When the body is grounded you can experience, through your senses, that which is beyond *Body-Mind* awareness. Ride the feelings out, clear your mind of all internal dialog. Claim control over your mind. Center your energy inwards.

Personal power comes from being in the **now**. Dis-empowerment comes from living in the past, or trying to run into the future. Your pathway must address the present. Only from the present can creation of any kind occur. The reason you enter into a state of confusion at any given moment is the sole result of being out of alignment with the **now**, for then perception is clouded, and there is no focus possible. The Master walks the middle road, through the center.

This great I AM energy, the God Force, is always in the center. You have heard it referred to as walking the middle road. It was never meant to be construed as the state of complacency. Consider it, rather, like a sliding scale. Lets make 10 positive -10 negative. Creation occurs in the center, at zero point. That is where neutral is, that is isness. Remember, the God Force is neither positive or negative. It simply is. " I AM that I AM." The Universal Law does not discriminate, it does not judge. It is of itself. It is available to anyone, even the Butterfly. If it is available to a mere Butterfly, why not to you? Are you any less worthy?

You are not less than the Butterfly. You are, however, still the Caterpillar, struggling to break out of the Chrysalis that you have slept in for seven and a half million years. You are struggling against a millennium of organized religions, governments, society, your parents, your traditions, your culture, and your friends saying, "It's hard out there alone. Come back into the fold. You know no one can make it alone. No one has all the pieces. You can't think for yourself. God is out there. Heaven is out there." These are patterns from your past. They are already lived Dreams. Although the present conditions may be different, the person within is still the same person, having the Dream over and over, and over.

Heaven is and has "always" been within you. God, the mighty I AM that I AM, is not outside of you. Heaven is not a piece of Real Estate out in space. The Father of all life is within. So if God, the Supreme Being, who ever or what ever you perceive God to be, lives in Heaven, where is that? Reason it out. Where is most pure mind? What is it? Where does it come from?

Developing Proper "Attitude" is essential to the path of the initiate. It can be one of the longest disciplines that we apply. We must re-adjust our perception of our entire reality to the original thought of Creator in order to continue down the pathway of knowledge. We must become one with it, then willfully live it out in our expression of every day life in the Human Drama. Only through developing Proper Attitude can the initiate expand beyond the boundaries of the limited collective consciousness. The reclaiming of personal power can only hope to be achieved by understanding what causes it, and how to correct the patterns of the consciousness that created the situation of dis-harmony in the first place.

As long as we continue to give our power to external sources, self realization, which is self empowerment can not occur. Enlightenment itself is a process of "remembering" what has always been there. It is a process of awakening from the Dream. Through the process of becoming the master of the Dream, by mastering self. Know thyself and you shall know God. You can only be enslaved, you can only be controlled, if you are in lack of knowledge. It is the lack of knowledge which keeps you dependent upon the external benevolence of some created God, and your destiny subject to the mysteries of fate. There is no fate, there is only destiny. Fate is the result of Manifestation, complete or incomplete. Destiny is the self realized, asserting itself in the Dream.

A day is coming where human kind will no longer need to express itself in terms of power. For the greatest power that can be experienced is experienced in the state of not being. The state of ISNESS. There, we no longer have the need to justify our existence. We will come to know God, the true Source. The very fact that you are is enough for God. Why then is this simple fact not enough for you? The Great Spirit that Dreams the Dream of life has never lost belief in what you could become. It is only mankind that has lost belief in himself. Only mankind can destroy himself.

Only Mankind can recreate himself. The pain that is being experienced by mankind is caused only from mass separation from the Source. It is the worst kind of pain... it is an illusion.

A Divine Concept - A Dream of Creation

We were created in absolute perfection. We are a divine concept. We are whole. We were created complete. There have been some errors of judgement. We are children growing. The Father knows that. Mothers know that. There have been genetic tamperings resulting from "outside" interference in our development as a species. There still remains the truth, even after seven and one half million years of self enslavement, self annihilation and blind devotion to ignorance. You can not ever bury the truth, for it is within the blueprint of life itself. It is the testimony to Epigenetics -- the plan of Creation. It is the will of the unknown God, the Great Mystery, the I AM that I AM.

You can never destroy life, no more than you can destroy a Dream in your slumber. You can stop dreaming, you can wake up, but you have no power to destroy the Dream itself. After all, Life is the Dream of creation itself. You can choose to participate, or not to participate. You can choose to know, or choose to walk in ignorance. You can choose to take on a dis-easement, or choose perfect health. You choose to live in self Joy, or self denial. You choose to be powerless or the child of the living God. It is your choice and that choice is all a result of your personal attitude. The difference between observing the light, or being the light, is attitude.

From the Lord God of My being, from the Father/Mother that is within me, to the Father/Mother that is within you, may the mighty I AM Presence enfold you within the Violet Flame of forever. May you be empowered to be all that you can be. May you walk evenly with all your brothers and sisters in the cosmos. May you realize your true relationship to all your relations here upon the Earth plane. May you come to see that all you walk upon, the Water you drink, the very breath you take, the Trees, the flowers, the four legged, and the fowl that fly through the sky, even yourself, are SACRED to this Great Mystery. You are the Dream of the Mother, you are the Dream of the Father. Know you are forever. Know you, child of God, that you are the Dreamer.

SO BE IT !

Coyote Moon

The Enchantress weaves her spells of mystery, the silence of the midnight blue sky. Grandmother Moon is a mystery all her own. Whatever she is, satellite to some, goddess to another, she will always remain a romantic mystery to me. Who is to deny that as she shines her light upon us from her home amongst the stars, in one moment she can bring together the lips of young lovers, leading them to a journey through tantric pathways of ecstasy. Yet, in that very same moment, in yet another part of the forest, another couple experiences mood swings into the deepest of dark emotions. The human drama is played out in scenes of agony as they lay begging for the night to end and to experience the release from the spell that comes with the first red rays of dawn.

She casts a clear yet eerie light that gives the desert landscape the feel of a Spielberg movie set. I am bathed in waves of silver blue as I feel a strange force in the light of her that shines upon my face. As if part of me were being pulled out of my body, and in some way beyond my expression I find myself merging with her molecular structure. I can feel a kind of pressure, or electrical sensation that seems to be in my brain. It is as if my electromagnetic frequencies were being manipulated. Like I am under the effects of a cosmic magnet.

The geometry of the evening is shaken by the sound of an owl in the distance calling to its mate. There is a surrealists energy to everything this evening. It is as if at any moment Don Genero himself could come walking out from behind one of the cedars. No thing is what it appears to be within our normal perception. I can not help but feel as if I am one with the whole of nature. Light spans taking momentary expressions in different forms within the holographic set. Yet in the same moment I can begin to feel myself loosing my grasp of reason as time slips from my awareness.

I can actually feel myself floating out of my body when all at once I am brought back like a boomerang as once again the geometry of the setting is altered. This time shattered by the song of Grandfather Coyote which pierces the silence. His song changes the nature of the evening to still another reality, and I am reminded by a familiar feeling.... ah yes, it is that time once again, the time of the Coyote Moon.

The trickster is moving across the land like a silent wave of power. You can't see it, but the feeling is everywhere. Change is afoot. The very nature of the light is surrealistic, giving the patches of normally pink granite sand the appearance of newly fallen phosphorescent snow. The wind calls to my attention as it sings through the pinions giving a gentle warning of a changing mood to the whole of reality. No thing is what it appears to be within the perception of ordinary reality. There is a *Quickening* that is occurring in the garden and mystery is afoot.

Prophecy has declared that the people of the Eagle and the people of the Condor will be awakened to a song coming from the heavens. In many places in North and South America the Children of the Sun are beginning to resonate to a quickening of the pulse of the heart beat of the Mother. The whole of nature is anxious, it is birthing time in the Alchemical Garden of the Gods. Life itself seems to be twisting and turning struggling to find new ways of expression. The air is thick with orgone energy as people gather from the tundra of Alaska to the mountain villages of Machu Picchu in Peru. They do not possess the pollution of technology, nor do they suffer from the analytical conflicts of intellect. They feel with a most pure mind the emotional swings of life in the throws of a birthing process.

There is a new world being born. Born from within. The Indigenous People of this land are having visions. The Gods are returning. Across the skies both day and night the light ships appear. The messengers have come. With the passing of each moment the prophecies of the ancients are being fulfilled. In their visions the people are seeing scenes of our galactic future. While here in our civilized urban societies we are lost in super technology. Imprisoned in our mountains of glass and steel, we still argue as to the reality of whether the visitors from other worlds exist or do not.

Hale-Bopp has crossed our skies. Each morning it was visible to the naked eye. The emperors of television media allowed us stories of only a tabloid nature; "How the comet will destroy the earth" while another proclaimed "We have no need to fear." Scientist struggled to rationalize public explanations of how the comet could change course over forty times in 18 months. But like Jupiter, they haven't got a real clue, just words and theories. People do not listen any longer, and the talk shows are broadcasting fear throughout the night, taken from the hands of the metaphysicians, placed into the arena of the media. Now millions will be kept from the truth.

The Indigenous People sit quietly, saying very little. For to them the truth is simple. It is time for the great shifting of realities. There are rumblings from within the Earth. The Earth movers are awakening, shaking the ground beneath our feet as they make their new tunnels. The Dragons have been seen in the skies. New forms of life are appearing in our oceans where life began, where it always has had it's beginnings. We are seeing animals that have long been gone from this Earth in our forests and mountains. There are new colors in the skies. The merging of dimensions has begun.

People are experiencing simultaneous realities and dimensional shifts. This is the time when our Elders told us we would experience *walking in two worlds*. There are indeed many leaving this plane. The lists of names of those who are passing over are growing. There are those who have been getting messages that this is not the time to perpetuate life forms as we have known them, so some of us have ceased to have children. Their are many souls disappearing from this plane, some in whole groups.

These are crazy times to be sure, filled with events that can only be talked about on the Art Bell Show. It seems we are too often struggling to find sure footing upon increasingly unstable ground. We seem to be fighting a paradigm here. Are you aware that on February 14th and 15th, 1997, as the giant Mer-Ka-Ba appeared in our heavens, we actually passed into the age of Aquarius? Well, what did you expect as one age passes and a new one emerges? Chaos always precedes Creation.

Our friction in life will not cease as long as we are trying to fit a living fluid reality into that which remains of a decaying, structured, artificial reality. We do not walk through reality in these times subject to fixed rules. The houses of dogma are crumbling. We are in truth creating reality with each passing moment. With each thought embraced by our emotions, we become the alchemists of our time, spinning the web of our emerging realities.

We are experiencing the dichotomy of mans law verses Universal Law. We are waking to the reality that we are Star Seed who have come to a world where much of what is taught is in direct conflict with the truth of the nature of reality. There is nothing wrong with your feelings, dear ones. Your intuitive perceptions are correct. It is in the teachings you have been spoon feed that the fault lies. Manipulated truth has a short life span, and the consciousness of the people must be continuously manipulated by servants of the shadow kings to prevent them from realizing the truth in the conspiracy. It is the dance of the tyrants.

The priesthoods of patriarchal dogmatism are on the run from their own lies. The collapse of religious, scientific, and social structures is frightening to these Lords of Illusion. The goal of the conspiracy is to continue to attempt to keep you in ignorance of ancient truths. We are a galactic people. None of us come from here. The Gods of old are our ancestors. We have been force feed illusions for generations in a desperate attempt to cover-up terrible acts of treason against our personal liberties and sovereign rights to know the truth about our heritage.

Reality as most of us have been taught is no more than a manipulation of the light, while irradiating the sources of knowledge. Every where people are beginning to see the truth. We are like children awakening from a deep sleep, or is it more likened to a drugged state of unconsciousness? But there is a strong attempt by the opposing forces to keep us in constraint. Our living conditions are being manipulated to help the tyrants break the back of our spirits through a campaign of economic tyranny.

In ever increasing numbers, people are seeking to find some relief from the pressure of change and their shifting relationships. Financial demands are overwhelming these days to say the least. One has to make ten times what they did in the 70's to live a similar life style to the families we grew up in. Yet the pay scale remains the same, and often less than it was twenty years ago. "We the People" is becoming as mythical as the Wilderness Family.

Diseases are taking us over and "modern medicine" is more and more helpless to find remedies. We are told that there are three to four new viruses appearing in the medical labs on a daily basis. What is it that we are not being told? Mutation of the species is becoming a science fiction reality as life forms seem to mutate before the very eyes of technological observers. In our third world countries whole towns fall victim to genetic experimentation, and are wiped out by outbreaks of illnesses such as the Ebola virus. Then we hear about school children being evacuated from their school, after a low flying aircraft flew over their school house. The children are rushed to a hospital as they somehow have come down with unexplainable rashes and coughing spells. When they arrive at the hospital the doctors have already pre-medicated themselves. How did they know?

A lot of what is causing us to contract these new diseases, whether they are mechanical, or organic in nature, is due to two simple but highly overlooked causes. Mental and Spiritual neglect. How is this so? There is a small mass located in the center of the skull called the hypothalamus which lies just below the thalamus on the midline at the base of the brain. This brain control center regulates or is involved directly in the control of many of the body's vital activities and drives that are necessary for survival: eating, drinking, body temperature regulation, sleep, emotional behavior, and sexual activity. It also controls visceral functions by means of the autonomic nervous system, interacts closely with the pituitary gland, and acts in coordination with the reticular formation. We breathe without thinking, our heart beats and our blood pressure regulates without conscious command, our cells regenerate without conscious mind application. Our eyes blink and are made moist by unconscious bodily functions. We have our own automated internal Body-Mind-Consciousness.

The pituitary acts in connection with the hypothalamus and merges the functions of our emotions and our intellect, then inputs information from our spiritual body. Creating, when conditions are in proper balance, a state of harmony within the body in which disease can not exist.

Whatever is happening within the body, whatever the experience, the pituitary gland is notified immediately by the hypothalamus through physical and non-physical systems of communication. The hypothalamus is the access terminal between Body-Mind-Spirit. The body then responds to two distinct information sources, conscious and unconscious thought input communicated through the nervous system activated by electromagnetic thought impulses. By the right use of our will and deliberate and aware thought form application we can reverse negative bodily reactions. Thought manifests the nature of reality. Therefore, by changing thought patterns consciously, by not neglecting positive thought forms, we are creating thought forms which aid the bodies own automatic immune systems to bring about a state of perfect health.

By changing our thought patterns, and consciously directing our emotional reactions we can create an environment of wellness. We can change the bodies reality from creating the state of decay and dying to one of creating the emotional attitude of perfect health. Most of us have lost our ability to communicate between emotions, the mind, and the body. And for the most part, we have separated the spiritual aspect of our being completely from body-mind reality. We get stuck in a mind set of separation.

We need to change direction now. The vibrations of the new consciousness will bring about situations where we are going to find it harder and harder to hide our shadow self. Becoming aware is the key, but it is not an easy path. We need to create an emotional environment where we can observe our behavior. Become the dreamer observing the dream, so to speak. Our immediate future holds life situations where we will experience extreme polarity within self. We will find that on one hand we experience the dark night of the soul, while at same time we feel the emergence of divine realization and bliss. We will experience love and hate in the same breath.

The reason for this dichotomy of emotional realizations is that we are being shown to search out and identify the dark side of ourselves. As initiates of the highest order, there is no way into the future without our dealing with the separation of the light and the dark that exist within us. When we deal with our shadow self as an education and embrace all parts of us as an emanation of the divine Source, the negativity will dissipate from our external reality.

We are learning to master emotions. We are moving from a consciousness that denies emotion, where we are taught to suppress our feelings, to hide the inner truth for the sake of an external image. The stress of living in this kind of denial is killing us. It is causing premature aging, heart problems, and an emotional psychosis that has infected the whole of society. Most have been taught from childhood to live a lie. To fit into the acceptable mold. To compromise the true desire for a substitute reality. So in many ways we have become the metaphor for "the picture of Dorien Grey." Remember the movie?

Your emotions can be hazardous to your health. By neglecting your spiritual reality you can surrender your exercise of divine will, and harbor feelings of anxiety, grief, anger and judgement depleting your body of its natural vitality and strength. Through neglect we become victims of Body-Mind-Consciousness rather than creating the state of perfect health. Science can not deny the link between emotional stress, the harboring of maligned thought forms and the onset of disease. In their most recent findings, scientists support it as absolute reality. This entire subject is discussed in detail in *Eye of the Shaman,* a book by the author, available soon in a limited edition manuscript form.

Amongst the Indigenous People of North and South America, most have not lost their connection to our galactic heritage. Even though much of our healing methods, which date back well over 30,000 years have either been destroyed or stolen, there are still many that remain intact. We have written records of science that could change the known reality. They include the cure for aids and methods of organ transplants, including the brain. They will remain inaccessible until such time as the ruling societies of the world cease their policies of genocide against the Indigenous People.

No offense to the *New Agers* but we too often seek answers to deep rooted problems in the exercise of something shallow. Too often we seek the answers externally, when the true remedy for the cause of imbalance lies within us. If we can change our patterns of thinking within, then we can truly manifest the desired results externally, or in the physical. But it is hard to break patterns. Especially when we can not identify them. We are all fighting this invisible enemy, and too often we resort to creating phantoms of reality to justify our state of mind. Phantoms are the way of the Coyote man, so let us spend some time together and dispel the myths and understand the reality of Coyote Medicine.

We are, in this time, choosing how to deal with our reactions as well as our reasoning abilities in a changing paradigm. This is a time of realization and awakening to our true nature. A time of learning to access our true abilities as we transmute into a new species of being. We are changing internally and that is causing the shifting of our outer realities. Yet we seem more concerned with the occurrences in outer-space than the true center and cause of change which is occurring in our own inner space. It is our inner spatial reality that is causing the whole of the known universe to react to our own, as of yet unrealized, powers of creation.

Presently we are merging with a new universe. This is not meant as a metaphor but as a hard fact reality. I discuss this subject in _Last Cry._ We must understand the full impact of our unraveling our true relationship and interactions with galactic beings, and what we are about to experience on a global level. We as Terrans re-uniting with our brothers from the stars will become a very tangible reality within our life time.

We are experiencing the opening of dimensional portals as a result of the birthing of this new universe. At this time there is not much which can be said about this new universe. It is an occurrence that is beyond words. For the sake of convenience we shall call it Telluria Patala. The birthing of this new universe is creating higher octaves of dimensional reality. This is causing every living thing in the known universe to raise its own vibration in order to come into harmony with the higher octave of creation that is presently emanating.

Thus, we here in third dimensional reality are about to shift into fourth and fifth dimensional experience. But we have a problem in seeing the truth in the actual impact of this. Mainly because we have yet to evolve beyond the point where we can see through the myth of religion to the truth of our divine spiritual nature. In other words, we fall too easily into the trap of fighting over the differences between our individual concepts of God the Creator rather than realizing the commonality of our truths.

Many still rely upon an addictive insistence, holding onto dogmatic, unsupported beliefs and remain in denial of truths that have and still exist in the physical which are tens of thousands of years old. As long as we are operating from beliefs rather than from our own knowing, we are hopelessly caught in the state of denial, which is the forced imprisonment of our own divine being. If God the Creator made all things, and God is in all things, then why do we keep denying the existence of God within ourselves. It is recycled ignorance.

We are light beings having a physical experience. We have created something new and this something new is filling the void with a new light. As a result of the birthing energy new consciousness, and new potentialities, are being birthed simultaneously. This new light is activating our pineal gland, which sits above the pituitary in the center of the head. When the pineal gland is activated, it stimulates the pituitary gland. The pituitary is sending messages to our entire glandular system, causing our bodies to alter and transmute within our very beings. We are waking up. We are moving from an unconscious state of existence to a totally awakened state of awareness which could be called super consciousness.

Earth is like an egg which is about to hatch. We are the consciousness within the egg. What will be birthed is a new consciousness. Right now we are very much like that little being within the darkness of the shell. As the shell continues to fracture, we will experience more and more of the light. Within our third dimensional reality, the light spectrum is expanding to twelve colors. These are now being seen in the new colors of the rainbow.

We are beings resonating to the twelve rays we discussed in the chapter, *Eye of the Shaman* in *Last Cry* which are activating twelve Chakras or seals with the body physical. These are necessary to reactivate the twelve strands of DNA that are in our cells. All of this is being accomplished through the raising of the vibratory frequencies of the birthing process of this new universe. These frequencies are enabling us to resonate to the higher octaves of creation. This is accomplished through tone, you know, those high pitched frequency sounds you hear in your ears? Well, these tones are causing harmonics which effect even the amino acids in our bodies to respond.

We need more minerals, we need more oxygen to fire up the engines of creation within the body physical and be able to hold the new higher frequencies. You are running out of the food supply that sustained you in the egg. You are too big to be contained within the shell any longer, you are being born. So I prefer to call this time the time of *Birth Changes* rather than Earth Changes. You are opening your eyes and seeing for the first time the true nature of the reality you dreamed.

One of the things you will experience over the next few years, is the true nature of your multidimensional existence. Many experiences of extraterrestrial interaction are actually the realizations of self in other dimensional existences. We live in a holographic world. Not always is what you see reality, and too often what you do not see is more real than flesh and bone. We have become addicted to the dream. We started to think it was reality, but it is a two-dimensional experience, and we are, my friends, multi dimensional beings. Children of the light, by the light, and in the light.

There is a war going on in our heavens. Upon this plane that war is invisible. Invisible because it is occurring within us. It is inter-dimensional in nature. It is an Armageddon, and the Armageddon is within. It is you battling your image. The final trial of the initiate where we learn to conquer ourselves, the limited self. The real essence of you and the chains of what you have been taught to envision yourself as. The image of the movie roll you think you are supposed to be. A role that never can be achieved.

We are experiencing a friction and a feeling of confinement. There is a longing for the feeling of Freedom of Spirit. We find ourselves bound like Michael Angelo's four Captives, struggling to be released from form. For in truth we are the living thoughts of creation, flowing like the sea from which we came, formless and ever changing. We are beings in the eternal river of life, initiates in the final initiation where we are learning to conquer the illusions of ourselves. We are overcoming the experience of living within a concept of limited existence -- and yes, birthing can be painful.

Our comfort zones are going to be disrupted, and our buttons pushed. We are going to learn to master our emotions, and discern true wisdom which is always born of the heart, from image thoughts born of the mind. Intelligence comes first to the heart, then it is moved through the mind. This is Chi energy evolved. For emotions are the sounds of creation resonating within the body physical. So let's start exploring our feelings instead of running from them. Stop reacting to reality, playing the victim can get old very fast. We all have frailties. When we cease judgement we allow ourselves to experience life without limitation, then we cease being reactionary and become causal.

Learn to become the master of your own reality by exploring where few have gone before... inner space the final frontier. Never impose your will upon another, but at the same time develop the ability to define your boundaries. Defend your Sacred Ground. Appreciate yourself, stop neglecting yourself, and denying your spiritual reality. It has never worked, has it? Your feelings keep pushing through, disrupting the whole plan to keep you in ignorance.

Learn the wisdom of the Cloud People. Change always, flow as freely as the wind, own the power of the silence, for then you are truly forever. And in embracing change you are constant and remain the same. Like the truth of Creator you become the living truth, limitless and free as the wind. What the wind touches is always alive. Freedom is a feeling. It is a state of mind and you are a thought in Creator's mind.

The purpose of Coyote Medicine in your life is to make you aware of your duality, your conflicts, that you may overcome them and become truth in your own reality. Coyote is the trickster who makes certain that that which is not false can enter Sacred space. Coyote Medicine is always for your best interest. Only truth can get you past the Coyote. There is no place we can hide in the light of the Coyote Moon.

Vision into Visions

Insights from Robert Ghost Wolf

Aho Mitakuyue Oyasin,

We see many things in ceremony. Not all we see is written in stone. Some things can be altered. Some things can be avoided. Other things worsen as the spirit of man declines.

Change your ways ~ change your experience. We can choose between two roads. One leads to life ~ the other leads to death. We choose our destiny every moment of every day by the way we choose to see the world and ourselves. Which road do you choose?

What I have chosen to share here is that which I see as inevitable, however the outcome is still mutable. In the flow of experiences, certain things can be altered by our consciousness. Some can not. If you see a storm coming, you can elect to find shelter, or you can chose to walk through the storm. The decision is yours. Either way, we are at a time when the Earth Changes must commence.

You can take from these works the drama, or the Pearls of Wisdom. It is with great personal sacrifice to my own serenity, the serenity of my family and those close to me that I make this information available to you.

The World has come to me, asking that I bring forth the truth. We are moving toward a climax, a culmination of events. The War of Valued Life is upon us. It is the Armageddon. It is a war of consciousness, not of tanks, missiles or Pony Soldiers.

The War of the Heavens is revealing itself as fact - not myth. Unless we change our consciousness and accept our Spiritual Heritage, there will be no hope for survival. We have far too long condemned; our selves, our neighbors, our dreamers and our seers. We can no longer live in denial of our Spirituality and hope to continue.

When we do not see the creator in all things we have lost our ability to laugh and know JOY and life is over for without JOY we no longer live our lives.

In the midst's of the chaos remember the words of a Great Master who once said...

" From the Lord God of your being, all things are possible... Behold God!"

Namasté ~

Ghost Wolf

Red Alerts - 1998 and Beyond

ne must remember, the Prophet who is most successful is the Prophet who spreads the word of his prophecies, and by doing so, keeps them from coming to fruition.

- ➤ There will be the rains that fall from the heavens. Balls of fire will fall upon the Earth leaving marks upon the Mother's Robe. Meteors, or debris will fall from space.

- ➤ Many areas will begin to notice changes in land formations. 1998 will be particularly devastating to Japan, England and Central America.

- ➤ Events will transpire that will facilitate the re-emergence of the USSR as a country once again, and the Prophecy of the Bear and the Lion shall begin to manifest.

- ➤ There are many viruses that resulted from the Desert Storm event. Many of these were carried here by women from the Middle East, specifically Iraq. These were death gifts from Saddam Hussein. These viruses have a gestation period of approximately 6 years. Then they begin to awaken. Check your time lines (remember Desert Storm?) as these viruses will begin to appear in epidemic proportions later in '98. The viruses will attack the respiratory system with killer flues and new strains of pleurisy. The kidneys, pancreas and flesh will also come under attack. Many of these viruses will erupt in the Southwest and on the East Coast. There are two ways the viruses are being deposited. One, the viruses are being deposited at airports and vacation resorts where the presence of those depositing them would be inconspicuous. Two, it will be found that the viruses are being deposited through the shipment of crude oil from Iraq. It then will be found that the viruses are contained within the additives in the fuel. The outbreak of these viruses will begin the quarantine of many urban areas. We are already seeing some of these viruses being birthed, but regard them with the same interest as an article in a Supermarket Tabloid.

- ➤ Over the last ten years we have seen the conversion of many inactive military compounds into holding camps. We have also seen the purchase by the US government of over 1,000 railroad cars which are equipped with shackling, so as to contain up to 100 prisoners per car. Are these not strange events? These are the encampments I see beginning to be utilized. We will see many being moved to these camps, for all those who oppose the new order will be so imprisoned. Reports of encampments that have and are being built by "the government" are and will continue to pour in. Just drive through Arizona between Tucson and Phoenix or by Gila Bend, through the California desert, around Umatilla, OR, or Fort Lewis near Yelm, WA to prove it to yourself! Other encampments exist, are being or will be constructed throughout the rest of the US. They are typified by wire fencing topped with razor wire and barracks type structures.

➢ We will see a huge increase in the amount of convicted felons. Unfortunately, this will not be done for the sake of justice. There will be a focus on felony convictions for young men 18 to 35. One should keep in mind that a felony conviction critically changes the rights of those convicted. Once convicted of a felony, one no longer has the right to bear arms nor do they has the right to vote. In essence, the ability to protect and be heard will be stripped from those who would be most physically able to do so. Those that oppose the new order will overfill the prisons.

➢ The discovery of a UFO under the city of Phoenix will become a cause of national disclosure of prior cover-ups regarding the UFO involvement. This discovery will lead to a chain of events that will open contact with beings from where these ships originated. Prominent world leaders will be forced to admit the agreements that have been long standing between our world governments and those ETs. A topic that will be disclosed is that these ships were pirated by our own military. This will evolve into a deeper understanding of what occurred in the Montauk experiments.

➢ The existence of Hybrid Humans will be revealed. Their part in the manipulation of social consciousness will be very evident to those who possess an immunity to their frequency signals.

➢ A major volcanic eruption will occur in or near Mexico City. This will start the chain of events that will have repercussions around the ring of fire. Japan and Indonesia will be hard hit as well. Then the earth quakes will intensify along the West Coast of America, up through the Cascades. Rainier will be very active and could blow in '98. If not, it will occur in '99.

➢ The attempted development by major industry upon the Moon will come to public light. This attempt will most likely be pioneered by Japan as they seek to resurrect a failing economy, and obtain Helium 3 from the surface of the Moon as an alternative to Fossil fuels. It should be understood that a piece of Helium 3 smaller than your fist would supply enough energy to power the city of Phoenix, AZ for conservatively 2 years. (Another of NASA's hidden secrets!)

➤ October and November of '98 will see the appearance of meteors falling to Earth, causing considerable damage. This correlates to the *Fire Rain* of the Indigenous prophecies, as well as to revelations. This event will precede the red dawn.

➤ We will see many crop failures due to El Nino. Expect rises in the prices of many agricultural products by as much as 85% between '98 and '99. Start drying your fruits, vegetables and herbs **now**, as well as starting plants indoors and stocking up on seeds!

➤ Radon Gas will become a significant problem in many dormant farming areas throughout the US, but particularly in the Northwest.

➤ Spiritual miracles will become more and more frequent amongst the Indigenous Peoples in North and South America as they continue to awaken and breath life into their ancient wisdoms.

➤ Attempts by evangelist groups and those who follow the *Dark Star* to stop the Indigenous People from awakening will intensify. Their efforts will be likened to those of the Salem Witch Hunts and the Spanish Inquisition. But in the end these attempts will fail as world governments fall into utter chaos due to financial failures and climatic disasters.

➤ There will be a major awakening in the third world countries of South America as to a humanity of equality, (the Great Society of the Golden Age,) where achievements and position in society will be based upon spiritual qualities. There will be many migrating to these areas, as the American Dream dissolves before the pressure of the New Order, and economic sanctions are levied by world bankers.

➤ The government will attempt to control all holistic practices, from the growing of herbs to the administering of Spiritual healing. A prime example is already taking root – CODEX – which is a UN program for bio-diversity requiring the regulation of herbs including spearmint and St. John's Wart, as well as hundreds of others.

➤ Humanity will break through many barriers that have blocked the realms of higher consciousness. Mankind will begin to awaken to their inner abilities and embrace Spirit. For in the midst of darkness the light shall come. Because of the increase in frequency that Earth is experiencing, the Seven Seals, as spoken of in the Bible, will be activated. The Seven Seals correlate directly to the Seven Seals of the body. The activation of these seals will trigger the amino acids. Once the amino acids are triggered, our dormant strands of DNA will awaken.

➤ Societies in the Western Hemisphere will begin to break away Spiritually and in conscious awareness from the war torn East. There will be a Spiritual awakening that will come from the land that will witness the beginnings of many cataclysms. This will be the beginning of a split in consciousness amongst Earth's Peoples.

➤ Food and medicines will be increasingly hard to come by with the severity of the winter storms and unnatural weather conditions. Further complications of these commodities will be compounded by government imposed restrictions at the dictate of the new order. (CODEX)

➤ We, in the Western Hemisphere will witness the beginnings of the split in consciousness of the People of the Earth. A simple explanation of this is that there will be those who choose to awaken and those who choose to remain asleep. We will discover many ancient cities, hidden chambers near existing temples and below existing cities, especially in South America. These discoveries will show indisputable evidence of our long running relationship the Ethereans. Our awakenings to the understanding of our true Spirituality and Galactic Heritage will cause many to turn away from the fundamentalist Christian Doctrines that were born of the Middle East. Those here in North and South America will reclaim their own connection to the teachings of the Pale Prophet, the True Christ. This connection will revolutionize all present concepts of Christianity, for it will be revealed that his life as well as his ministry continued for a lifetime before his final ascension, which occurred here in North America.

➤ **Red Alerts will be posted at our web site as we are able to make them publicly available. You are welcome to view these postings at http://www.wolflodge.org/**

Works to Review

The following list of books and productions are those I recommend for your further edification. Many have been mentioned within "Winds of Change" and will be so noted by an asterisk (*). *Robert Ghost Wolf*

- Alphabet of the Heart – Dan Winter

- Angels Don't Play This HAARP ~ Advances in Tesla Technology – Dr. Nick Begich – Jeane Manning – ISBN# 0-9648812-0-9 *

- Awakening to Zero Point ~ The Collective Initiation – Gregg Braden – ISBN# 0-9648990-4-3 *

- Book Of Hopi, The – Frank Waters *

- Communion and The Secret Schools - Whitley Strieber *

- Day After Roswell, The – Col. Corso *

- Fire in the Sky – Travis Walton *

- I Am America Maps – Lori Toye *

- Last Waltz of the Tyrants – Judy Pope Koteen *

- My Healing Path ~ The Wheel of Life – Sherry Takala – Library of Congress # 97-090760

- For a complete listing of books and tapes available on the Montauk Project, send a SASE to: Sky Books, Box 769, Westbury, NY 11590-0104 (Highly recommended)

Books by the Author

- Eye of the Shaman ~ The Nagal Returns with the Gift of Kryahgenetics ~ The Alchemy of Self Transformation – Robert Ghost Wolf – Laura Lee Mistycah – Currently in production

- Last Cry ~ Native American Prophecies ~ Tales of the End Times – Robert Ghost Wolf – ISBN# 0-9660668-5-5

- Project Stargate – Heaven and Earth – The Games People Play – Robert Ghost Wolf and the Mountain Brotherhood – Currently in Production

- Sacred Circles – Robert Ghost Wolf – Currently in production

HU-MAN ENVIRONMENTAL LIVING PROGRAM

One of the questions we hear most often at Wolf Lodge, is "How can I help? I'm just an individual." We are all aware that the world needs all the 'HELP' it can get right now! With the coming of the Millenium we are faced with finding new ways to facilitate that which is needed for everyday living. The Mountain Brotherhood in association with the Wolf Lodge Cultural Foundation has created the H.E.L.P. program to gather a Human Potential Force consisting of some of the world's most accomplished professionals to further our understanding and application of the Earth sciences. The research afforded through H.E.L.P. will focus on the applications of herbology and other modalities of natural healing. Through our expanded under-standings, we as a species will be able to enhance the utilization of natural forces, the energy of Earth's elements and frequencies to develop our planet as a healthy and abundant global community. Our goal is to educate People in effective methods of sustainable agriculture, living architecture and energy harmonics.

Proposed Pacific Northwest research and development site for H.E.L.P.

We are Spiritual Beings having a human experience. If we are to survive the anticipated events of the coming *Shift* we must raise our own consciousness to include our voluntary participation with planetary harmonics working in cooperation with nature as we enter the new millenium. H.E.L.P. will enable research based upon Native American spiritual under-standing, respect and preservation of Mother Earth and the cooperative blending of modern technology.

The wealth of information, technological advances and discoveries in healing brought forth through the efforts of H.E.L.P. will serve to better Hu-manity on a global level. Through published works and research projects, H.E.L.P. will promote the philosophy of reuniting the Sacred Hoop… reuniting all with each other on a basis of respect, harmony and hu-man integrity.

By helping H.E.L.P., you will be helping hu-manity on a global level while at the same time, helping yourself. We will all benefit from the work done on behalf of us all. To contribute to the H.E.L.P. fund, donations can be sent to Wolf Lodge Cultural Foundation, P. O. Box 10196, Spokane, WA 99209, or called in to 509-623-2496. You can make this dream a reality – HE.L.P. us dream it … become part of the dream!

Robert Ghost Wolf and the Mountain Brotherhood